"A man hath no better thing under the sun, than to eat, and to drink, and to be merry."
　　　　　　THE BIBLE, ECCLESIASTES CHAPTER VIII, VERSE 15.

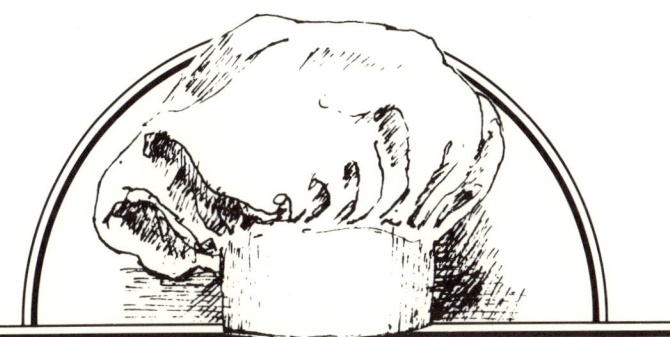

Chefs' Secrets from Great Restaurants in Louisiana

By
The Louisiana Restaurant Association

PELICAN PUBLISHING COMPANY
GRETNA 1986

Thanks to the members of the Louisiana Restaurant Association, the staff, and Hal Moser, contributing production editor, for making this book possible.

Cover photography courtesy of Taylor California Cellars, Gonzales, California.

First printing, May 1984
Second printing, November 1986

The recipes in this book have been submitted by restaurants and have been or are currently served in the restaurant. The Publisher and Editors accept no responsibility for recipes that seem to be unsatisfactory.

Copyright© 1984 Marmac Publishing Company, Inc.
6303 Barfield Road, Suite 208, Atlanta, Georgia 30328

ISBN: 0-939944-25-1
Library of Congress Number: 83-063105

All rights reserved, including the right to reproduce this book in whole or in part in any form without permission from the publisher.

Publisher and Executive Editor, Marge McDonald
Senior Editor, Susan Hunter Smith
Recipe Editor, Elise Griffin
Illustrations by Jan Chaput, Atlanta, Georgia
Cover photography by Conway-Carter Photography, Atlanta, Georgia
Manufactured in the United States of America

Restaurants featured are members of the Louisiana Restaurant Association.

TABLE OF CONTENTS

RESTAURANT LOCATOR MAP 6
FOREWORD 9
INTRODUCTION .11
COLOR PHOTOGRAPHS. 17
APPETIZERS. 25
GUMBOS, SOUPS, SALADS 39
MEATS, GAME. .71
POULTRY 93
SEAFOOD. 111
VEGETABLES, BREADS 171
DESSERTS, BEVERAGES 187
CULINARY COMPLEMENTS 219
    WINES. 220
    BASIC STOCKS & SAUCES. 226
    GLOSSARY 228
    EQUIVALENT MEASURES. 231
INDEX BY FOODS AND RECIPE NAME 232
INDEX BY RESTAURANT 237
ORDER FORM. .239

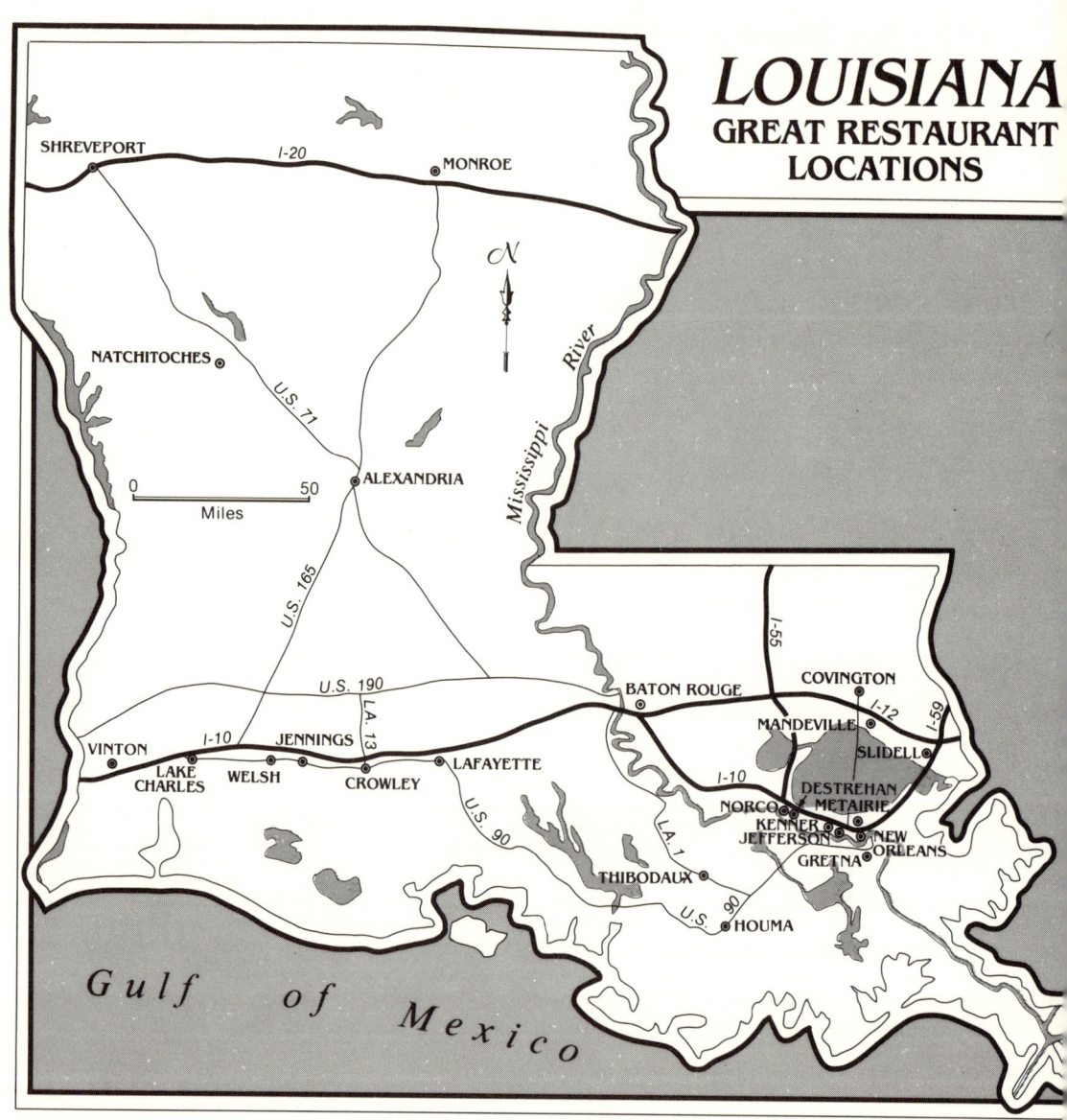

L.R.A.

Of all the heritage and traditions for which Louisiana is noted, its cuisine possesses the most alluring characteristic. Due to historical influences of diverse cultures, combined with the natural resources of the geographical terrain, Louisiana has developed a culinary art not found elsewhere. The Louisiana Restaurant Association is proud to have gathered these secret recipes from the kitchens of great restaurants throughout the state of Louisiana and place them together in one book. Some of these recipes have been passed down from generation to generation and feature a wide range of gustatory styles.

This book captures Cajun cooking as well as the Creole cuisine of New Orleans. For this book to be complete, the foods of central and northern Louisiana have also been included. I hope you will enjoy the experience of cooking with these recipes. I know you will enjoy the food.

Come. Taste the charm of Louisiana.

Jim Funk
Executive Vice-President
Louisiana Restaurant Association

"If ever I cease to love...May sheepsheads grow on apple trees...
May oysters have legs and cows lay eggs, If ever I cease to love."
MARDI GRAS OFFICIAL SONG

FOREWORD

Louisiana is a state that is blessed with extraordinary natural resources, including richly productive fisheries, teeming wildlife, a climate conducive to growing exceptionally flavored fruits and vegetables, and soil that is naturally rich in nutrients and minerals. In short, Louisiana provides a perfect setting for food and cooking—and, unquestionably, Louisiana has unique food.

In the last few years, I have begun referring to the various types of cuisine in Louisiana—including Cajun and Creole—as "Louisiana cooking." With the continued growth in national and international attention directed at regional American cuisine, Louisiana cooking has secured its place at the top level of regional foods in the nation. Even our restaurants that are "known" only in their immediate neighborhoods have at least one really great dish.

In Louisiana there is an inherently deep appreciation for good cooking, based in part on the exceptional fish, seafood, meats, vegetables, and fruits available in the state. Creativeness with food and good cooking has always been an important source of pride to Louisiana people and this is reflected in our restaurants. Good cooking is a part of our tradition in Louisiana.

This is a book of recipes from Louisiana's diverse restaurants. I feel certain that with Louisiana's heritage of creative cooking, and its emphasis on food as an important part of life—nutritionally, socially, and emotionally—you will find recipes in the book that will be exciting and different for you.

Paul Prudhomme
Chef and owner of K-Paul's Louisiana Kitchen

Paul Prudhomme was born and reared in Acadian country, with its two hundred year heritage of French cooking. Craig Claiborne, food writer for the **New York Times**, deems Prudhomme "a celebrated, internationally known chef who just happens to have been born in the United States." Prudhomme is the recipient of the coveted French award, the **Republique de Francaise's Merite Agricole 1883**, was Chef for the First Anniversary Dinner for **Food and Wine Mazagine**, and his restaurant, K-Paul's Louisiana Kitchen, was selected one of the top ten restaurants in the country by **Nation's Restaurant News**, 1983.

"He may live without books,—what is knowledge but grieving?
He may live without hope,—what is hope but deceiving?
He may live without love,—what is passion but pining?
But where is the man that can live without dining?"

OWEN MEREDITH

INTRODUCTION

Cooking styles of Louisiana figure prominently in early and present-day American cuisine. While many parts of the country have culinary specialties, only in Louisiana do we find a distinctive and all-encompassing regional cuisine comparable to the regional traditions of Europe.

This regional excellence is identified by two key culinary words, Creole and Cajun. The intrinsic excitement of both cuisines is attested to by the number of menus in the United States and around the world which list Creole and Cajun dishes.

Creole refers to a person of French or Spanish descent born in the American colonies. Creole cooking is historically centered in the urban development of the great port city of New Orleans. There the mixing of French and Spanish culture and foods began in the eighteenth century and was further enriched by the contributions of native American Indians and Haitian refugees, fleeing from the revolutions in the 1790s on their island home. It is no accident that certain Creole dishes are derivations of cooking from the Caribbean Islands. World-class restaurants, which were first established in New Orleans in the nineteenth century, have maintained for over a century the high levels of achievement which make their names and Creole cooking a password to dining eminence.

In the rural southern parishes of Louisiana, Cajun cooking became dominant as French Acadian farmers and fishermen, migrating from Canada and France in the eighteenth century, settled in the bayous west of New Orleans. Cajun culture is virtually intact and still flourishing after two hundred years. Cajun is an alteration of the word "Acadian." Although Creole and Cajun cooking use many of the same foodstuffs, seafoods, and game, the approaches to preparation are different from one another. Generally speaking, the Cajun cooking of the country is more pungent, robust, and more highly seasoned than the discrete, refined Creole cookery of New Orleans.

The northern and central portions of Louisiana, a zone where the west and the south meet, intermingle the specialties of both regions. Chili, grits, and gumbo are commonly found listed on the same menu.

UNIQUE ORIGINS

The uniqueness of Louisiana's culinary heritage can be traced to the state's origins and long history. New Orleans, located at the mouth of the mighty Mississippi River, was the capital of the expansive French colony of Louisiana and was founded by Jean Baptiste LeMoyne, Sieur de Bienville, in 1718. The city was named after Philip, Duc d' Orleans, Regent of France, and quickly became the premier French-speaking city on the North American continent. Between its founding and 1803, when New Orleans and the rest of Louisiana became part of the fledgling United States of America through the Louisiana Purchase, New Orleans experienced four decades each of French and then Spanish rule, culture, and tastes. New Orleans was a French settlement from 1718 to 1762, came under Spanish rule until just after 1800, and finally became an American territory in 1803.

There was another cultural ingredient added to the creole melting pot in the 1880s—the influence of the many early Italians who came to New Orleans in the late nineteenth century. There are many Italian-inspired dishes on Creole menus and there is a whole class of restaurants which can genuinely be called Creole-Italian.

A WEALTH OF SEAFOOD

Despite all these strong culinary traditions, Louisiana would not be the gourmet hotbed it is were it not for the vast wealth of raw materials at the disposal of its cooks. The system of bayous and marshes which extend from the Gulf of Mexico to as far as a hundred twenty miles inland constitute the richest natural seafood hatchery on the continent. It provides a quality and quantity of fish and shellfish great enough to keep luscious fresh seafood on the tables of Louisiana restaurants all the time.

The inventory of Louisiana's native fish is a bit different from other parts of the country. Local fish have almost completely crowded universals, such as sole, haddock, perch, scrod, and bass, off Louisiana menus, replacing them with four Gulf fish—trout, redfish, flounder, and pompano.

The speckled trout served in Louisiana is not fresh-water trout. A denizen of the shallow, salty waters of the Gulf Coast and Lake Pontchartrain, speckled trout (or sea trout) has a light texture. Trout fillets figure prominently in the best Creole seafood houses. They are usually fried or sauteed, and moistened with one of the innumerable versions of meuniere sauce or melted butter with toasted almonds.

Redfish is related to trout, but is a bigger, firmer fish which lends itself well to broiling or grilling. It is authoritative enough to support some very rich sauces, and for that reason it has become very popular among chefs in recent years. Redfish generally fills the role sea bass would in other parts of the country.

Flounder is Louisiana's answer to sole. It is prepared in every imaginable way, but stuffing it with a crabmeat dressing is a popular practice. Pompano is the most expensive and sought-after Louisiana fish. It has a fine texture and a rich, elegant flavor which is best appreciated in its simple broiled form. However, many restaurants prepare more elaborate pompano dishes, the most famous of which is pompano en papillote, in which the fish and its sauce are cooked in a parchment bag.

An extremely popular fresh-water fish in Louisiana is catfish. The classic service of this inimitable fish is deep-fried with a side order of hushpuppies. Catfish houses are found throughout the state, some of its most fervent adherents in Des Allemands, Manchac, and Baton Rouge.

Shellfish are even more important to Louisiana's cuisine than fish with fins. The big names are oysters, shrimp, crabs, and crawfish, the small crustacean native to Louisiana waters.

There is probably no place in the world where more oysters are consumed per person than in southeast Louisiana. The supply is extremely abundant all year round and the size and quality is superb. Most oysters are downed in their raw form right off the shell with a sauce of catsup, horseradish, hot sauce, and lemon juice.

Most seafood restaurants sport oyster bars or "raw" bars. Oysters are also fried on their way to becoming parts of seafood platters or sandwiches. Two favorites of the many varieties of baked oyster dishes are oysters Rockefeller and oysters Bienville.

Louisiana shrimp are very familiar to most American diners, for Louisiana supplies a great portion of the shrimp eaten in the United States. In Louisiana fresh shrimp are available in every size and are prepared in many imaginative ways; this book contains many recipes which demonstrate the epicurean versatility of shrimp.

Louisiana crabs are similar to those enjoyed on the east coast of the United States. In fact, the two areas supply each other's needs during their respective off-seasons. Crabs are boiled whole and served up by the dozen or they are picked apart and made into casseroles, sauces, and stuffings.

JAMBALAYA, CRAWFISH PIE, FILE GUMBO

If there is one shellfish which epitomizes the eating habits of Louisianians, it is without question the modest crawfish. Called "crayfish" by those beyond the state or the South, crawfish are central to Cajun cuisine, which dotes on them in the most enthusiastic way from the time they first appear around Thanksgiving until they wander off to lay their eggs in June. Crawfish look like tiny lobsters, three to six inches long. They congregate in the marshes and especially in the Atchafalaya River floodway. In good years they can be picked up by the hundreds as they attempt to cross roads at night.

The flavor of a prime crawfish is almost too good to be believed. In France, they are essential to some of the most complex and beguiling sauces in the world. In Louisiana, they are the seafood component of many dishes—most of them spicy. Crawfish etouffee is a thick stew of the whole tails, served over rice. Crawfish bisque is a thick soup, usually served with a few crawfish heads stuffed with a fine dressing. Crawfish are also popular in many other dishes and sauces. Many thousands of crawfish are boiled in a spicy liquid and then eaten by the dozen over newspaper-covered tables, especially during the Cajun "feast before sleeping," a fête do do, where Cajun music, dancing, drinking and eating are celebrated.

Guests are presented a bowl of gumbo preceding many a seafood feast in Louisiana. Gumbo is an original Louisiana dish, the African word for okra being "gombo." There are as many variations of this thick, robust, spicy soup as there are cooks who make it, but most gumbos fall into one or two categories. Seafood or okra gumbo is chock-full of crabs, shrimp, and oysters, with the okra as a thickening agent. Chicken or filé gumbo is usually a smokier affair with pieces of chicken or turkey and sausage—commonly andouille, the thick, garlic ham sausage that is a specialty of the river parishes between New Orleans and Baton Rouge. Filé is powdered sassafras leaves, an herb discovered by the Choctow Indians; it is dusted over the top of the bowl of gumbo as it is served, and gives the gumbo its distinctive herbal aroma. There is no law that says that you cannot have a gumbo with chicken, oysters, filé, *and* okra—or any other combination of the basic ingredients. Gumbo is traditionally served over rice.

Rice is locally grown, a staple of Louisiana cooking and preferred as a starch over potatoes. It is certainly at the center of two Louisiana classics, red beans and jambalaya. Red beans and rice is the universal Monday lunch platter special in New Orleans restaurants. The firm red kidney beans are served in a sauce well-seasoned with smoked sausage over fluffy long-grain rice. Rice is even more dominant in jambalaya, which is classically cooked outside in giant kettles over an open fire. Jambalaya is the Cajun's answer to paella, a smoky mixture of rice, sausage, chicken, shrimp, and seasonings with more than a little oil.

There are thousands of Louisiana culinary delights to be found in the state's restaurants and in this cookbook. I will mention just one more, the specialty of Louisiana's oldest community, Natchitoches, on the Red River in the central part of the state—a spicy fried meat pie. This pie is shaped like a half-moon and filled with any of a wide variety of meats and spices. It resembles the Latin American empanada, but it tends to be very juicy inside and very spicy. The Natchitoches meat pie has begun to spread to other parts of the state, but there is no better place to savor it than in the city of its origin.

THE DISTINCTIVE CREOLE/CAJUN TOUCHES

If you are planning on cooking in the Louisiana styles and you have never tried before, the question that is probably on your mind at this point is, "What makes a Creole dish Creole or a Cajun dish Cajun?" That is a tough question to answer. Both Creole and Cajun cooking are so broad, are so related, and have so many sub-styles that it is hard to designate exactly which step is the one which gives the magic touch of authenticity.

But we can give you at least one generality—*more*. Creole and Cajun food is generally *more* highly flavored than most American and European dishes. Four things in particular are liberally used to heighten flavors—salt, pepper, oil, and garlic. It should be immediately pointed out, however, that you can have an authentic Creole dish without these elements. You will rarely come across a bland Creole dish, and never come across a flavorless real Cajun dish. In the hands of the best cooks, the Creole and Cajun methods produce gustatory sensations of almost unbelievable intensity, without masking the identity of the main ingredient.

Creole recipes most frequently begin with the most important instruction in Creole preparation, "first make a roux." A roux is a mixture of flour and oil, butter, or shortening. This mixture is cooked over medium heat to the desired degree of brown for the dish in question, and serves as the thickening medium for the sauce or soup. It is in the roux that the onions are browned and to which the chicken, beef, or seafood is later added as the dish builds. The roux is quintessential to Creole cooking.

An indispensable ingredient in both Creole and Cajun cooking is cayenne, both as a powder and as the main flavoring ingredient of Louisiana hot sauce, the premium brand of which is Tabasco. Louisiana cooks have to make a conscious decision *not* to use cayenne in a dish, so natural is the urge to put it in everything. Not much is used, but a pinch goes a long way.

The spice levels in Cajun cooking are even higher than they are in Creole food. The Cajun cuisine evolved as a method of making palatable the then less-desirable fish such as crawfish and catfish; many poor Cajun families had to sell the best of their catch to make a living. Now crawfish and other Cajun specialties have assumed a place of honor as a regional cuisine. Long, slow, moist cooking methods are an earmark of Cajun dishes which offer as memorable a taste as can be found anywhere in the world.

More can be said about the great foods of Louisiana, but no amount of explanation can equal the experience of tasting them, in the state's many landmark restaurants or in your own kitchen, using the following recipes gathered from the best dining establishments in all parts of Louisiana. Bon appétit and, as the Cajuns say, "laissez le bon temps rouler!" (let the good times roll!)

Tom Fitzmorris
Editor/Publisher,
The New Orleans MENU Magazine

FILLET OF SNAPPER ROME
Delmonico
Page 128

TURTLE SOUP
Kolb's
Page 48

CRABMEAT A LA JULIA
Emery's
Page 165

LINZER TORTE
Mayer's Old Europe
Page 197

COQUILLES SAINT-RAMON
Tivoli
Page 148

SPANISH SHRIMP
Saffron
Page 166

CRABMEAT AU GRATIN
The Restaurant Angelle's
Page 115

TURTLE SOUP
Delmonico
Page 49

BAYOU EGGPLANT
The Red Onion
Page 176

BOUDIN PIZZA
Mister Jay's
Page 76

SHRIMP ITALIAN
Jackson Street Pizza
Page 162

HOUSE SALAD
Kolb's
Page 63

**BREAD PUDDING
WITH RUM SAUCE**
Chez Pastor, Page 192

BROILED REDFISH
Covington Depot
Page 132

BREAD PUDDING SOUFFLE
Commander's Palace
Page 190

ESCARGOT ROQUEFORT
Winston's
Page 34

OYSTERS MARAS
Mr. B's
Page 147

CRAB RAVIGOTTE
Winston's
Page 32

TROUT MEUNIERE
Ralph & Kacoo's
Page 140

POITRINE DE VEAU FARCIE DE GASCOGNE
The Plimsoll Club, Page 81

SNAPPER FONTENOT
Chez Pastor
Page 129

SHRIMP AND OYSTER FETTUCINI
Benedict House
Page 154

PUFF PASTRY WITH CARAMEL SAUCE,
Saffron, Page 200

DUCKLING BALLOTINE
The Landing of Lafayette
Page 102

SAUERBRATEN
Mayer's Old Europe
Page 73

CANARD AUX ANANAS REVE DE BALMAIN
The Plimsoll Club, Page 101

STEAK SUPREME
Chez Pastor
Page 72

CABBAGE ROLLS
Don's Seafood Hut
Page 150

ROAST VEAL SHANKS
Willy Coln's Chalet
Page 82

VEAL AU CITRON
Commander's Palace
Page 79

**CARRE D'AGNEAU
A LA MONGOLIAN**
Winston's, Page 75

OYSTERS TRUFANT
Commander's Palace
Page 145

SAUTEED SHRIMP
Emery's
Page 165

KAISER SCHNITZEL
Kolb's
Page 83

ESQUIRE SALAD
Paddlewheel Express
Page 64

HICKORY GRILLED WISCONSIN DUCKLING
Mr. B's
Page 106

CAJUN CRAWFISH PIZZA
Mister Jay's
Page 122

SEAFOOD GUMBO
Don's Seafood Hut
Page 40

TROUT DELMONICO
Delmonico
Page 141

OYSTERS HEBERT
Tivoli
Page 144

SCHWARZWALDER KIRSHTORTE
Willy Coln's Chalet
Page 199

STREGA SALUTE
Valentine's
Page 212

QUAIL WITH WILD MUSHROOMS
Saffron
Page 107

VEAL CHOP FRANCISCO
Tivoli
Page 80

PATE DE POISSONS MARIE-FRANCE
The Plimsoll Club, Page 35

CRAWFISH BISQUE
Bon Ton Cafe
Page 50

CORN AND SHRIMP SOUP
Paddlewheel Express
Page 53

SHRIMP CHIPPEWA
Mr. B's
Page 169

APPETIZERS

RIVERVIEW RESTAURANT

Marriott Hotel, 555 Canal St., New Orleans, LA 70140; (504) 581-1000.

Sunday brunch is a very popular meal in this rooftop restaurant. Expect a great assortment of breakfast foods on the buffet table, complimentary Champagne, and live jazz. At the omelette station, the chef prepares your favorite omelette with fresh ingredients. If you haven't already woken up in the clouds on Sunday morning, this restaurant can do the trick for you. The view and cuisine are inspiring.

STUFFED ARTICHOKE BOTTOMS

2 medium eggplants, peeled, cut into 1-inch cubes
1 cup salad oil
1 small rib celery, chopped
1 small yellow onion, chopped
$1/2$ small green pepper, chopped
4 ounces small shrimp, peeled and deveined
1 tablespoon olive oil
Salt to taste
Freshly ground black pepper to taste
Dash Tabasco sauce
Pinch dry mustard
Pinch thyme
1 bay leaf
4 anchovy fillets, finely chopped
1 tablespoon chopped parsley
$1/2$ cup bread crumbs
8 artichoke bottoms (canned, frozen, or freshly cooked)

Hollandaise Sauce, Riverview
$1/2$ cup butter
3 egg yolks
Juice of $1/2$ lemon
Pinch salt
Dash Tabasco Sauce
1 teaspoon chopped parsley

To make Stuffing: Deep fry eggplant cubes in oil until golden brown and drain on paper towel. In a medium skillet heat the 1 cup of salad oil and saute the celery, onions, and green pepper until transparent. Add shrimp and spices and let simmer for 5 more minutes. Add anchovies, parsley, and bread crumbs; cook and stir for 2 minutes. Remove from heat and allow to cool.

Place artichoke bottoms with a few drops of water and olive oil in baking dish. Top artichokes generously with filling. Bake at 350 degrees F. for 7 to 9 minutes.

To serve top each artichoke with Hollandaise Sauce and serve immediately.

To make Hollandaise Sauce: Place cold butter in small, heavy saucepan; add egg yolks, lemon juice, salt, and Tabasco. Stir constantly over moderate heat until butter melts and sauce thickens. Add chopped parsley. Makes about $3/4$ cup.

MAKES 4 SERVINGS

ANTOINE'S

713 St. Louis St., New Orleans, LA 70130; (504) 581-4422.

In a city of old, established restaurants, Antoine's is the grandaddy of them all. It has been on the scene in its present location, owned by the same family, since 1840. That makes it the oldest continuous restaurant operation in America — one that dates back to a time when the very idea of going out to eat was a rather novel one. Antoine's wears its age gracefully and preserves the best of its past in its many antique rooms and in its style of Creole-French cookery.

HUITRES BIENVILLE *(Oysters Bienville)*

Bienville Sauce
1/4 cup butter
1 1/2 cups minced green pepper
1 cup minced green onions
2 cloves garlic, minced
1/2 cup white wine
1/2 cup chopped pimiento
2 cups bechamel sauce (see Basic Sauces)
2/3 cup grated American cheese
1/2 cup bread crumbs
Salt and white pepper to taste

Oysters
36 raw oysters on the half shell
6 pie pans filled with rock salt

Note: The purpose of the rock salt is to retain heat even after the oysters are brought to the table. Be careful that the salt doesn't get into the oyster shells or into the bienville sauce.

To make bienville sauce: Melt the butter and saute the green pepper, green onions, and garlic until they are limp. Add white wine and bring to a boil. Add pimiento, bechamel sauce, cheese, and bread crumbs. Add salt and pepper to taste and simmer 20 minutes or until the sauce is very thick. Makes 5 cups.

To prepare oysters: Place 6 raw oysters on the half shell on each of the six pie pans filled with rock salt. Cover each oyster with bienville sauce and bake at 400 degrees F. for 10 minutes or until the oysters and sauce are very hot and begin to brown on top. Serve immediately.

Note: Jean Baptiste LeMoyne, Sieur de Bienville, an early colonial governor of Louisiana, was born in Montreal, Canada, in 1680 and died in Paris in 1768. He was the eighth of eleven sons of Charles LeMoyne. In 1698, Pierre Le Moyne, Sieur d'Iberville, the brother of Bienville, set out to begin a colony at the mouth of the Mississippi. But it was not until 1718 that Bienville, with the help of eighty French exiles, cleared some wilderness near the mouth of the river and established La Nouvelle Orleans.

Former Antoine's Chef Pete Michel, along with Roy Alciatore created this dish several decades ago in honor of Bienville.

MAKES 6 SERVINGS

ARNAUD'S

813 Bienville St., New Orleans, LA 70112; (504) 523-5433.

Since the restaurant was founded in 1918, lunch at Arnaud's has been a rigorously-kept tradition of New Orleans businessmen. A slate of some half-dozen specials are served in the restaurant's classic tile-and-beveled-glass main dining room. Meanwhile, for those with less time, lunch is served in Arnaud's Grill Room, a congenial atmosphere with a live pianist. And after dinner, or lunch, it is fun to take a tour of Arnaud's Mardi Gras museum, with its many elaborate gowns and costumes.

OYSTERS SUZETTE

1/2 pound bacon, minced
2 green peppers, minced
1 medium white onion, minced
2 celery ribs, strings removed and minced
1/4 cup minced pimiento
1/2 cup fish stock or oyster liquor (see Basic Stocks)
1 tablespoon lemon juice
1 dash Angostura bitters
1/8 teaspoon thyme
2 tablespoons butter
2 tablespoons flour
36 oysters
36 washed oyster shells

Garnish: 3 lemons, halved

Saute the bacon with the green peppers, onion, and celery for 5 to 7 minutes until the bacon fat is melted. Pour off the fat. Add pimientos, fish stock or oyster liquor, lemon juice, bitters, and thyme. Boil for 5 minutes.

Prepare the roux in a separate small saucepan by cooking the butter and flour together for 5 minutes, stirring occasionally to insure even cooking. Blend the roux with the vegetable mixture and stir until thickened.

Place 1 oyster on each shell and top with 1 tablespoon of the sauce. Bake at 400 degrees F. for 15 minutes.

Serve 6 oysters on a plate garnished with half a lemon.

MAKES 6 SERVINGS

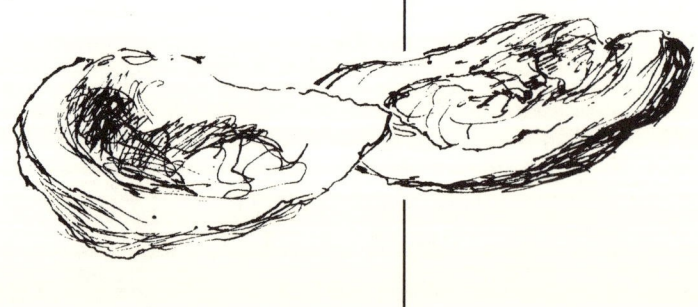

BRENNAN'S

417 Royal St., New Orleans, LA 70130; (504) 525-9711.

Until Brennan's opened in 1946, the restaurant community in New Orleans was dominated by Frenchmen. Owen E. Brennan showed what the Irish could do in the way of classic dining — combine it with a sense of fun and friendship. In assembling that happy amalgam the Brennans know no peers. From the renowned "Breakfast at Brennan's" to the classic French-Creole dinner, Brennan's is pure joy and very, very New Orleans.

OYSTERS ROCKEFELLER

36 oysters in shell
6 individual pans filled with rock salt
1 1/2 cups butter
3/4 cups finely chopped green onions
3/4 cups finely chopped white onions
1/2 cup finely chopped parsley
1 cup finely chopped celery
1/4 cup finely minced garlic
1/4 cup finely chopped anchovies
1/2 cup cooked bacon crumbs
1 1/2 cups oyster liquor
1/4 cup Pernod or Herbsaint (see Glossary)
5 cups cooked chopped spinach
2 tablespoons Worcestershire sauce
1/4 cup Italian bread crumbs

Drain the oysters thoroughly, saving liquor. Clean and dry the shells. Place the oysters on the half shells and set the shells six to a pan on the rock salt.

Meanwhile melt the butter in a large skillet. Saute the onions, parsley, celery, garlic, anchovies, and bacon. Cook on medium heat for 20 minutes. Add oyster liquor, Pernod or Herbsaint, spinach, and Worcestershire sauce. Cook 10 minutes more and add Italian bread crumbs.

Spoon about 2 1/2 tablespoons of sauce over each oyster, then bake at 450 to 475 degrees F. for 12 to 15 minutes, until the sauce is browned on top. To serve, set the pans on dinner plates.

MAKES 6 SERVINGS

RALPH & KACOO'S

7110 Airline Hwy., Baton Rouge, LA 70805; (504) 356-2361.

The Baton Rouge Ralph & Kacoo's is decorated with century-old cypress. The nautical theme of the decor is carried out with an assortment of antiques and oil paintings. The restaurant is one of Baton Rouge's most popular and has grown several times since it was founded. The most recent addition was the large, attractive Patio Room. In the lounge is a large painting of a ship and a copper-top bar. Catfish and hush puppies at their best are the specialty, along with a full menu of seafood and steaks.

STUFFED MUSHROOMS

1 pound whole mushrooms (15 to 20)
1 cup butter
1 cup chopped onions
1/2 pound cooked shrimp, peeled, deveined and chopped
1 teaspoon salt
2 teaspoons pepper
2 chicken bouillon cubes, crushed
1/3 cup grated Parmesan cheese
2 cups bread crumbs
1 pound lump crabmeat, chopped
2 teaspoons chopped parsley
1/4 cup white wine
1/4 cup melted butter

Remove stems from mushrooms; chop stems and reserve caps.

Melt butter on low heat. Add onions and saute for 5 minutes. Add the mushroom stems, shrimp, salt, pepper, and bouillon cubes. Cook for 10 minutes, stirring constantly.

Remove skillet from heat and stir in cheese, bread crumbs, crabmeat, and parsley.

Stuff mushroom caps with a ball of stuffing. When ready to serve, place in a buttered baking dish. Mix white wine and melted butter and pour over stuffed mushrooms. Bake at 350 degrees F. for 15 minutes.

This recipe may also be used as an accompaniment to beef dishes.

MAKES 15 to 20 MUSHROOMS

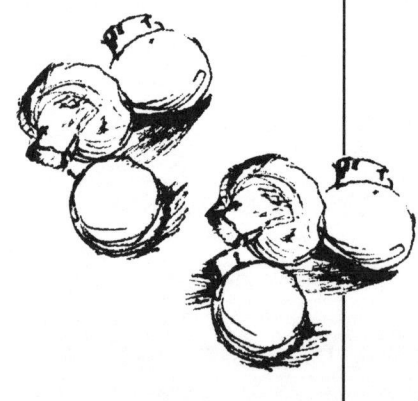

30   APPETIZERS

ARNAUD'S

813 Bienville St., New Orleans, LA 70112; (504) 523-5433.

What comes to the minds of most Orleanians at the mention of Arnaud's are tile floors and shrimp Arnaud. The first is the atmospheric trademark of the 65-year-old restaurant; different patterns of tile appear on the floors of the many rooms in the enormous building. The second is the classic way to start a lunch or dinner here. Unusual essays in trout, redfish, and pompano lead the seafood portion of the menu; poultry, veal, and beef get their own highly original treatments as well.

MARINATED SHRIMP

5 pounds shrimp, cooked and peeled
6 thinly sliced white or red onions
6 bay leaves
1 1/4 cups salad oil
3/4 cup white vinegar
1 1/2 teaspoons salt
2 1/2 teaspoons celery seed
1 bottle capers and juice
Tabasco sauce to taste

Place layers of shrimp, onions, and bay leaves in enameled or pyrex pan. Continue until all are used.

Combine remaining ingredients and pour over shrimp; cover tightly and refrigerate.

Prepare at least 24 hours before serving. Turn from bottom with spatula several times while marinating.

Serve in very shallow serving dish with as little liquid as possible.

MAKES 10 SERVINGS

WINSTON'S

New Orleans Hilton, Riverside and Towers,
2 Poydras St., New Orleans, LA 70140; (504) 561-0500.

Winston's is the first-class restaurant of the Hilton, and occupies a prime space on the second floor of the airy atrium. In the garden-like setting, with its plush couch seating, fresh flowers, rare wood accents, and antiques are served classic French and Creole dishes. The menu is read by the "butler," who with your "maid" serves you dinner in fine style. The best meats, fresh seafood, and fresh herbs are used to create a memorable meal.

CRAB RAVIGOTTE

½ teaspoon salt
Pinch of pepper
2 tablespoons capers
1 teaspoon chopped parsley
1 tablespoon mustard
1 onion, finely chopped
2 tablespoons vinegar
5 tablespoons oil
7 ounces lump crabmeat

In large bowl combine salt, pepper, capers, parsley, mustard, and the onion.

While beating vigorously with a whisk, pour in the vinegar and oil a little at a time.

Add the crabmeat and serve on lettuce or in individual serving dishes.

MAKES 2 SERVINGS

Photograph, Page 20

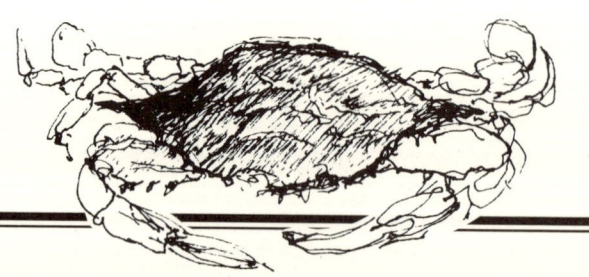

THE COURT OF TWO SISTERS

613 Royal St., New Orleans, LA 70130; (504) 522-7261.

Few restaurants anywhere can match the classic loveliness of the Court of Two Sisters. The dining rooms are arranged about the leafy center courtyard in authentic French Quarter style. Naturally, the courtyard also provides the prime tables for dining, cooled by the breezes through the plants and trees. The menu at dinner features traditional Creole dishes, many of them unique Court of Two Sisters' creations.

ESCARGOT AUX CHAMPIGNONS

3/4 cup butter, softened
1 teaspoon minced green onions
2 cloves garlic, minced
1 teaspoon minced parsley
1/2 teaspoon salt
1/4 teaspoon pepper
1 tablespoon heavy cream
1 tablespoon vermouth
24 fresh mushroom caps
24 canned, drained and washed escargot

Cream the softened butter with the green onions, garlic, parsley, salt, pepper, cream, and vermouth.

Remove the stems from the mushrooms. Stuff each mushroom cap with an escargot. Place in baking pan. Cover with spoonful of the butter mixture. Broil for 6 to 8 minutes.

MAKES 6 SERVINGS

WINSTON'S

The New Orleans Hilton, Riverside and Towers.
2 Poydras St., New Orleans, LA 70140; (504) 561-0500.

One finds unexpected pleasures at this flagship restaurant of the luxury Hilton hotel on the riverfront. But something one does not find is a menu. The daily offerings are recited by your "butler," who with your "maid" serves you in an unusual English style. There are three to five choices in every course of the prix-fixe dinner; the dishes change from night to night according to what the chef has found of special interest that day.

ESCARGOT ROQUEFORT

2 cups salted butter, room temperature
1 1/2 teaspoons finely minced garlic
1 tablespoon chopped Italian parsley
1 teaspoon Dijon mustard
1 ounce brandy
1 ounce Pernod (see Glossary)
1 1/2 ounces Roquefort cheese
1 ounce dry white wine
Salt and pepper to taste
36 canned escargot

In a mixing bowl beat together the butter, garlic, parsley, mustard, brandy, and Pernod.

In a sauce pan melt Roquefort with wine over low heat. When cheese is melted, add to butter mixture and stir.

Divide escargot between 6 individual serving dishes with sides. Spoon sauce over each dish.

Bake at 350 degrees F. for 10 minutes.

MAKES 6 SERVINGS

Photograph, Page 19

THE PLIMSOLL CLUB

International Trade Mart, New Orleans, LA 70130; (504) 529-1701.

The Plimsoll Club sits high atop the International Trade Mart, overlooking the busiest bend in America's mightiest channel of trade, the Mississippi River. It is named for the two marks which are seen on the sides of ships. A private club, it offers to its members and their firms an incomparable location for dining and entertaining, one which has been enjoyed by heads of state and dignitaries from around the world.

PATE DE POISSONS MARIE-FRANCE *(Marie-France's Seafood Pâté)*

4 cups ground fish meat (redfish, salmon, scallops, shrimp, or equal parts)
1 egg white
1 tablespoon salt
1 teaspoon white pepper
Dash cayenne pepper
3 cups plus 1 tablespoon heavy cream, divided
2 cups bread crumbs
2 eggs
2 teaspoons chopped parsley
1 teaspoon chopped onion
1 teaspoon chopped garlic
1 tablespoon Cognac
2 cups fresh asparagus tips

Mix the ground seafood with the egg white, salt, and peppers. Add 3 cups of the heavy cream, a little at a time.

In another bowl, mix the bread crumbs, eggs, parsley, onion, garlic, Cognac, and the tablespoon of heavy cream. Stir until blended well.

Place a scant three fourths of the fish mixture $1/2$ inch thick on the bottom and 2 long sides of a buttered loaf pan. Add half of the bread crumb mixture and half of the asparagus tips. Repeat the layers and top with remaining fish mixture. Cover with buttered foil or parchment paper.

Place pan in a larger pan filled with water to reach 2 inches up the sides of the loaf pan. Bake at 200 degrees F. for 2 hours. Serve hot or cold.

MAKES 12 SERVINGS

Photograph, Page 24

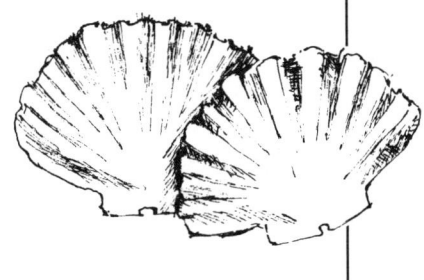

FLAMINGOS CAFE

1625 St. Charles Ave., New Orleans, LA 70130; (504) 523-6141.

One of the most memorable things about having a meal at this gaily-decorated and renovated mansion is the menu itself. It is thirty-two pages long and makes for highly entertaining reading. Each dish is described by anecdote, as are the many specialty drinks. (For example, it is noted that with one of the drinks you get your ear pierced.) Needless to say, this purveyor of quiche and other things is a lot of fun.

FLAMINGOS COUNTRY PATE

- 1/2 cup dried mushrooms
- 1/4 cup sherry (not cooking sherry)
- 1 pound boneless pork shoulder or other lean pork
- 1 pound boneless veal
- 1 pound unsmoked pork fat
- 1 1/2 pounds chicken livers
- 12 cloves garlic (yes 12)
- 3 eggs
- 1/4 cup heavy cream
- 1/2 cup Cognac or brandy
- 4 teaspoons salt
- 5 teaspoons pepper
- 1 1/2 teaspoons ground allspice
- 1 1/2 teaspoons cinnamon
- 1 1/2 teaspoons whole thyme, crushed
- 1/8 teaspoon ground bay leaf or 4 whole bay leaves tucked around the sides of the pâté before baking
- 1/2 cup flour
- 1/3 cup shelled pistachio nuts, coarsley chopped
- 12 strips thick-sliced bacon

Note: This is a hearty and flavorful pâté which should be made several days before using and can be made up to two weeks ahead.

Soak mushrooms in sherry for 20 minutes and grind together with a medium-coarse blade in food grinder with pork, veal, and pork fat. Do not use food processor as it becomes too fine. Keep all juices from meat and any extra sherry and add to ground meat. Puree chicken livers in blender with garlic, eggs, cream, and Cognac. Add one third of the mixed meat mixture and puree until fine.

Mix together the ground meat, pureed liver mix, and spices in a large bowl using hands to mix well (it's messy). Sprinkle in flour and pistachio nuts and mix well.

Line the bottom and sides of a 4-inch by 8-inch loaf pan with strips of bacon, letting some overhang the sides in order to flip them on top of the pâté. Pour pâté mix into pan and cover fully with bacon strips. Cover the top with a buttered double thickness of foil and place in a larger pan with water coming one half way up the pâté pan. Bake at 400 degrees F. for three hours, replacing water bath if necessary.

After three hours, remove pâté from oven, uncover, and replace foil with a single sheet of foil. Weight top with a brick until cooled. Cover the cooled pâté well and chill in refrigerator for several days.

To remove, dip the baking pan in hot water to melt the fat. Wrap the pâté well and it will keep for weeks. Slice thinly, serve with small sour pickles (cornichons) and crackers or lightly toasted bread.

MAKES 20 TO 30 SERVINGS

RESTAURANT SCLAFANI

1301 North Causeway Blvd., Metairie, LA 70001; (504) 835-1718.

Sclafani's was one of the first major restaurants to open in the old New Orleans suburb of Metairie, and it has retained a consistency of food and a popularity among its customers ever since. Opened by Peter Sclafani Sr. in the forties, Sclafani's is now under the management of son and chef Frank Sclafani. The dining rooms are enormous, highlighted by a central fountain; there are also attractive rooms for private parties. The service is an easy-going touch of a neighborhood restaurant in this major dining establishment.

CAPONATA

1 bunch celery, finely diced
1 green pepper, finely diced
4 cloves of garlic, finely minced
1 cup olive oil
4 cups drained and chopped canned tomatoes, (reserve liquid)
1/4 cup sugar
1/4 cup wine vinegar
1/4 teaspoon crushed dried red pepper
1/4 cup raisins
1/4 cup capers, drained
2 unpeeled eggplants, diced in 1/2-inch squares (total weight 2 pounds)
1/4 cup bottled Italian sour peppers, cut into strips and seeds removed
1/2 cup bottled cocktail pearl onions
1 cup broken green olives, in liquid
1 cup broken black olives, drained
Salt to taste

Put prepared celery, green pepper, and garlic in baking casserole. Casserole should be at least 4 quarts in size, with sides 3 inches high.

Stir in olive oil. Cook at 400 degrees F. for 15 minutes.

Put reserved tomato juice into separate pot and let come to brisk boil. While boiling, add chopped tomatoes and cook for 2 minutes. Take tomatoes off heat, stir in sugar until melted.

Add tomato mixture and all remaining ingredients to casserole in oven. Cook for 15 minutes. Salt to taste. Refrigerate until needed.

Note: Serving suggestions:
Cold — served as an appetizer with crackers.
Cold — served as center of antipasto.
Hot — served as side dish to main course.
Hot — served as topping on pizza for main course.

MAKES 8 TO 10 SERVINGS

TREY YUEN

600 North Causeway Approach, Mandeville, LA 70448; (504) 626-4476.

Just as Oriental pilgrims travel hundreds of miles to worship at holy temples, so do the faithful come from all over Southeastern Louisiana to dine at this startlingly beautiful, expansive gourmet Chinese restaurant on the North Shore of Lake Pontchartrain. For Orleanians, this means a twenty-mile trip across the world's longest bridge, but many make the voyage daily. The food is a superb testimony to the Wong brothers' long record of culinary excellence.

SPRING ROLLS

6 ounces pork, shredded
1 1/2 teaspoons soy sauce
1 teaspoon cornstarch
2 tablespoons oil, divided
1/2 teaspoon minced garlic
4 ounces bamboo shoots, finely shredded
6 to 8 medium dried black mushrooms, pre-soaked and shredded
1 pound cabbage, finely shredded
2 tablespoons sherry wine or rice wine
1 teaspoon salt
3 tablespoons light soy sauce
1 teaspoon sesame oil
2 teaspoons sugar
1/2 teaspoon white pepper
1/2 cup chicken stock (see Basic Stocks)
2 green onions, finely chopped
2 teaspoons cornstarch dissolved in 2 tablespoons water
20 spring roll wrappers (available in oriental markets)
1 egg, beaten

Oil for frying

Marinate pork in soy sauce and cornstarch.

Heat wok or heavy skillet, adding half of oil until hot. Add pork and stir-fry for 30 seconds. Remove pork and drain oil.

Reheat wok/skillet; add remaining oil. Add pork, garlic, bamboo shoots, black mushrooms, and cabbage. Sprinkle with sherry. Add all seasonings along with stock and stir for 2 minutes. Add green onions and cornstarch mixture and cook until thick. Remove filling mixture and place in colander to cool and drain for minimum of 2 hours.

Wrapping the spring rolls: Place about 2 tablespoons of filling just below the center of the wrapper; spread it lengthwise. Fold nearest edge over the mixture, then begin to roll it up fairly tightly. After wrapping is partially rolled, turn in both edges and continue to roll away from the body and seal it with beaten egg.

Deep-fry spring rolls in oil until golden brown. Drain and serve immediately.

MAKES 20 SPRING ROLLS

GUMBOS · SOUPS · SALADS

DON'S SEAFOOD HUT

4309 Johnston St., Lafayette, LA 70503; (318) 981-1141.

As one of the leading seafood establishments in Lafayette, Don's has registered incredible growth in its first decade of business. The restaurant features not only a complete line of Louisiana seafood, imaginatively prepared, but also a host of Cajun and Creole specialties. And from December through June, diners delight to a host of crawfish specialties cooked in the exciting way you will never find outside the Cajun country. Don's also has an excellent lounge with raw oysters on the half shell.

SEAFOOD GUMBO

5 cups cooking oil
4 cups flour
6 quarts of water
2 pints oysters, liquor reserved
1 cup chopped onions
1 cup chopped celery
2 cloves garlic, finely chopped
1 teaspoon salt
1 teaspoon red pepper
2 chicken bouillon cubes
2 pounds shrimp, peeled
1 pound crabmeat
1 tablespoon Kitchen Bouquet (see Glossary)

In large kettle, heat oil until hot. Add flour one cup at a time and stir constantly. When all the flour has been added, stir over medium heat to make a dark brown roux (see Glossary). Roux will take about 45 minutes to turn a deep brown.

In a separate pot, combine water and oyster liquor, vegetables, salt, and pepper. Bring to a boil and simmer 30 minutes. Add chicken bouillon cubes and roux. Simmer another half hour. Add oysters, shrimp, and crabmeat and cook gently an additional 30 minutes. Add Kitchen Bouquet.

MAKES 10 TO 12 SERVINGS

Photograph, Page 23

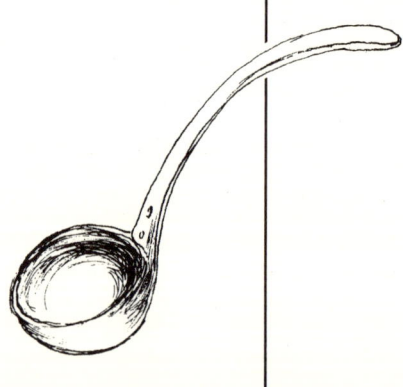

K-PAUL'S LOUISIANA KITCHEN

406 Chartres St., New Orleans, LA 70130; (504) 522-3818.

In the few years since Paul Prudhomme opened his own cafe in the French Quarter, he has become one of America's best-known and most-copied chefs. A Cajun through and through, Prudhomme takes a no-holds-barred approach to his native cuisine, particularly as regards spice levels. His all-purpose seasoning is a mixture of his own making called Cajun Magic, which he packages in various combinations for meat, fish, and chicken. The spice, like K-Paul's cooking, is, to quote his motto, "Totally Hot!"

CAJUN SEAFOOD GUMBO WITH ANDOUILLE SMOKED SAUSAGE

Seafood Seasoning mix (or substitute Seafood Magic)
2 bay leaves, broken in small pieces
2 teaspoons salt
1/2 teaspoon white pepper
1/2 teaspoon ground red pepper (preferably cayenne)
1/2 teaspoon black pepper
1/2 teaspoon dried thyme
1/4 teaspoon dried oregano

2 cups chopped onions
1 1/2 cups chopped green peppers
1 cup chopped celery
3/4 cup vegetable oil
3/4 cup all purpose flour
1 tablespoon minced garlic
5 1/2 cups seafood stock (see basic stocks)
1 pound andouille or smoked pork sausage (see Glossary)
1 pound medium shrimp, peeled
12 medium to large oysters in their liquor
3/4 pound crabmeat
2 1/2 cups hot Basic Cooked Rice (see p. 173)

Note: to serve as a main course, mound 1/4 cup rice in the middle of each serving bowl. Spoon 1 cup gumbo over the rice. Serve half this amount in a cup as an appetizer.

To prepare seasoning mix: Combine all seafood seasoning mix ingredients. Set aside.

Combine the onions, green peppers, and celery in a medium size bowl and set aside.

Heat the oil in a large heavy skillet (preferably not a non-stick type) over high heat until it begins to smoke; about 5 minutes. Gradually add the flour, whisking constantly until roux is dark red-brown to black, about 2 to 4 minutes, being careful not to let it scorch. Immediately add half of the vegetables and stir well (switch to a spoon, from whisk, if necessary). Continue stirring and cooking 1 minute. Then add the remaining vegetables and cook and stir 2 minutes. Stir in the seasoning mix and continue cooking 2 minutes, stirring frequently. Add the garlic and stir about 1 minute more. Remove from heat.

Meanwhile, place the seafood stock in a 5 1/2-quart pot or large Dutch oven. Bring to a boil. Add roux mixture by spoonfuls to the boiling stock, stirring between additions. Bring mixture to a boil. Add the sausage and return to a boil; continue boiling 15 minutes, stirring occasionally. Reduce heat and simmer 10 minutes more. Add the shrimp, undrained oysters, and crabmeat. Return to a boil over high heat, stirring occasionally. Remove from heat and skim any oil from the surface. Serve immediately.

MAKES 10 ENTREE SERVINGS OR 20 APPETIZER SERVINGS

THE GUMBO SHOP

630 St. Peter St., New Orleans, LA 70116; (504) 525-1486.

We probably don't have to tell you what the specialty at the Gumbo Shop is, but you might be interested to know that the restaurant serves two different kinds of gumbo: seafood and chicken andouille. Both are dark brown, thick with roux and lustily spicy. The seafood gumbo contains okra, shrimp, crabs, and rice. The very similar chicken andouille gumbo employs a sausage, made in the river parishes, of ham and garlic with big pieces of chicken. Get a cup of both and learn gumbo from the top down!

CREOLE SEAFOOD OKRA GUMBO

2 to 3 pounds unpeeled shrimp
1 hambone
2 quarts water
2 tablespoons oil
1 quart okra (cut into $1/2$-inch pieces)
$2/3$ cup oil
$1/2$ cup flour
2 medium onions, chopped
1 green pepper, chopped
2 ribs celery, chopped
2 cloves garlic, chopped
$1/4$ cup parsley
1 (16-ounce) can stewed tomatoes
2 small boiled crabs
2 bay leaves
2 tablespoons Worcestershire sauce
$1/2$ teaspoon black pepper
$1/2$ teaspoon cayenne pepper
Salt to taste
6 cups cooked rice

Peel and devein shrimp, saving shells. Set shrimp aside in refrigerator.

Boil shrimp shells and hambone in the water for several hours to make a stock. Strain and set aside.

In heavy skillet, heat 2 tablespoons oil and saute the okra until all ropiness is gone, about $1/2$ hour. Set aside.

In large (6-to-8 quart) heavy pot, make a dark brown roux (see Glossary) with the oil and flour. Add onions, green peppers, celery, garlic, and parsley and saute until tender. Add tomatoes and cook 15 minutes. Add sauteed okra, ham-shrimp stock, crabs (broken in quarters), bay leaves, Worcestershire sauce, black pepper, and cayenne pepper. Bring to slow boil and simmer for about 2 hours, stirring occasionally. Add salt to taste. Add the peeled shrimp and continue cooking until shrimp are done.

Serve over steamed rice. This dish is best if cooked a day in advance and refrigerated overnight, then reheated until hot.

MAKES 6 SERVINGS

CORINNE DUNBAR'S

1617 St. Charles Ave., New Orleans, LA 70130; (504) 525-0689.

Nothing is ordinary about Corinne Dunbar's. There are no waiters or waitresses, but maids who serve you. You are admitted into the parlor not as a diner, but as an expected dinner guest at a private party. There is no menu; you are served the complete Creole dinner of the evening. All of this has been going on in the one hundred forty-year-old mansion for fifty years, ever since Corinne Dunbar turned her talents at entertaining guests to the service of the public.

GUMBO GOUTER

1 tablespoon shortening
1 large eggplant, peeled and diced
3 green peppers, chopped
$1/2$ pound okra, sliced
2 large onions, chopped
1 clove garlic, minced
1 (16-ounce) can tomatoes
$1/2$ teaspoon sugar
Salt and pepper to taste
$1/2$ cup water
Salt pork (optional)
2 cups cooked peeled shrimp (optional)

Melt shortening in sauce pan. Add all ingredients, except shrimp. Cover tightly and simmer $1 1/2$ hours. Stir often to avoid sticking.

Add shrimp just before removing from heat. Serve as vegetable dish.

May also be served as main course when shrimp is added.

MAKES 6 SERVINGS

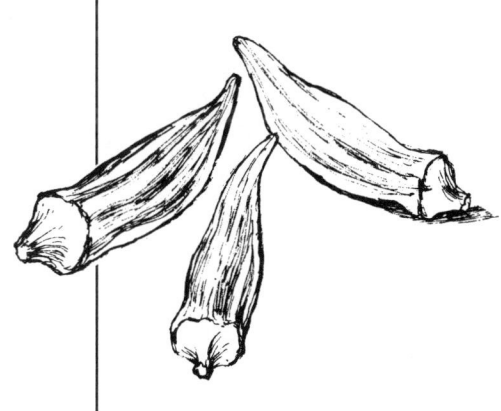

JEFFREY'S RIVERSIDE RESTAURANT
915 River Rd., Norco, LA 70079; (504) 764-9904.

Two elements dominate the scene in Norco, the Mississippi River and the oil refineries. Both aspects of Norco life are reflected in Jeffrey's decor. Posters and paintings depict local plantation homes and the Oz-like wonder of the industrial plants. The feel of the restaurant is airy and casual, and the location on the historic Great River Road makes the restaurant a rendezvous point for the people of the river parishes.

ANDOUILLE FILE GUMBO

3 quarts water
3 pounds andouille sausage, cut into 1/2-inch slices (see Glossary)
1/2 cup butter
3 medium onions, finely chopped
1 small green pepper, finely chopped
1/2 cup vegetable oil
3/4 cup flour
1 quart fresh oysters and liquor
3 bunches green onions, finely chopped
2 sprigs parsley, finely chopped
Salt to taste
Red and black pepper to taste
1 tablespoon filé powder (see Glossary)

Rapidly boil andouille in stock pot with the water, for 15 to 20 minutes. Remove andouille; set aside. Reserve stock.

In a skillet melt butter and saute all vegetables, except green onion tops.

In a separate heavy pot heat oil; gradually add flour, stirring constantly, until roux is the color of peanut butter. Add vegetables; mix well and cook 5 minutes.

Add andouille and combine with the stock. After mixture reaches boiling, cook 45 to 60 minutes on medium-low heat until it reaches the consistency of light cream. During last 10 minutes of cooking add oysters. During last 5 minutes of cooking add green onion tops and parsley. Season to taste with salt and pepper. If desired, add pinch of filé to each portion when serving.

Note: For maximum flavor, allow to stand for 1 or 2 hours or overnight. Reheat to boiling and serve with steamed rice.

MAKES 12 SERVINGS

BOUDIN KING

906 West Division St., Jennings, LA 70546; (318) 824-6593.

The item for which the Boudin King is named is an ubiquitous Cajun treat—boudin, a spicy sausage of rice and pork in a casing,. Proprietor Ellis Cormier is one of Acadiana's premier purveyors of the unique treat, but boudin is not the only thing on tap in his restaurant. Catfish, crawfish, and other Cajun seafood dishes, as well as authentic gumbos, fill out the menu of taste-tempting delights.

CHICKEN GUMBO

2/3 cup all purpose flour
2/3 cup cooking oil
1 (3-pound) chicken cut for frying
Salt and pepper to taste
3 tablespoons cooking oil
1 cup chopped onions
1/2 cup chopped green onions
1/4 cup finely minced parsley
2 quarts hot water
Salt to taste
Black and cayenne pepper to taste
3 cups cooked rice

Make a roux by mixing the flour and the 2/3 cup oil in a heavy pot. Stir constantly over a moderate heat until flour is a rich dark brown. Remove immediately from heat, continuing to stir until temperature is low enough for browning to stop.

Salt and pepper chicken and fry in the 3 tablespoons oil until golden brown. Remove from frying pan. Add onions to the same oil and cook until onions are lightly browned.

Place browned chicken, sauteed onions, green onions, parsley, and water into a large pot. Season to taste with salt and pepper. When water comes to a boil, add roux. Stir well, lower heat and simmer, uncovered, 1 1/2 to 2 hours.

Serve over cooked long grain rice.

MAKES 6 TO 8 SERVINGS

THE GUMBO SHOP
630 St. Peter St., New Orleans, LA 70116; (504) 525-1486.

The word "gumbo" derives from an African word for okra, which is one of the principal ingredients of a good seafood gumbo. The dish arrived in New Orleans with the first wave of freed slaves from Haiti, and was immediately taken up by the French Creoles of the city. It has since been a staple of New Orleans cuisine, and is found in as many forms as there are gumbo cooks. The Gumbo Shop has two different gumbos, and an array of other local platters.

CHICKEN ANDOUILLE GUMBO

1 (2 1/2-pound) chicken
3 quarts water
1 1/2 pounds fresh okra
2 tablespoons oil
1/2 cup oil
1/2 cup flour
1 large onion, chopped
1 large green pepper, chopped
2 ribs celery, chopped
2 cloves garlic, minced
1 (16-ounce) can tomatoes
1 pound andouille sausage, sliced (see Glossary)
1 bay leaf
1 teaspoon thyme
1 teaspoon basil
1 teaspoon cayenne pepper
1 teaspoon black pepper
2 teaspoons salt
1 tablespoon filé powder (see Glossary)
4 cups cooked rice

Cut chicken into 8 pieces, cover with the water, and simmer for approximately 1 hour, until chicken is tender and easily removed from the bones. Pour off stock into large bowl and set aside. Allow chicken to cool, remove meat from bones and set aside.

Meanwhile, slice okra and saute in the 2 tablespoons of the oil until all ropiness is gone (about 1/2 hour).

In a heavy pot, combine the 1/2 cup oil and 1/2 cup flour. Cook over medium heat, stirring frequently, to make a dark brown roux. Add onion, green pepper, celery, and garlic and saute until vegetables are tender. Add sauteed okra, tomatoes, and sliced andouille sausage. Cook for about 15 minutes. Add bay leaf, thyme, basil, pepper, and salt.

Add the chicken stock, mix well, and bring to a slow boil. Simmer for approximately 1 1/2 hours with the pot loosely covered, stirring occasionally. Add cooked chicken and simmer an additional 15 minutes.

Remove from heat. Skim off excess fat. Slowly stir in filé. Do not reboil after adding in filé as this tends to make the gumbo stringy.

Serve over cooked rice.

MAKES 4 SERVINGS

BRENNAN'S

417 Royal St., New Orleans, LA 70130; (504) 525-9711.

The pink stucco building on famous Royal Street in the heart of the French Quarter houses Brennan's in classic New Orleans style. The structure was built in 1801 and saw many uses until it was taken over by the Brennans in 1946. With an exquisite New Orleans courtyard and many small dining rooms, it is one of the most beautiful venues imaginable in which to take a meal. Pip, Ted, and Jimmy Brennan, the current proprietors, have created a setting and style to match Brennan's renowned fare.

TURTLE SOUP

3 pounds turtle meat
5 quarts water
2 bay leaves
2 teaspoons Italian seasoning
1 tablespoon salt
1/2 cup chopped white onion
1/2 cup finely chopped green pepper
1/2 cup finely chopped celery
1 1/2 cups finely chopped parsley
1 lemon, thinly sliced
1 teaspoon paprika
1/2 cup tomato paste
1 teaspoon caramel color (or Kitchen Bouquet)
1/4 cup Worcestershire sauce
1 cup sherry
1 cup flour
3/4 cup butter
1 teaspoon salt or to taste
1 teaspoon black pepper
2 cups finely chopped hard boiled eggs

In a large saucepan or kettle combine the turtle meat, water, bay leaves, Italian seasoning, and the 1 tablespoon salt. Bring to a boil over high heat, then lower the heat slightly and cook until the turtle meat is quite tender. Add more water while cooking as necessary to maintain about 3 quarts of liquid at all times. Strain and reserve the 3 quarts of stock. Cut the turtle meat into small cubes and set aside.

Add all chopped vegetables, lemon slices, paprika, tomato paste, caramel color, Worcestershire sauce, and sherry to stock in a large saucepan. Cook over low heat for 20 minutes or until vegetables are very tender.

In a separate pan, add flour to melted butter stirring to a smooth consistency. Add this roux to stock while stirring, along with turtle meat, salt and pepper and eggs. Simmer for 15 minutes and serve at once.

MAKES 8 SERVINGS

KOLB'S

125 St. Charles Ave., New Orleans, LA 70130; (504) 522-8279.

Kolb's is one of New Orleans' oldest restaurants, having been founded by Conrad Kolb in 1899. It has remained in the same classic German premises ever since. The building dates back to 1845, and was the original home of the Louisiana Jockey Club. The fascinating system of ceiling fans was manufactured for New Orleans' first world's fair, the Cotton Centennial in 1884, after which they were installed at Kolb's. The restaurant is a perennial favorite of New Orleans businessmen.

TURTLE SOUP

1 small white onion, chopped
1/2 cup chopped celery
1/4 cup oil
1 bay leaf
1 (12-ounce) can whole tomatoes, crushed
1 (12-ounce) can tomato paste
3/4 pound turtle meat, cut into cubes
1 tablespoon ground ginger
1 cup flour
3 tablespoons sugar
3 quarts beef bouillon
4 chicken bouillon cubes
4 beef bouillon cubes
1 cup sherry
1/2 cup Burgundy
Juice of 1/2 lemon
2 hard boiled eggs, chopped

Saute onions and celery in oil. Set aside. In a large kettle combine bay leaf, tomatoes, tomato paste, and turtle meat. Add the onions and celery and simmer 1 hour.

In separate container, combine ginger, flour, sugar, bouillon, bouillon cubes, wine, and lemon juice. Add to turtle mixture and cook and additional 20 to 30 minutes until hot. Add chopped eggs.

MAKES 14 SERVINGS

Photograph, Page 17

DELMONICO

1300 St. Charles Ave., New Orleans, LA 70130; (504) 525-4937.

Delmonico has held an important position on the Avenue near Lee Circle since the beginning of the century. Its two main dining rooms display a wonderful antique charm. Behind the bar, in the rear room, is a mural painted by John McCrady depicting life on the Mississippi River. The four private dining rooms are in constant use by uptowners, who consider Delmonico to be almost their "clubhouse."

TURTLE SOUP AU SHERRY

2 pounds turtle meat, finely diced
2 quarts water
2 ribs celery, sliced
1 onion, chopped
1 clove garlic, minced
1/4 teaspoon salt
1/4 cup olive oil
1/4 cup vegetable oil
1/4 cup all purpose flour
1 1/2 cups chopped leeks or green onions
1 cup chopped tomato
Salt to taste
8 teaspoons dry sherry
4 hard boiled eggs, chopped

Combine turtle meat, water, celery, onion, garlic, and salt in a 4-quart kettle; heat to boiling. Reduce heat and simmer 30 minutes, skimming top if necessary.

Heat oils in a medium skillet until warm. Stir in flour; cook over low heat, stirring constantly, until flour is browned. Add leeks and tomato; cook, stirring frequently, until leeks are lightly browned.

Stir flour mixture into hot broth; cook until thickened and bubbly. Add salt to taste, stir in additional water if soup is too thick. Ladle soup into serving bowls. Stir 1 teaspoon sherry into each, and top with chopped egg.

MAKES 8 SERVINGS

Photograph, Page 18

BON TON CAFE

401 Magazine St., New Orleans, LA 70130; (504) 524-3386.

The Bon Ton Café has been in existence in New Orleans' coffee-merchant district since the early years of this century. But the restaurant began to achieve real prominence when Alvin Pierce and his talented wife and cook Alzina took over in 1953. They assembled a menu of Creole and Cajun specialties which have made the Bon Ton one of the hardest places in the downtown area to find an empty table.

CRAWFISH BISQUE

Bisque Gravy
1 cup flour
1 cup plus 2 tablespoons vegetable oil, divided
1 cup chopped onions
1/4 cup chopped green onions (white and green parts)
2 teaspoons finely chopped garlic
1/4 cup chopped green pepper
5 1/2 cups water
1 tablespoon salt (or more)
1 teaspoon black pepper
1 pound peeled crawfish tails
1/2 cup crawfish fat
1/3 cup finely chopped parsley

Stuffed Crawfish Heads
2/3 cup finely chopped onions
1 tablespoon chopped green onions (white and green parts)
1 teaspoon finely chopped garlic
2 tablespoons vegetable oil
3/4 pound peeled crawfish tails finely chopped
1/4 cup crawfish fat
3 tablespoons chopped parsley
1/2 teaspoon salt
1/4 teaspoon black pepper
1/2 cup bread crumbs
30 crawfish heads, cleaned for stuffing (see Note)
2 eggs, beaten
Flour to coat
Vegetable oil for deep-frying
6 hard boiled eggs, halved lengthwise

To Make Bisque Gravy: Make a roux by combining the flour and a cup of oil and stirring the mixture over low heat in a heavy skillet until well mixed and golden brown, approximately 20 minutes. Stir constantly, being careful not to burn the roux.

Using the remaining 2 tablespoons of vegetable oil in a large saucepan, saute the onions, green onions, garlic, and green pepper until they are limp, approximately 2 to 3 minutes. Add roux to the vegetables and mix well. Add the water, salt, and black pepper, and cook for 45 minutes, stirring often.

Add the crawfish tails and fat, and simmer for 1 hour over low heat, stirring occasionally. Stir in the parsley.

To Make the Stuffing for Crawfish Heads: Saute the onions, green onions, and garlic in 2 tablespoons of vegetable oil until the vegetables are limp, approximately 2 to 3 minutes. Add the chopped crawfish tails and crawfish fat and stir until well mixed. Simmer over low heat for 15 minutes. Add the chopped parsley, salt, and black pepper. Remove from the heat and let cool. Add the bread crumbs, and combine well.

Stuff each cleaned crawfish head with 1 tablespoon of the stuffing. Dip the crawfish heads in the beaten eggs, and coat thickly with flour. Deep-fry the crawfish heads in hot oil for 2 to 3 minutes or until they are golden brown, turning them with a slotted spoon. Drain the crawfish on a paper towel, keeping them warm until ready to serve.

CRAWFISH BISQUE *(Continued)*

Taste the bisque gravy for seasoning before serving and make adjustments if necessary.

To serve, ladle the bisque gravy into a tureen or individual bowls. For each portion add 5 stuffed crawfish heads and 2 hard-boiled egg halves.

Note: You can buy professionally cleaned crawfish "heads" or body shells, or you can clean them yourself. After removing the tails, cut off the top of the head including the eyes. Scoop the shell clean, and pick out the fat (be sure to save the fat and use it in the bisque gravy). Discard any intestinal matter. Soak the cleaned heads in baking soda and water, and rinse. If heads are unavailable, the Bon Ton forms meatballs out of the stuffing, dips the balls in egg batter, and deep-fries.

MAKES 6 SERVINGS

Photograph, Page 24

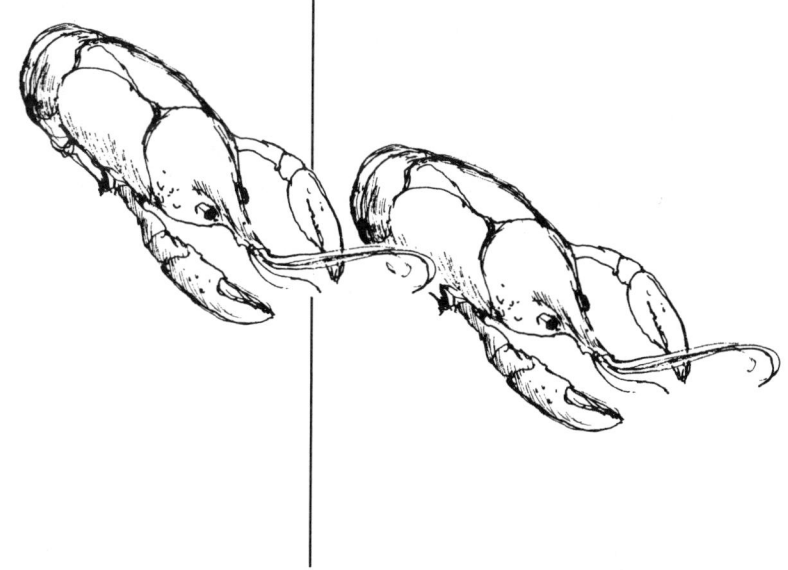

MARTI'S

1041 Dumaine St., New Orleans, LA 70116; (504) 524-6060.

Until Marti's opened in the early seventies, such Creole classics as red beans and rice, pannee veal, grilled andouille, and dirty rice were the exclusive purvey of neighborhood lunch restaurants. Marti Shambra thought that the food was good enough to be served in a comfortable dining room with good service, after as well as before dark, and with an eye to polish. And that's the story of Marti's—giving the best of everyday Creole food its due.

CHILLED CRAWFISH CURRY

2 pounds peeled crawfish tails
Water to cover
1/2 cup butter
1/2 cup oil
2 medium onions, chopped
1 bunch green onions, chopped
4 cloves garlic, minced
3 cups flour
1/2 rib celery, finely minced
1/2 teaspoon thyme
4 teaspoons mild curry powder
2 teaspoons salt
1 teaspoon white pepper
1 teaspoon paprika
1 cup tomato paste
Dash Worcestershire sauce
1 cup chopped fresh tomatoes

Boil the crawfish in water for 7 to 8 minutes. Remove them but reserve the water. Chop half of the tails and reserve the other half whole.

In a Dutch oven, melt the butter and blend in the oil. In it saute the onions and green onions. When softened, add garlic and saute until the onions are clear. Then stir in the flour and cook over low heat for 1 minute. Do not allow it to brown. Add the chopped crawfish, celery, thyme, curry powder, salt, pepper, paprika, tomato paste, and Worcestershire. Let this mixture cook for 3 minutes over low heat, stirring.

Now add the water reserved from the crawfish tails and enough water or fish stock to make three gallons. Add the tomatoes and bay leaves. Stir well and bring to a boil. Reduce heat and simmer mixture 10 minutes or more if a thicker sauce is desired. Remove bay leaves. Add the whole crawfish tails and allow the mixture to cool.

Store covered overnight in the refrigerator to allow flavors to blend. Serve chilled.

MAKES 24 SERVINGS

PADDLEWHEEL EXPRESS

One American Place, Baton Rouge, LA 70802; (504) 387-4943.

Personality is a strong suit at the Paddlewheel Express, a restaurant in the most modern part of downtown Baton Rouge, but with the antique charm of the old steamboat days. Proprietor Fred Kimball, a restaurateur for over 25 years, is well-known to his regular customers. He can be seen comparing notes on skiing and canoeing, asking how the kids are doing in school, discussing the fortunes of the LSU Tigers, and, of course, collecting compliments on the great lunches and salads his restaurant serves.

CORN AND SHIMP SOUP

1/4 cup butter or margarine
2 tablespoons flour
1 small yellow onion, chopped
1 quart water
1/2 tablespoon salt, or to taste
1 teaspoon red pepper
1/2 cup whole crushed tomatoes
2 chicken bouillon cubes, crushed
2 1/2 cups whole kernel corn
1 1/2 cups raw shrimp, peeled and deveined

Melt butter or margarine in soup pot. Add flour and chopped onion and saute 10 to 15 minutes.

Add water, salt, pepper, tomatoes, and bouillon cubes and simmer 15 minutes over medium heat.

Add corn and shrimp, simmer another 30 minutes, then serve piping hot.

MAKES 6 SERVINGS

Photograph, Page 24

CAFE RANI

315 N. Vermont, Covington, LA 70433; (504) 893-4383.

This pleasant little bistro is run by a talented chef, Gary Darling. It is named for the chef's daughter, and the premises are a charming touch of Louisiana culture. The dining rooms are decorated with posters from the many Louisiana festivals. The style of cooking is New American, with some borrowings from the French and Creole cuisines. The menu changes every day to reflect the freshest food on the market.

OYSTER ARTICHOKE SOUP

2 cups butter
1 cup chopped onion
1 cup chopped celery
¼ cup minced parsley
2 teaspoons minced garlic
¼ cup flour
2 quarts oysters, liquor reserved
Water or chicken stock (see Basic Stocks)
3 cans artichoke hearts, coarsely chopped
2 cups cream
1 tablespoon salt
2 tablespoons white pepper
1 tablespoon cayenne pepper, or to taste
1 teaspoon thyme

In large kettle, melt butter and saute onion, celery, parsley, and garlic, about 5 minutes until tender. Add flour and cook 5 minutes.

Set aside 1 quart of whole oysters and mince the remaining quart of oysters, reserving liquor. Add water or chicken stock to liquor to make 3 quarts liquid.

Add artichoke hearts, oyster stock, minced oysters, cream, salt, pepper, cayenne, and thyme to sauteed vegetables. Bring to boil. Reduce heat and simmer 10 minutes. Add whole oysters just before serving.

MAKES 8 SERVINGS

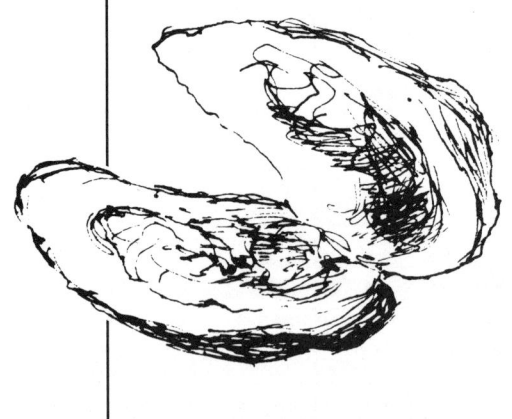

THE PEPPERMILL

3524 Severn Ave., Metairie, LA 70002; (504) 455-2266.

The flowery rooms of this restaurant, with their hanging greenery and huge wicker chairs, attract a fiercely loyal clientele. They enjoy the fresh seafood, particularly those dishes involving crabmeat, the baby white veal, and the prime steaks. The cooking style is an interesting hybrid of Creole and Italian, the creations of Josie Riccobono, whose family has been in the restaurant business in New Orleans for over sixty years. The atmosphere is convivial and casual, and an easy enjoyment is assured.

OYSTER AND ARTICHOKE SOUP

2 quarts oysters in their liquor
1 onion, finely minced
3 ribs celery, finely minced
2 to 3 leeks, minced, or 8 to 10 minced green onions
2 cloves garlic, finely minced
1/2 cup butter
1/4 cup olive oil
4 tablespoons flour
1 (14-ounce) can artichoke hearts coarsely chopped, and liquid
6 cups chicken stock (see Basic Stocks)
2 bay leaves
Pinch oregano and thyme
Salt and pepper to taste

Poach oysters in oyster liquor until their edges begin to curl. Remove from liquor and chop oysters coarsely. Strain liquor and set aside.

Saute onion, celery, leeks, and garlic in butter and oil until onions are transparent (do not brown). Add flour and cook approximately 5 minutes stirring constantly.

Then add artichokes with liquid, chicken stock, oyster liquor, bay leaves, oregano, thyme, salt, and pepper. Simmer 15 minutes. Add oysters and simmer 10 minutes longer. Correct seasonings and serve in heated soup bowls with hot French bread and whipped butter.

MAKES 8 SERVINGS

LA COQUILLE

One Shell Square, New Orleans, LA 70139; (504) 523-7259.

The name of this restaurant is French for "the shell"—a reference to the skyscraper (the tallest in New Orleans) in which it is housed. While most restaurants treat lunch as a secondary meal, La Coquille puts its best foot forward at noon—since lunch is the only meal it serves. The menu offers as wide a variety at lunch as most menus do at dinner. It includes a wealth of seafood dishes, as well as unusual steak and veal creations. La Coquille is a very popular restaurant; tables fill up early.

BONGO BONGO *(Oyster and Spinach Soup)*

3 cups oysters, in their liquor
1 bay leaf
Pinch thyme
1/2 cup butter
1 rib celery, diced
1 onion, diced
1 green pepper, diced
2 bunches fresh spinach, chopped
1/2 cup flour
1/2 cup white wine
3/4 teaspoon chopped garlic
2/3 cup heavy cream
Salt and pepper to taste

Poach the oysters in their liquor with bay leaf and pinch of thyme, until their edges curl. Remove and cut the oysters into large dice. Remove the bay leaf and measure the stock. Add enough water to make 1 quart of stock and set aside.

Melt the butter in a heavy sauce pan over medium heat. Add celery, onion, green pepper, and spinach and saute until tender. Sprinkle in flour and cook for 5 to 8 minutes. Then add the wine, garlic, and reserved oyster stock and let simmer for 20 minutes. Add the cream, the diced oysters, and season to taste.

MAKES 6 SERVINGS

THE OAKS PLANTATION

Avenue of Oaks, Old River Rd., Destrehan, LA 70047; (504) 764-1798.

A seven-acre plot of land on the mighty Mississippi River, twenty miles upstream from New Orleans, is the homestead of Judge and Mrs. Joel Chaisson and the site of an exciting new restaurant. The Oaks Plantation features live lobster, prime steaks, and seafood in its rustic dining rooms. It looks like a barn from the outside, but inside everything gleams with brass or is lush with greenery

POTATO/CHEESE/LOBSTER SOUP

4 cups potatoes, peeled and diced
$1/4$ cup grated carrots
2 quarts chicken stock (see Basic Stocks)
$1 1/2$ cups finely chopped onions
$1/2$ cup finely chopped shallots
2 ribs celery, finely chopped
$1/2$ cup clarified butter, divided (see Glossary)
1 cup coarsely chopped cooked lobster (see Note)
4 tablespoons flour
$1 1/2$ cups grated Cheddar cheese
$1/2$ cup heavy cream
Dash Tabasco sauce
2 tablespoons finely chopped parsley

Boil potatoes and carrots in chicken stock until tender.

In a skillet, saute until transparent the onions, shallots, and celery in $1/4$ cup of the clarified butter. Add this mixture to the stock along with the lobster.

In same skillet used for seasonings, stir and cook flour and remaining clarified butter for 5 minutes without browning. Add to soup and mix well.

Lower heat and add grated cheese. When melted, add cream and Tabasco. Serve hot, sprinkled with finely chopped parsley.

Note: Variation: chopped ham may be substituted for lobster.

MAKES 10 SERVINGS

RIVERVIEW RESTAURANT

Marriott Hotel, 555 Canal St., New Orleans, LA 70140; (504) 581-1000.

A well-named restaurant, this. From the top-floor perch which this restaurant occupies, there's a superb view in all directions, and the river finally looks the way it does on a map. The menu emphasis is on polished versions of New Orleans and continental dishes. The seating is unusually comfortable, with the celebrated view available from virtually any table. The adjacent lounge features live music, and is a favorite last stop for Orleanians.

CREME OF LEEK CHANTILLY

1 bunch leeks
1/4 cup butter
1/2 cup chopped onions
1/2 cup unsifted flour
2 cups chicken stock (see Basic Stocks)
2 cups milk
1/8 teaspoon ground nutmeg
Salt and white pepper to taste
1/2 teaspoon monosodium glutamate
Garnish: 1 cup heavy cream, whipped

Cut off tough part of leeks and split stalk lengthwise into halves. Slice green part of stalk into 1-inch pieces. Wash thoroughly twice in cold water.

Saute green parts of leek and onions in butter until transparent. Stir in flour and cook, but do not brown. Add cold chicken stock, milk, and spices. Whisk and bring to boil; lower heat and simmer 45 minutes stirring occasionally.

Meanwhile cut washed white parts of leeks into thin slices. Strain hot mixture through a colander. Add white parts of leek to strained mixture and cook on medium heat for 5 more minutes.

Spoon into 4 dishes and top each cup of soup with spoonful of whipped cream.

MAKES 4 SERVINGS

THE VERSAILLES

2100 St. Charles Ave., New Orleans, LA 70140; (504) 524-2535.

Most chef-owned restaurants tend to be on the modest side in both size and appointments. Not so The Versailles. It occupies three large dining rooms and a hotel-scale kitchen. The favored room is the St. Charles Avenue and its historic streetcar. More classic in style is the Trianon Room, with its red velvet walls and crystal chanderliers. The Sun King lounge is a tribute to Louis XIV, after whom Louisiana is named.

CREME OF LEEK CHANTILLY

3 or 4 medium size leeks, finely chopped, (white part only), greens reserved
$5^{1}/_{2}$ cups water
1 tablespoon minced garlic
4 tablespoons unsalted butter
5 tablespoons all purpose flour
2 chicken bouillon cubes
2 bay leaves
$1/_{2}$ cup heavy cream
Salt and white pepper to taste

Garnish: 1 cup heavy cream, whipped

Boil leak greens in $5^{1}/_{2}$ cups water for 30 minutes to make a stock. Drain and reserve stock.

Cook chopped leeks and garlic gently in butter until they begin to turn clear. Add flour, stirring constantly. Cook the roux 10 minutes over low heat (do not brown). Add leek stock in three stages, mixing thoroughly each time. Add bouillon cubes and bay leaf and simmer gently 25 to 30 minutes. Finally add heavy cream with salt and pepper to taste and simmer 10 more minutes.

To serve, ladle boiling soup into hot cups or bowls. Garnish each serving with a dollop of freshly whipped cream.

MAKES 6 SERVINGS

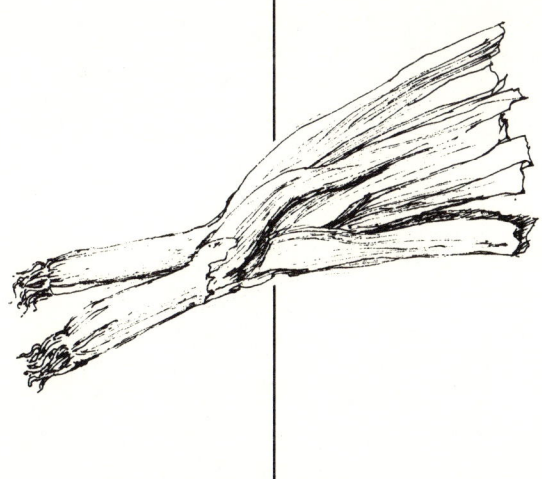

CORINNE DUNBAR'S

1617 St. Charles Ave., New Orleans, LA 70130; (504) 525-0689.

The story of Corinne Dunbar's is as fascinating as the restaurant itself—an 1840s townhouse on St. Charles Avenue, where diners feel more like guests in a private home than patrons in a restaurant. But that's the way Corinne Dunbar wanted it. An elegant Creole lady forced by circumstance to work, she opened her home to the public and served them with fine family recipes in a lovely antique setting. That was fifty years ago, and the tradition remains.

RED BEAN SOUP

1/2 pound dried red kidney beans
Water to cover
2 tablespoons butter
1 small onion, chopped
1 quart water
2 cloves garlic, chopped
2 ribs celery, chopped
2 bay leaves
2 sprigs fresh thyme or 1/4 teaspoon dried thyme
1 teaspoon Worcestershire sauce
1/2 pound ham, finely ground
Salt and pepper to taste
4 tablespoons dry sherry

Garnish: *finely chopped hard boiled egg, 4 lemon slices*

In a large pot soak beans in water to cover overnight. Drain beans and discard soaking water.

In a skillet melt butter and saute onion until brown. Add 1 quart water to beans along with garlic, celery, bay leaves, thyme, and Worcestershire sauce. Simmer about 3 hours. Strain mixture through course strainer, mash with large spoon, and return to water. Add ham, salt, and pepper and reheat to blend flavors.

To serve, place 1 tablespoon sherry in bottom of each soup cup. Pour soup and garnish with chopped egg and lemon slice.

MAKES 4 SERVINGS

FLAMINGOS CAFE

1625 St. Charles Ave., New Orleans, LA 70130; (504) 523-6141.

This is one of the wildest-looking restaurants you are likely to ever encounter. It is a renovated St. Charles Avenue three-story house, the leitmotif of which is the pink bird of the name. Nobody knows for sure how many representations of flamingos there are in Flamingos, but one thing is for sure — they are everywhere. You will see neon flamingos, flamingo murals, "Flamingo" on the juke box, newspaper clippings about flamingos, on and on, in a dining room glowing with bright pink and green walls. Unforgettable!

FLAMINGOS COLD CUCUMBER SOUP "JORDAN"

3 cucumbers, peeled and diced
1 bunch green onions with tops, chopped
3 3/4 cups canned chicken stock, fat removed
1 teaspoon freshly ground black pepper
1 teaspoon garlic salt
1 tablespoon cornstarch, mixed with small amount of water
3/4 cup heavy cream
1 cup sour cream
2 tablespoons fresh or freeze-dried chives
Garnish: cucumber slices and additional sour cream

Simmer chopped cucumbers and onions with tops in chicken stock until the cucumbers and onions are tender. Add spices and cornstarch and simmer until slightly thickened. Cool.

Add cream, sour cream, and chives. Mix in blender or food processor until smooth. If additional color is wanted, a drop of green food color may be added. Chill until cold, overnight if possible.

Remix or shake before serving. Garnish with cucumber slice and dollop of sour cream atop.

MAKES 8 SERVINGS

MIKE & TONY'S

10270 Airline Highway, Baton Rouge, LA 70816; (504) 292-6751.
1934 Scenic Highway, Baton Rouge, LA 70816; (504) 357-7573.

The two locations of Mike & Tony's, both essential Baton Rouge restaurants, are different in all ways except in the food, which is great at both addresses. The Airline Highway location is the more elegant and comfortable of the two, but many prefer the old-style Baton Rouge hospitality of the Scenic Highway restaurant. Since 1940, Mike & Tony's has been a favorite.

CREAMY BROCCOLI SOUP

6 tablespoons butter
6 tablespoons all purpose flour
3 quarts chicken stock (see Basic Stocks)
Cayenne pepper to taste
3 pounds chopped broccoli
2 cups half and half, heated

Melt butter over low heat. Blend in flour, stirring until well blended. Remove from heat; add chicken stock and cayenne pepper while stirring. Add chopped broccoli and mix well.

Heat to boiling, stirring constantly. Reduce heat and simmer slowly 15 minutes stirring occasionally. Add hot half and half. Serve hot.

MAKES 12 SERVINGS

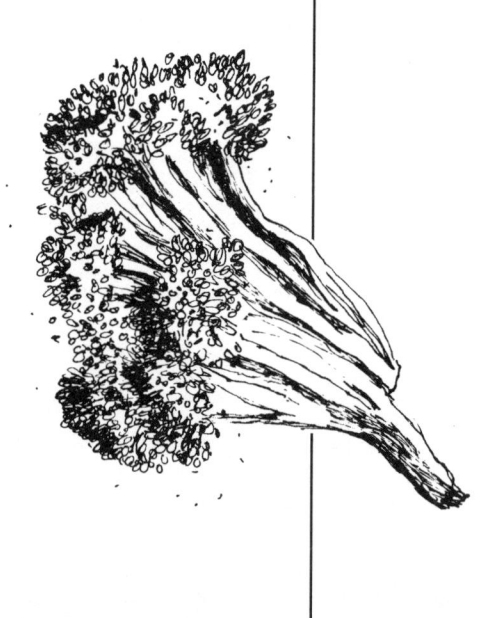

KOLB'S

125 St. Charles Ave., New Orleans, LA 70130; (504) 522-8279.

One thing's for sure about Kolb's — once you have been there, you will never forget it. This gigantic restaurant has two big dining rooms, both decorated with classic German accents. Most striking in the main dining room is an antique ceiling fan system which is driven by an elaborate system of interconnected belts. One of these leads to a crank which "Ludwig" turns day and night. There is an assortment of posters of Germany and a large collection of beer steins.

KOLB'S HOUSE SALAD

1 cup creole mustard
¼ cup tarragon vinegar
¼ cup salad oil
1 tablespoon sugar
¼ cup water
2 tablespoons lemon juice
1 medium head iceburg lettuce, broken
3 large tomatoes, cut in wedges
3 avocados, peeled and sliced

In a bowl combine mustard, vinegar, oil, sugar, water, and lemon juice.

Pour over lettuce, tomatoes, and avocados before serving.

MAKES 6 SERVINGS

Photograph, Page 18

PADDLEWHEEL EXPRESS

One American Place, Baton Rouge, LA 70802; (504) 387-4943.

Amid the skyscrapers which continue to grow in burgeoning downtown Baton Rouge, this restaurant is located on the plaza level of one of the city's most modern buildings. The decor of Paddlewheel Express recreates the world of Mark Twain, the world of sternwheel steamboats, southern belles, and colorful calliopes. The Mississippi River is right outside the door. The restaurant is popular with downtown office workers and tourists alike.

ESQUIRE SALAD

2 heads iceberg lettuce, torn into bite-size pieces, large outside leaves reserved
3 tomatoes, cut in bite-size pieces
1/4 cup grated Parmesan cheese
1/2 cup ripe olives, sliced
1/2 cup bleu cheese dressing
1/4 cup chopped parsley
Salt and pepper to taste

Line salad bowl or salad plates with large outside lettuce leaves.

Combine all ingredients and toss in large bowl. Place tossed salad into lined salad bowl or plates.

Serve chilled.

MAKES 6 SERVINGS

Photograph, Page 22

ANTOINE'S

713 St. Louis St., New Orleans, LA 70130; (504) 581-4422.

Antoine's has occupied its place on St. Louis Street in the French Quarter since its 1840 founding. It is an enormous property, with three floors of public and private rooms. A tour of just the first-floor rooms is fascinating. There is, for instance, the Mystery Room, where a painting of a girl at her dresser changes into something else before your eyes. The Rex and Comus Rooms are named after the two most famous Mardi Gras krewes, and have a grandeur appropriate for those kings.

FONDS D'ARTICHAUTS BAYARD *(Hearts of Artichoke Bayard)*

6 cooked artichokes
18 anchovy fillets
1 cup minced celery
1 cup minced parsley
1 cup minced green onion
1 teaspoon salt
1/2 teaspoon ground white pepper
3 cups chopped lettuce
6 slices tomato, halved
1 hard boiled egg, chopped
1 1/2 cups vinaigrette sauce
3 teaspoons caviar

Vinaigrette Sauce
1/2 teaspoon salt
1/4 teaspoon finely ground white pepper
1/2 teaspoon dry mustard
1/3 cup vinegar
1 cup olive oil

Scrape the meat from the leaves of the cooked artichokes. Retain the meat and the hearts and discard the rest. Mince 12 of the anchovy fillets and mix together with the celery, parsley, green onions, salt, pepper, and the artichoke scrapings. Form the mixture into six balls, equal in size, and squeeze out the excess moisture.

Cover each of six chilled salad plates with 1/2 cup chopped lettuce. Place an artichoke heart in the center of each plate and top each with a ball of the minced vegetable mixture. Garnish with two halves of a slice of tomato. Chill.

To make vinaigrette sauce: put all ingredients into a bottle and shake to mix. Store at room temperature. Makes 1 1/2 cups.

To serve, pour 1/4 cup vinaigrette sauce over the top of each bayard and sprinkle with chopped egg. Top each one with one anchovy fillet formed into a ring and filled with 1/2 teaspoon caviar.

MAKES 6 SERVINGS

LA SAVOIE

94 Friedrichs Ave., Metairie, LA 70005; (504) 831-1108.

This new restaurant is in the beautiful setting of oak-tree-lined Old Metairie. The trees in the area of the restaurant, are lit elegantly with tiny white bulbs. La Savorie is quartered in a handsomely-redecorated house; the dining room is divided into a number of intimate areas. All of them are within eyeshot of two tables which hold the evening's selections of appetizers and desserts.

SALAD SAVOYARD

Dressing
1 tablespoon Dijon mustard
2 ounces wine vinegar
1/2 cup olive oil
1 egg
Salt and pepper to taste

1 whole chicken breast
1 tablespoon butter
1 ounce port wine
1 head bibb lettuce
1 cucumber, sliced
1 tomato, diced
1 carrot, shredded
4 mushrooms, sliced

To make dressing: Combine all dressing ingredients in a blender or food processor until well mixed.

Debone and skin chicken breast. Pound and flatten between plastic wrap to about 1/8-inch thickness. Slice into bite-size strips. Quickly saute chicken strips in pan with butter and port wine, less than 1 minute. Add dressing to pan and keep warm.

To serve divide lettuce between plates, top with cucumbers, tomatoes, carrots, and mushrooms. Pour warm chicken and dressing equally over each plate and serve.

MAKES 4 SERVINGS

THE COURT OF TWO SISTERS

613 Royal St., New Orleans, LA 70130; (504) 522-7261.

One could hardly get a more intense taste of New Orleans than by partaking of the Court of Two Sisters' daily Jazz Brunch. The buffet has become a popular French Quarter institution, with all manner of Creole food. The experience is further spiced up by the strolling jazz musicians, who cut loose with the sounds for which New Orleans is famous. When it all happens in the classic courtyard, the meal becomes incomparable.

AVOCADO ROMANOFF

3 ripe avocados
6 lettuce leaves
2/3 cup sour cream
1 1/2 to 2 ounces black caviar
6 pimiento strips

Halve the avocados, remove the pits, and peel. Place each avocado half on a lettuce leaf, and fill each cavity with sour cream.

Circle the sour cream in each avocado with a line of caviar. Lay a pimiento strip over the sour cream.

MAKES 6 SERVINGS

THE EMBERS STEAK HOUSE

700 Bourbon St., New Orleans, LA 70116; (504) 423-1486.

You don't have to wonder about the quality of the steaks or the excitement of their preparation at the Embers; you can check that out through the St. Peter Street window before you walk in. There, over the glowing flames, high-quality beef is char-broiled to exacting specifications. The sight and aroma is mouth-watering, and the finished product delivers on its promise. The rustic dining room has exposed rough-hewn beams and unfinished brick walls, highlighted by a large fireplace, creating a warm clubby ambience.

FRENCH DRESSING

1 small onion, chopped
1 clove garlic, minced
2 1/2 tablespoons tomato soup
2 1/2 tablespoons water
1 1/2 teaspoons sugar
1/2 cup salad oil
1/4 cup vinegar
6 tablespoons chili sauce
1/2 teaspoon dry mustard
1/2 teaspoon pepper
1 teaspoon salt
1 1/2 teaspoons Worcestershire sauce
Pinch celery seed
2 drops Tabasco sauce

To make french dressing: Combine all ingredients in a large jar and shake well. Refrigerate.

Allow to age for two weeks before serving.

Serve with your favorite lettuce and greens.

MAKES 2 CUPS

ROQUEFORT CHEESE DRESSING

10 ounces imported Roquefort cheese
12 ounces cream cheese, room temperature
2 tablespoons mayonnaise
1/2 cup white vinegar
1/2 cup salad oil
2 tablespoons sugar
1 1/2 teaspoons salt
1 teaspoon pepper

To make roquefort cheese dressing: Blend all ingredients with electric mixer until smooth and fluffy. Refrigerate.

MAKES 2 CUPS

SAZERAC

Fairmont Hotel, University Place, New Orleans, LA 70140; (504) 529-7111.

This ultra-elegant restaurant with full French service is named for what has been claimed to be the original cocktail, the Sazerac. Made with whiskey, absinthe substitute, and Peychaud's bitters, the drink is prepared with a flair by the bartenders in the Sazerac lounge. The word cocktail, in fact, seems to have developed hearabouts as a corruption of the French word coquetier, which referred to the egg cup in which Monsieur Peychaud served his elixir.

L'ETOILE DE MELON AU JAMBON FUME

1 cantaloupe
3 ounces proscuitto ham, thinly sliced
1 Boston lettuce (heart)
1 Belgian endive, julienned (see Glossary)
1 small bunch watercress

Dressing:
1/2 cup walnut oil
1 tablespoon raspberry vinegar
Salt and pepper to taste

Cut the melon in half lengthwise, and remove seeds. Take one half of the melon and cut 5 triangles in order to make a star shape, removing skin. Wrap each melon triangle in proscuitto ham slices, leaving the tip of each triangle exposed for color. Set aside.

On a chilled salad plate arrange the heart of boston lettuce in the center, then arrange watercress around boston lettuce. Place melon triangles around the edge of plate, in order to form star shape. Place julienne of endive in center of Boston lettuce. Chill until serving time.

To make Dressing: Mix ingredients together and pour over salad just before serving.

MAKES 1 SERVING

"Who doth ambition shun
 And loves to live i' the sun,
 Seeking the food he eats,
 And pleased with what he gets."
                WILLIAM SHAKESPEARE

MEATS · GAME

CHEZ PASTOR

1211 Pinhook Rd., Lafayette, LA 70501; (318) 234-5189.

Sunset is a special time at Chez Pastor. Diners jockey for the tables nearest the large windows to watch the sun go down—then they turn their attentions to the extensive menu of Cajun, Creole, and continental specialties. Meanwhile, greenery hangs down in lush profusion from the exposed beams above, and flowery tablecloths host lovely platters of deftly-wrought, highly original cuisine. Owners Pat and Maugie Pastor carry on the celebrated gustatory traditions of *les Acadiens*.

STEAK SUPREME

1 cup flour
2 cups butter
2 cups chopped onions
3 teaspoons chopped garlic
6 teaspoons seasoned pepper
4 cups chicken stock (see Basic Stocks)
3 cups canned sliced mushrooms, drained
3 cups red wine
8 (8-ounce) tenderloin filets

Brown flour in a heavy skillet stirring continuously. Set aside.

In a large pot, melt butter over low heat. Add onions, garlic, and pepper. Saute until onions are clear. Add browned flour, mix well. Stir in stock and mushrooms. Cook until sauce thickens, about 3 minutes. Add red wine and simmer 5 more minutes.

Broil filets to desired degree of doneness. Serve sauce over broiled filets.

MAKES 8 SERVINGS

Photograph, Page 21

MAYER'S OLD EUROPE

2998 Pontchartrain Dr., Slidell, LA 70458; (504) 649-1426.

Mayer's Old Europe ranks in the top tier of restaurants in the fast-growing community of Slidell. It is a dining room which offers well-tuned dining pleasures, with the unusualness and authenticity of German, Austrian, and Hungarian cooking. It is a dining room marked by warmth, both that of the antique-decorated forty-year-old house and that of the congenial, professional serving staff, lovely waitresses in unique long, aproned dresses.

SAUERBRATEN

4 cups vinegar
2 carrots, sliced
2 onions, sliced
12 juniper berries
6 whole cloves
2 bay leaves
1 tablespoon salt
1 teaspoon pepper
5 pounds eye of round roast
$1/4$ cup oil
1 carrot, minced
1 onion, chopped
1 rib celery, chopped
1 bay leaf
$1/4$ teaspoon thyme
2 tablespoons tomato paste
3 cups beef bouillon
$1/2$ cup red wine
2 tablespoons sugar
2 tablespoons soy sauce
$1/2$ cup flour
$1/2$ cup crumbled ginger snaps

In a non-metallic container, combine vinegar, sliced carrots, sliced onions, juniper berries, cloves, bay leaves, salt, and pepper. Add meat, cover, and store in refrigerator 4 or 5 days.

Remove from refrigerator and dry meat thoroughly, reserving marinade.

Heat oil in large Dutch oven. Add meat and brown well on all sides. Remove from pan. Add minced carrot, chopped onion and celery, bay leaf and thyme to Dutch oven. Saute until vegetables are soft. Add tomato paste and stir until well blended with vegetables. Add bouillon, wine, 1 cup of strained marinade, sugar, soy sauce, and meat.

Cover and bake at 350 degrees F. about $2 1/2$ hours or until meat is tender. Remove meat from casserole and keep warm.

Skim fat from gravy. Thicken with flour, add crumbled ginger snaps, and serve over sliced meat.

MAKES 10 TO 12 SERVINGS

Photograph, Page 21

L.R.A.

The Natchitoches meat pie was born in the town of Natchitoches, the oldest permanent settlement in the Louisiana Purchase Territory, founded in 1714 by Louis Juchereau de St. Denis, and named after the Natchitoches tribe of Caddo Indians living on the Red River. Translations of the word have included "chestnut eaters," "chinquapin eaters" and "paw-paw eaters." Each chef and home cook has his own secret version of the Natchitoches meat pie. The Louisiana Restaurant Association offers the one below as a tribute to this local favorite dish.

NATCHITOCHES MEAT PIE

Filling
1 teaspoon vegetable shortening
1 pound ground beef
1 pound ground pork
1 cup finely chopped green onions, including tops and bottoms
1 small green pepper, chopped fine
1 tablespoon salt
1 teaspoon black pepper
1 1/2 teaspoons red pepper
1 clove garlic, minced
1/3 cup all purpose flour

Pastry
4 cups all purpose flour
1/3 cup vegetable shortening
2 teaspoons salt
1 teaspoon baking powder
1 egg, beaten
1 cup water or milk

Oil for frying

To make filling: Melt vegetable shortening in large heavy pot. Add meats, onions, green pepper, salt, black and red pepper, and garlic. Cook over medium heat, stirring often, until meat is done. Add flour and stir until well mixed. Remove from heat. Drain in colander to remove excess grease.

To make pastry: Sift flour into large mixing bowl. Cut in vegetable shortening. Add salt and baking powder.

In separate bowl beat egg and mix with water or milk. Add to dry ingredients until easy consistency to roll.

Pinch off small pieces of dough and roll thin on a floured board. Cut in 5-inch or 6-inch circles. Use saucer or lid for cutting guide.

To assemble: Place a heaping tablespoon of filling off center on the pastry round. Fold pastry over and crimp edges together with fork. Deep-fry in oil at 350 degrees F. until golden brown.

Note: pies can be frozen in plastic bags for later use. If frozen, do not thaw; fry frozen.

MAKES ABOUT 18 PIES

WINSTON'S

New Orleans Hilton Riverside and Towers,
2 Poydras St., New Orleans, LA 70140; (504) 561-0500.

Most diners who enjoy an evening in the atrium dining room of the Hilton's Winston's remember the "butler" and "maid" service and the recited menu. But gourmets are impressed by the original combination of Nouvelle French cooking with Creole cooking styles. The menu changes daily to reflect what the markets are offering at peak and what ideas the chef has to surprise and delight his charges. All is served in plush, flowery comfort.

CARRE D' AGNEAU A LA MONGOLIAN

1 (3-pound) rack of lamb
Salt and pepper to taste
1/2 pound fresh apricots, peeled and halved
1/4 cup sugar
2 ounces brandy
1/4 cup honey
1 teaspoon freshly grated ginger
1 teaspoon fresh tarragon, chopped
2 tablespoons bottled teriyaki sauce

Garnish: *fresh apple slices, apricot halves, and strawberries*

Trim off excess fat from rack and season lightly with salt and pepper. Roast rack at 350 degrees F. for 15 minutes.

Meanwhile in a sauce pan cook apricots, sugar, and brandy for 10 minutes. Add remaining ingredients to sauce.

When lamb has reached desired doneness, glaze with sauce and surround with fresh apple slices, apricot halves, and strawberries.

MAKES 2 SERVINGS

Photograph, Page 22

MISTER JAY'S

1604 Hwy. 90 W., Vinton, LA 70668; (318) 589-7300.

This popular restaurant, in the Southwestern Louisiana town of Vinton, has some great specialties. Pizzas are made from those two Cajun favorites, boudin and crawfish. More familiar pizzas are also available, as are Italian pasta dishes, sandwiches, hamburgers, and the delicious boudin burger. The decor is a rustic Cajun cowboy look, with a casual, friendly atmosphere. The restaurant is just off I-10 at the last exit before you get to Texas; you can use exits 7 or 8.

ORIGINAL LOUISIANA CAJUN BOUDIN PIZZA

4 cups boudin, removed from casing (see Glossary)
1 (12-inch) pizza crust, unbaked
1/2 cup grated mozzarella cheese
Louisiana pork cracklin's (see Note)

Spread boudin evenly over pizza crust, leaving 1/2-inch edge. Spread cheese over top. Bake at 500 degrees F. for 17 minutes, adding the cracklin's after 10 minutes. Cut into 8 pieces and serve.

Note: Cracklin's are salt pork or fatback, cut into small cubes, and fried until brown and crispy.

MAKES 8 SERVINGS

Photograph, Page 18

THE GUMBO SHOP
630 St. Peter St., New Orleans, LA 70116; (504) 525-1486.

The Gumbo Shop features two different kinds of gumbo, right at the top of its menu. But that is just the beginning of the New Orleans specialties this old Creole café serves. It is one of the few restaurants where you can get red beans and rice anytime, not just on Mondays. There is also a bit of seafood, poor boy sandwiches, salads, daily plate lunch and dinner specials, and desserts.

RED BEANS AND RICE WITH SMOKED SAUSAGE

1 pound dried red beans
Water to cover
1 large onion, chopped
1 green pepper, chopped
1 rib celery, chopped
1 clove garlic, minced
1 1/2 pounds smoked sausage, sliced
1/2 pound smoked ham shanks
1 bay leaf
1 teaspoon thyme
1/2 teaspoon sage
1 teaspoon black pepper
Pinch cayenne
Salt to taste

Rinse and sort beans. Place the beans in a large kettle and cover with water. Allow the beans to soak overnight.

Drain beans and put them along with all the remaining ingredients, except the salt, in cold water to cover. Simmer, covered, for approximately 2 1/2 hours or until beans are tender, adding water if necessary. Add salt to taste.

To thicken the gravy, remove about 3 tablespoons of beans and mash to a paste. Return the paste to the pot, stir well, and simmer an additional 15 minutes.

Serve over steamed rice.

MAKES 6 SERVINGS

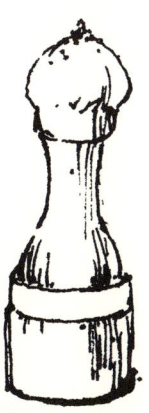

MENEFEE'S

1101 N. Rampart St., New Orleans, LA 70116; (504) 566-0464.

This beautiful new restaurant, built in an old mansion, has two stories of distinguished architecture. Most striking are the neon sculptures placed in effective positions around the restaurant. Also interesting is a corner behind the banquettes on the second floor where the floor parts to admit the sounds of the pianist who plays for those in the lounge. The menu is a compilation of Continental classics with some Creole touches and the chef's own creative twists.

VEAL MENEFEE

1 1/2 pounds veal
1 cup wild rice, prepared according to directions
2 cups chopped spinach, drained
2 tablespoons pine nuts
Salt and pepper to taste
Flour for dredging
Butter

Orange Sauce
1 (8-ounce) can orange juice concentrate
1 cup brown sugar
1/2 cup ground veal
1/2 teaspoon cinnamon
1/2 cup water
1/2 cup Grand Marnier
7 tablespoons cornstarch

To make veal: Cut veal into 6-ounce portions. Pound until very thin. Mix rice, spinach, and pine nuts to make stuffing. Season with salt and pepper. Place stuffing on veal, roll up, and secure with toothpicks or tie with thread. Dredge veal in flour and saute in butter until browned. Remove from pan and cook at 350 degree F. until done, approximately 20 minutes.

To make sauce: Combine orange juice, brown sugar, veal, and cinnamon in a sauce pan and bring to a boil.

In a small bowl combine water and Grand Marnier; stir in cornstarch. Add to orange juice mixture and cook over medium heat until thickened.

Serve the veal rolls on a bed of wild rice and cover with sauce.

MAKES 6 SERVINGS

COMMANDER'S PALACE

1403 Washington Ave., New Orleans, LA 70130; (504) 899-8221.

Founded in 1880 by Emile Commander, this restaurant has been an important part of the New Orleans dining scene ever since. Commander's Palace has now risen to national prominence. The foodstuffs are all fresh and of extremely high quality, prepared imaginatively in a very elegant Creole style. Guests are served in the traditional dining room downstairs and the incomparably beautiful Garden Room among the oaks upstairs. Private parties may be hosted in the Wine Cellar Room.

TENDERLOIN OF VEAL AU CITRON WITH PATE DE FOIE GRAS

Creole meat seasoning
- 1/2 cup salt
- 1/4 cup plus 2 tablespoons granulated garlic
- 1/4 cup plus 2 tablespoons black pepper
- 1 tablespoon cayenne pepper
- 2 tablespoons paprika

Tenderloin of Veal
- 2 veal tenderloins, about 3 pounds
- 6 ounces canned Pâté de Foie Gras
- 1/2 cup butter
- 1/4 cup chopped shallots
- 2 teaspoons finely chopped fresh tarragon
- 1/4 cup finely chopped fresh parsley
- Juice of 5 lemons
- 9 ounces dry white wine
- 2 cups heavy cream, whipped

To make Creole Meat Seasoning: Combine all ingredients, mixing thoroughly. Pour into large glass jar. Keeps indefinitely. Makes 1 1/2 cups of meat seasoning.

To make Tenderloin of Veal: Make a hole lengthwise in the veal tenderloins with a sharpening steel. Stuff the hole with foie gras. Sprinkle 1 teaspoon seasoning over the veal.

Heat a large skillet and add butter. When butter is foaming hot, add veal and saute for 10 minutes, turning so that it browns evenly on all sides. Remove meat from skillet.

To skillet add shallots, tarragon, parsley, lemon juice, and wine; cook over moderate heat, stirring in all the bits of veal glaze from bottom and sides of skillet. Cook the sauce until reduced and slightly thickened. Gradually whisk the whipped cream into the sauce.

Slice meat and arrange on a warm platter. Top with the sauce and serve immediately.

MAKES 6 SERVINGS

Photograph, Page 21

TIVOLI

The Brent House, 1516 Jefferson Hwy., Jefferson, LA 70121; (504) 835-5411.

Ochsner Clinic, on whose grounds the Brent House stands, is one of America's premier medical facilities, drawing patients from all over the western hemisphere. Brent House serves the lodging needs of patients and guests of Ochsner Medical Institutions. Brent House has three dining facilities: a coffee shop for quick snacks and sandwiches with counter service, the Tivoli Cafeteria, open for breakfast and lunch, and the main cafeteria.

MILK-FED VEAL CHOP FRANCISCO

1 (8 to 10 pound) rack of veal, untrimmed
3 ribs celery
2 bay leaves
2 teaspoons thyme
3 peppercorns
4 tablespoons flour
1 cup tomato sauce
1 quart water or veal or beef stock
1/4 cup butter
4 shallots chopped
1/2 pound mushrooms, julienned (see Glossary)
8 slices cooked beef tongue, julienned
4 pitted black olives, julienned
1 cup white wine
Flour to coat
Salt and pepper to taste
1/4 cup cooking oil
1/4 cup chopped parsley

From sides of rack cut 12 boneless chops, 4 to 6 ounces each after trimming, or have your butcher do this. Set chops aside, reserve 2 to 3 pounds of bones. Place bones in roasting pan and brown at 400 degrees F. with celery, bay leaves, thyme, and peppercorns. When well browned, dust with flour. Add tomato sauce and water or stock. Bring to boil and let simmer 2 hours. Strain stock and set aside.

In sauce pan melt the butter and add shallots, mushrooms, tongue, and olives. Add white wine and strained stock. Let boil to reduce for an hour, stirring occasionally.

Dust chops with salt and pepper. Heat skillet with oil over moderate heat. Add chops and saute until golden brown on both sides. Serve with sauce spooned over and chopped parsley on top.

MAKES 6 SERVINGS

Photograph, Page 24

THE PLIMSOLL CLUB

International Trade Mart, New Orleans, LA 70130; (504) 529-1701.

As befits a gourmet dining establishment set up to encourage international trade through hospitality, the Plimsoll Club boasts decorations from around the world. Most impressive and famous are a pair of doors which once adorned a Spanish castle; these 400-year-old masterpieces now guard the entrance to the Galvez Room. Behind the bar is a 15th-century Belgian tapestry and in the exquisite Versailles Room are nine chandeliers from France and Germany.

POITRINE DE VEAU FARCIE DE GASCOGNE
(Gascony Style Stuffed Veal Belly)

2 cups ground pork
1 cup bread crumbs
2 eggs
1 tablespoon poultry seasoning
2 tablespoons heavy cream
Salt and pepper to taste
4 pounds veal shoulder or veal front belly
1 onion, chopped
1 carrot, chopped
1 rib celery, chopped
2 tablespoons melted pork fat (lard)
2 cups water
2 bay leaves
1 pound egg noodles
2 cups white sauce (see Basic Sauces)
1 egg yolk, beaten
2 tablespoons grated cheese ($\frac{1}{2}$ Swiss, $\frac{1}{2}$ Parmesan)
2 tablespoons melted butter

In a bowl mix together the ground pork, bread crumbs, eggs, poultry seasoning, cream, salt and pepper.

Debone the veal shoulder or belly and make a pocket. Stuff the pocket with the mixture. Sew the opening closed very carefully and tightly. (A large embroidery needle threaded with dental floss works well.)

In a roasting pan combine onion, carrot, and celery. Put the stuffed veal on top of the vegetables. Add pork fat, water, and bay leaves and bake at 300 degrees F. for 2 hours.

Cook the noodles al dente (see Glossary). Place noodles around veal in roasting pan.

Prepare 2 cups of white sauce and add beaten egg along with the cheese and butter. Pour sauce over roast veal and noodles. Bake at 250 degrees F. for $1\frac{1}{2}$ hours.

MAKES 6 SERVINGS

Photograph, Page 20

WILLY COLN'S CHALET
2505 Whitney Ave., Gretna, LA 70053; (504) 361-3860.

This restaurant exudes the charm of an Alpine chalet, both inside and out. The authentic European design was hand-built by chef-owner Willy Coln, who operates the small first-class gourmet restaurant with his wife and hostess Erna Coln. One of the highlights of the culinary year in New Orleans is Willy Coln's Oktoberfest, a month of special German menus with live music, bright decorations, and "gemütlichkeit."

ROAST VEAL SHANKS

2 (3 1/2-pound) milk-fed veal shanks
Salt and pepper to taste
1 cup diced celery
1 cup diced carrots
1 cup diced onions
2 cups beef or meat stock or canned bouillon
1 cup packed julienned carrots (about 2 medium carrots), (see Glossary)
1 cup packed julienned zucchini (about 1 medium zucchini)
1 cup packed julienned onion (about 1 medium onion)
1 cup packed julienned cauliflower floretes
24 small whole mushrooms
1/4 cup butter
Salt and black pepper to taste

Rub the veal shanks thoroughly with salt and pepper. Place the shanks in a roasting pan, and place the pan in a 450 degrees F. oven. Roast the shanks uncovered for 1/2 hour.

Add the diced celery, carrots, and onions to the pan, and pour in 1 cup of the stock. Cover the pan, and cook the shanks at 300 degrees F. for another 1/2 hour.

Remove the pan from the oven. Add the second cup of stock, and baste the shanks with the pan juices. Return the shanks, uncovered, to the oven, and cook them for approximately 1 1/2 hours, basting every 1/2 hour.

Remove the shanks from pan. Strain the juices and vegetables from roasting pan, reserving the juices and discarding the vegetables. Remove the fat as it rises to the top of the strained juices.

In a large frying pan, saute the julienned carrots, zucchini, onion, cauliflower and the mushrooms in the butter for 4 to 5 minutes over medium high heat. The vegetables should be served al dente (see Glossary) or crispy. Add salt and pepper to taste. Serve the vegetables over the warmed veal shanks. Serve the juice on the side.

MAKES 6 SERVINGS

Photograph, Page 21

KOLB'S

125 St. Charles Ave., New Orleans, LA 70130; (504) 522-8279.

Kolb's is the restaurant Orleanians think of when they think of German cuisine. On the scene since 1899, the very extensive menu includes all the classics of German cuisine at reasonable prices. Every October Kolb's explodes into a month-long festival of gaiety as the restaurant celebrates the traditional German harvest celebration of Oktoberfest. Every night there is a live oom-pah-pah band during the Oktoberfest, and the restaurant takes on the air of a Munich beer hall.

KAISER SCHNITZEL

Veal Stock
1 pound veal trimmings and bones
2 cups butter
2 medium onions, diced
2 medium carrots, diced
2 celery tops
1 bay leaf
3 to 4 parsley sprigs
1 cup dry white wine
3 cups water
1/4 cup butter
4 tablespoons flour
1/2 pound raw, peeled, and deveined small shrimp
1/2 cup half and half
Salt and white pepper to taste

Cutlets
6 (2-ounce) cutlets of milk-fed veal, flattened
6 (2-ounce) cutlets of pork loin, flattened
1/4 teaspoon salt
1/8 teaspoon white pepper
3/4 cup all purpose flour
2 eggs, beaten with 1/2 cup water
1 cup plain bread crumbs
1 cup butter, divided

To make the veal stock: Brown the veal trimmings and bones in the butter. Add the diced onions and carrots and saute for 4 to 5 minutes. Add the celery tops, bay leaf, parsley, and wine, and reduce the liquid by half. Add the water and simmer the stock for 1 hour; strain and reserve.

Make a roux by melting 1/4 cup butter in a sauce pan and adding the flour. Cook, stirring constantly, over medium low heat until the roux is medium brown in color, approximately 15 minutes. Slowly add 2 cups veal stock, and cook 2 to 3 minutes. Add the raw shrimp and simmer for 10 minutes. Add the half and half, and season with salt and pepper. Do not boil the sauce once the half and half has been added.

To prepare the cutlets: Sprinkle the cutlets with salt and white pepper. Keep the veal cutlets separate from the pork cutlets. Dredge the veal cutlets in flour, then dip them in the egg-water mixture, and finally coat them with bread crumbs. In a large frying pan melt 1/2 cup of butter, and saute the veal cutlets until they are golden brown. Follow the same procedure for the pork cutlets using remaining 1/2 cup of butter for sauteing.

Place one of each cutlet on serving plates and cover with the warm sauce.

MAKES 6 SERVINGS

Photograph, Page 22

THE VERSAILLES

2100 St. Charles Ave., New Orleans, LA 70140; (504) 524-2535.

The highly-thought-of creations of Versailles chef-owner Gunter Preuss are matched by the Versailles' proficiency in staging private dinner parties. The Versailles has become the exclusive purveyor of such affairs for a host of large Louisiana companies and New Orleans groups. Chef Preuss is always ready to concoct something unusual for the guests and serve it with letter-perfect style and panache.

VEAL VERSAILLES

18 silver dollar size medallions of milk-fed veal
Salt, pepper, lemon juice to taste
1 cup all purpose flour
4 or 5 beaten eggs
3 tablespoons clarified butter (see Glossary)
3 cups Crawfish Versailles (see page 121)
1 cup brown sauce (see Basic Sauces)
Chopped parsley

Season medallions with salt, pepper and lemon juice. Dip in flour, shaking off any excess. Immerse in beaten eggs.

Heat butter in a saute pan until hot. Put medallions into butter and saute over high heat until golden on each side, 1 to 2 minutes.

For each serving put 1 medallion on plate, cover with 1/2 cup heated Crayfish Versailles, then put 2 more medallions over this.

Ladle about $1^{1}/_{2}$ tablespoons brown sauce over and sprinkle with chopped parsley and serve.

MAKES 6 SERVINGS

RESTAURANT SCLAFANI

1301 North Causeway Blvd., Metairie, LA 70001; (504) 835-1718.

In New Orleans there is a great intermingling of the Italian and Creole styles of cooking. Nowhere is this more obvious than at Sclafani's, with its gigantic menu encompassing not only Italian fare from the familiar to the exotic but also a broad range of local fresh seafood, gumbos, shellfish, steaks, and Creole chicken dishes. Every day brings with it a new list of daily specials at very reasonable prices. They make Sclafani's a favorite family restaurant in Metairie.

VEAL BRACIUOLINI

2 cups seasoned Italian bread crumbs
3 eggs, beaten
6 tablespoons minced ham
2 green onions, chopped
2 hard boiled eggs, quartered
4 (4-ounce) veal cutlets, pounded thin
Oil to coat
Dash oregano
1 pound spaghetti, cooked
Tomato sauce (see Basic Sauces)

Mix together bread crumbs, eggs, ham, and green onions. Divide into 4 stuffing portions.

Place two quarters of hard boiled eggs onto each veal cutlet, add stuffing, and roll like a jelly roll. Secure edges with toothpicks.

Place in oiled baking pan and coat veal lightly with oil. Sprinkle with dash of oregano. Cover with foil and bake at 375 degrees F. for 20 minutes. Pour off excess oil and add tomato sauce.

Cut veal into 1-inch rounds and serve over cooked spaghetti with tomato sauce spooned over.

MAKES 4 SERVINGS

THE ROYAL RESTAURANT AND PUB

Travelodge, 2502 Port Dr., Jennings, LA 70546; (318) 824-6550.

Every night in this pleasant little restaurant near I-10, the main attraction is fresh Louisiana seafood. This nightly special brings in fans of the fish from all around the area to the comfortable wooden tables and chairs or the casual booths of the Royal Restaurant and Pub. But the menu goes well beyond catfish. Try the alligator barbecued or with sauce piquante, a local favorite.

ALLIGATOR SAUCE PIQUANTE

5 lbs. alligator meat, diced in 1 1/2" squares
Salt, pepper, and red pepper to taste
1/2 cup cooking oil
2 medium onions, chopped
2 cloves garlic, chopped
1/2 cup chopped parsley
1/2 cup chopped green onions
1 can tomatoes
1 tablespoon cornstarch
3 cups water
6 tablespoons Bayou Bengal Sauce

Season alligator meat with salt and peppers.

Heat cooking oil and add meat. Fry until brown. Place meat and all other ingredients in a Dutch oven.

Cook over low heat for 2 1/2 to 3 hours. Stir and add water occasionally to prevent sticking. Finished dish should be thick and reddish brown.

Serve over steamed rice.

MAKES 10 TO 12 SERVINGS

THE ROYAL RESTAURANT AND PUB

Travelodge, 2502 Port Dr., Jennings, LA 70546; (318) 824-6550.

This restaurant is convenient not only to the people of Jennings in Southwestern Louisiana but also to the heavy east-west traffic on I-10. Close to Exit 65, this medium-size eatery serves good food at reasonable prices. Perhaps the most popular meal here is the noon buffet, which features a variety of freshly-prepared items. At all meals there is a well-stocked salad bar for your greens-crunching pleasure.

BARBECUED ALLIGATOR

2 to 3 lbs. alligator meat, diced in 1½-inch squares
6 tablespoons Bayou Bengal Sauce
⅓ cup cooking oil
½ cup barbecue sauce of your choice
1 cup water
Salt and pepper to taste

Marinate alligator in a heavy pot in Bayou Bengal Sauce for 2 to 3 hours. Keep meat in marinade and add oil, barbeque sauce, water, salt and pepper.

Place the pot over red hot coals (no flames), stirring occasionally. Cook about 1 hour or longer to insure tenderness.

MAKES 4 TO 6 SERVINGS

LES CHEFS DE CUISINE DE LA LOUISIANNE

Louisiana is a rich hunting area for game. A wealth of wild animals live in the Cajun backcountry, within bayous and swamps—fox, rabbit, raccoon, possum, deer, alligator. Chef Kurt Wolf of the Chefs' Association offers an assortment of game recipes, including the one below for those with a craving for a taste of the wild.

FOX STEW

1 1/2 pounds fox, cut into bite-size chunks
1/4 cup flour
2 tablespoons butter
1 medium onion, sliced
1 tablespoon chopped parsley
1/4 cup Burgundy
1 cup diced carrots
1 bay leaf
1 cup whole mushrooms
Salt and pepper to taste
1/2 cup water
Cooked, buttered rice

Garnish: chopped parsley

Place meat in a paper or plastic bag with flour and shake to coat the meat.

Heat the butter in a large skillet. Add meat and brown on all sides over medium-high heat. When all sides are brown, add remaining ingredients and bring to a boil. Once the liquid is boiling, stir, cover, and reduce heat to simmer. Cook from 1 to 1 1/2 hours, until the meat is tender.

Serve over hot buttered rice. Garnish with parsley.

MAKES 4 SERVINGS

BEGUE'S

Royal Sonesta Hotel, 300 Bourbon St., New Orleans, LA 70130; (504) 586-0300.

Begue's is the premier restaurant of the luxury Royal Sonesta Hotel in New Orleans' French Quarter. Behind doors leading to a classic leafy courtyard, this restaurant features elaborate service of not only traditional French dishes but also an assortment of authentic Creole dishes. An unusual aspect of Begue's is the large number of wines available by the glass both in the lounge and at the table. Every evening the service staff provides letter-perfect French service to pleased patrons.

LE LAPIN EN MATELOTE *(Rabbit Stew with Red Wine)*

1/4 pound bacon, cut into 1-inch pieces
1 (3-pound) rabbit, cut into pieces
2 onions, chopped
2 tablespoons tomato puree
3 tablespoons flour
1 pound fresh mushrooms
1 quart red wine
2 cloves garlic, chopped
3 bay leaves
1/4 teaspoon thyme

In a large deep skillet or a sauce pan, cook bacon until crisp. Add rabbit, onion, tomato puree and cook over medium heat until rabbit is lightly browned.

Add flour, stirring constantly to mix. Add mushrooms, wine, and remaining spices. Simmer covered for 30 minutes or until tender.

Cooking time may vary slightly depending on tenderness of rabbit.

MAKES 4 TO 6 SERVINGS

LES CHEFS DE CUISINE DE LA LOUISIANNE

The Louisiana backwoods are the natural habitats of the raccoon, the small furry animal with ringed tail. Cajuns serve up the raccoon in a wonderful stew. Try this recipe by Chef Kurt Wolf.

ROAST RACCOON

1 raccoon, cut into serving pieces
Flour to coat
3 tablespoons cooking oil
4 small onions, chopped
1 beef bouillon cube
1 cup water
1 tablespoon steak sauce
4 to 6 medium size potatoes, cut into large chunks
4 to 6 carrots, chopped
4 to 6 ribs celery, chopped
Salt and pepper to taste

Dust the raccoon pieces with flour and brown on all sides in hot cooking oil. Place the pieces in a roasting pan with the onions, bouillon cube, water, and steak sauce. Cover and roast at 350 degrees F. until the meat starts to become tender, from 45 minutes to 1½ hours, depending on the age of the animal.

Add the potatoes, carrots, and celery, sprinkling them with salt and pepper. Cover the pan and roast until done, about 1 hour.

Thicken the sauce or serve it as is with meat.

MAKES 4 TO 6 SERVINGS

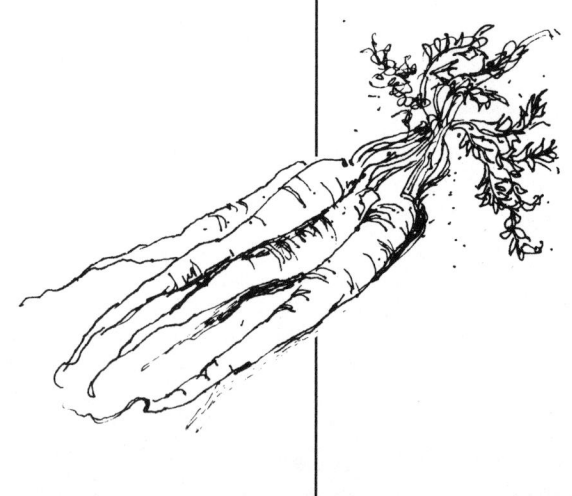

LES CHEFS DE CUISINE DE LA LOUISIANNE

When the deer hunter returns from the hunt with his trophy, be prepared with Chef Kurt Wolf's following recipe. The taste of deer meat is tangier than beef.

VENISON LASAGNA

2 pounds ground venison
1/4 cup cooking oil
1 quart tomato sauce (see Basic Sauces)
1/2 pound mozzarella cheese
1 pound ricotta cheese
2 eggs, beaten
1 teaspoon parsley flakes
Salt and pepper to taste
1 pound lasagna noodles (cooked 5 minutes)
1 cup grated Parmesan cheese

Brown venison in oil in a large skillet. Add tomato sauce and heat to the boiling point.

Cut 12 thin slices of mozzarella for topping and shred the rest. Mix shredded cheese with ricotta cheese, eggs, parsley, salt, and pepper.

Grease two 12-inch by 8-inch baking pans (or one large one). Ladle a cup of meat sauce into the bottom of each pan. Layer with noodles, then cheese mixture. Repeat twice. Top with mozzarella slices and sprinkle with Parmesan cheese.

Cover with foil and bake at 350 degrees F. for 30 to 40 minutes or until bubbly.

MAKES 8 SERVINGS

LES CHEFS DE CUISINE DE LA LOUISIANNE

This roast venison recipe from Chef Kurt Wolf will introduce the novice game cook to the pleasures of deer meat, slowly simmered in wine, with herbs and vegetable seasonings. The venison with pan juices spooned on top will be outstanding.

DUTCH OVEN VENISON

4 pound shoulder roast of venison
Flour seasoned with salt and pepper
3 tablespoons cooking oil
1 onion, sliced
1 green pepper, sliced
1 garlic clove, minced
1 (16-ounce) can tomatoes
1 tablespoon sugar
$1/2$ cup dry red wine
$1/2$ teaspoon thyme
1 parsley sprig
4 whole cloves
20 peppercorns
2 bay leaves, crushed
12 juniper berries, crushed

Roll roast in seasoned flour and brown in hot cooking oil in a Dutch oven. When brown on all sides, remove the roast from the pot.

In the same pan saute the onion, green pepper, and garlic over moderate heat for 5 minutes, stirring often. Add tomatoes, sugar, wine, and thyme to the Dutch oven and heat.

Place the parsley, cloves, peppercorns, and bay leaves on a piece of double-thickness cheese cloth, and tie with a string into a bag. Add the bag to pot.

When the mixture is boiling, add the browned roast and baste with sauce. Cover and cook at 350 degrees F. for about $2^{1/2}$ hours, until tender. Baste several times with pan juices during the roasting, slice thinly, and serve with pan juices.

MAKES 4 SERVINGS

POULTRY

BIENVILLE'S COURTYARD

9701 Lake Forest Blvd., New Orleans, LA 70127; (504) 241-2636.

In New Orleans East, the newest section of the old city, is a brand-new restaurant that looks like an old classic from the French Quarter. Bienville's Courtyard is a lovely patio-style dining room with a wealth of greenery and fountains. The lighting is from poles fashioned after those on Canal Street. The air is gently stirred by antique ceiling fans. Other decorative features include eggplant-hued slates similar to those found throughout the Vieux Carré, and Quarter-style balconies.

CHICKEN BIENVILLE

8 ounces boneless chicken breast
1/4 cup white wine
1/4 cup flour
Salt and white pepper to taste
1/8 teaspoon sugar
1/8 teaspoon garlic powder
3 tablespoons unsalted butter
2 tablespoons chopped green onions
2 ounces cooked and peeled baby shrimp
2 tablespoons sliced mushrooms
6 tablespoons dry sherry
1 cup béchamel sauce (see Basic Sauces)

Dip chicken breast in white wine. Combine flour and seasonings and roll chicken in seasoned flour. Heat butter in skillet and saute chicken 5 to 7 minutes or until done. Remove chicken and keep warm.

Place onions, shrimp, and mushrooms in same skillet and saute to soften, adding more butter if necessary. Add sherry and heat. Ignite to flambé. When flames die out, add béchamel sauce to pan and heat through. Spoon sauce over chicken breast to serve.

MAKES 1 SERVING

K-PAUL'S LOUISIANA KITCHEN

406 Chartres St., New Orleans, LA 70130; (504) 522-3818.

In just a few years, Chef Paul Prudhomme, who owns this incredibly popular French Quarter bistro, has invented more instant local culinary classics than anyone else in memory. He boldly cooks seafood and roux in an extra-hot skillet, liberally sprinkling dishes with "Cajun Magic," K-Paul's own mixture of potent hot seasonings. The menu here changes daily and always has surprises.

CHICKEN AND TASSO JAMBALAYA

Seasoning mix (Poultry Magic may be substituted)
2 bay leaves
2 teaspoons red pepper (preferably cayenne)
1½ teaspoons salt
1½ teaspoons white pepper
1 teaspoon thyme
½ teaspoon black pepper
¼ teaspoon sage

Jambalaya
2 tablespoons unsalted butter
½ pound chopped tasso or other smoked ham (preferably Cure 81), (see Note)
2 cups boneless chicken, cut into bite-size pieces
1 cup chopped onion, divided
1 cup chopped celery, divided
1 cup chopped green peppers, divided
1 tablespoon minced garlic
½ cup tomato sauce
1 cup peeled and chopped tomatoes
2½ cups chicken stock (see Basic Stocks)
1½ cups uncooked rice (preferably converted)

Note: Tasso is a local highly spiced smoked ham. This dish is very spicy with red, black, and white pepper. If your taste buds are feeling conservative, cut the pepper amounts in half.

To make Seasoning mix: Combine the seasoning mix ingredients in a small bowl and set aside.

To make Jambalaya: Melt the butter in a 2-quart sauce pan over high heat. Add the tasso or ham and cook until meat begins to brown, about 3 minutes, stirring frequently. Add the chicken and continue cooking until chicken is brown, about 3 to 5 minutes, stirring frequently and scraping the bottom of the pan. Stir in the seasoning mix and ½ cup each of the onions, celery, green peppers, and all of the garlic. Cook until vegetables start to get tender, about 5 to 8 minutes, stirring and scraping pan bottom as needed.

Stir in the tomato sauce and cook about 1 minute, stirring often. Stir in the remaining ½ cup each of the onions, celery, and green peppers, and the tomatoes. Remove from heat. Stir in the stock and rice, mixing well.

Transfer mixture to an ungreased 8-inch by 8-inch baking pan. Bake uncovered at 350 degrees F. until rice is tender but still a bit crunchy, about 1 hour. Remove from oven. Stir well and remove bay leaves. Let sit 5 minutes before serving.

To serve, mold Jambalaya in a ring mold, cup, or decorative mold. Allow about 2 cups as a main course or about 1 cup as an appetizer. Eat as is or top with creole sauce (see Basic Sauces).

MAKES 4 SERVINGS

CAROUSEL CAFETERIA

3110 Louisville Ave., Monroe, LA 71201; (318) 325-7794.

Now in its fifth year of operation, the Carousel is owned and managed by the Garrett family. The main dining room is bedecked in eye-pleasing earth tones, from bright yellow walls to rust and orange curtains, to wine-colored carpeting. A white-painted brick wall surrounds the serving line; accented by wrought iron. Four chandeliers and a fireplace add another few touches of elegance and warmth. **Restaurant Hospitality** magazine ranks the Carousel as the 191st best restaurant in America and the best in north Louisiana.

CHICKEN BREASTS WITH POTATO STUFFING

2 large onions, finely chopped
2 cups celery, finely chopped
1 cup melted butter, divided
2 quarts mashed potatoes (boiled without salt)
4 eggs, slightly beaten
2 cups herb-seasoned bread stuffing
1 cup minced parsley
2 teaspoons salt
1/2 teaspoon pepper
16 whole chicken breasts, boned and split
1 teaspoon salt
1/4 teaspoon pepper
1/2 teaspoon paprika

Saute onion and celery in 1/2 cup of the butter, just until tender; add to mashed potatoes. Stir in eggs, stuffing, parsley, salt, and pepper. Place stuffing in a buttered baking pan.

Arrange chicken breasts on top of stuffing. Mix remaining butter, salt, pepper, and paprika and brush over chicken. Bake at 375 degrees F. 35 to 40 minutes or until chicken is tender and browned.

MAKES 16 SERVINGS

CORINNE DUNBAR'S
1617 St. Charles Ave., New Orleans, LA 70130; (504) 525-0689.

In a city of unique restaurants, there are few with the charm of Corinne Dunbar's. Located on the streetcar line on St. Charles Avenue in an 1840s mansion, it serves a prix-fixe menu of Creole specialties in what looks much more like a private dining room than a restaurant. The dinner consists of nine courses and changes from day to day. This method of operation has made Dunbar's one of America's best-known restaurants, praised by many national magazines.

CHICKEN BREAST MAITLAND

8 whole chicken breasts
Salt and pepper to taste
2 cups chicken stock, (see Basic Stocks)
¼ pound bulk pork sausage
1 small white onion, chopped
1 teaspoon Kitchen Bouquet
1 tablespoon flour, mixed with 1 tablespoon water
¾ cup chopped pecans
2 tablespoons sherry

Salt and pepper chicken. Place in a roasting pan with 1 cup of the chicken stock. Cook uncovered at 350 degrees F. for 15 minutes. Cover pan and cook about 15 more minutes.

Meanwhile cook sausage in a skillet and remove. In the same skillet brown onion well in remaining sausage grease. Combine remaining 1 cup chicken stock, sausage, and onions and puree in a food processor or blender. Stir in Kitchen Bouquet and flour mixture. Place in a sauce pan and cook until thickened.

Stir in pecans and sherry. Remove chicken to serving dish and spoon sauce over.

MAKES 8 SERVINGS

TREY YUEN

600 North Causeway Approach, Mandeville, LA 70448; (504) 626-4476.

Trey Yuen is a hard restaurant to miss; it looks like a gigantic Oriental temple in the middle of the piney woods on the North Shore of Lake Pontchartrain. It's no less striking inside. An architectural gem built more or less in the round, it incorporates a great many details bought by the Wong brothers from China. The statuary and art are authentic; the rare fish in the tank just inside are fascinating to behold. The atmosphere, combined with the great food, makes the restaurant one of the most popular in the state.

LEMON CHICKEN

Marinade
1 teaspoon sherry
1 teaspoon light soy sauce
1/4 teaspoon salt
1 tablespoon cornstarch
1/2 beaten egg

Chicken
1 whole chicken breast halved, skinned and boned

Sauce
Juice of 1 lemon (reserve peel)
1 teaspoon dry mustard
1 teaspoon dry sherry
1 1/2 tablespoons sugar
1/4 teaspoon salt
1 tablespoon vinegar
1/2 cup water
2 teaspoons cornstarch mixed with 2 tablespoons water
1/2 tablespoon oil

Flour to coat
1/2 cup oil

To make marinade: Combine all marinade ingredients in a small bowl.

Add chicken to marinade and marinate for 20 minutes.

To make sauce: Combine all ingredients for sauce and set aside.

Remove chicken from marinade and roll in flour to coat.

Heat wok or heavy skillet. Add the 1/2 cup oil. Stir-fry chicken until both sides are golden brown. Remove from skillet, chop into bite-size pieces, and place on a serving dish.

To skillet add sauce and reserved lemon peel to reheat. Remove lemon peel. Pour sauce over chicken and serve.

MAKES 2 SERVINGS

CHRISTIAN'S

3835 Iberville St., New Orleans, LA 70119; (504) 482-4924.

Christian's, generally conceded to be one of the city's greatest culinary organizations, is located in an old church. From that fact one might conclude that the place is either a theme restaurant or a born-again eatery, but the name is actually that of proprietor Christian Ansel, who operated a Metairie restaurant of the same name before moving into the 1904 structure in 1976. The rest is happy coincidence. The bench seats are pews, the waiter's station was constructed from an old altar, and the food is heavenly.

CHICKEN BLACKBERRY VINEGAR

Chicken
2 chickens, halved, breast and backbones removed
1 tablespoon butter
1 1/2 cups demi-glace (see Glossary)
6 tablespoons butter

Blackberry Vinegar
1/4 cup blackberries
1/2 cup white vinegar

Saute the chicken in butter and remove from pan. Drain butter and pour in the blackberry vinegar. Return the chicken to the pan with the demi-glace. Bring to a boil. Whisk in the 6 tablespoons butter, 1 tablespoon at a time.

To serve spoon the sauce over chicken.

To make blackberry vinegar: Soak the berries in the vinegar and pass the mixture through a food mill. Discard the seeds. Makes 3/4 cup blackberry vinegar.

MAKES 4 SERVINGS

ARMANDO'S MEXICAN CUISINE

3229 Williams Blvd., Kenner, LA 70062; (504) 443-3831.

Armando's is one of the most handsome Latin American restaurants in the New Orleans area. The large dining room is resplendent with plants, fountain, and colorful and authentic Mexican decorations. All of this is designed to enhance your enjoyment of true Mexican cuisine. The sauces are made on the premises daily, and they combine with the restaurant's excellent beef, chicken, and cheese to make rousing south-of-the-border treats.

POLLO EN VINO TINTO *(Chicken in Red Wine)*

2 cups margarine
7 Spanish onions, chopped
8 medium green peppers, chopped
6 tomatoes, chopped
1 quart hot water
6 1/2 cups crushed tomatoes
3 tablespoons salt
1 1/2 tablespoons chopped garlic
1 1/2 tablespoons white pepper
3 tablespoons seasoned chicken stock base (available at spice counters)
1 1/2 tablespoons monosodium glutamate
3 cups red wine
9 pounds deboned chicken

Melt margarine in a large kettle. Add onions, peppers, and tomatoes. Stir and cook until vegetables begin to get tender, about 15 minutes. Add all remaining ingredients, except chicken, and simmer until vegetables are soft. Add chicken and simmer an additional 10 minutes.

This is wonderful for large entertaining.

MAKES 50 SERVINGS

THE PLIMSOLL CLUB
International Trade Mart, New Orleans, LA 70130; (504) 529-1701.

The International Trade Mart towers above the river at the foot of Canal Street, and it offers a view of the nation's second-busiest port unequalled anywhere else in the city. Near the top of the building is the Plimsoll Club, the gourmet restaurant where businessmen in international trade can be seen entertaining dignitaries from around the world. The professional staff is highly skilled in providing distinctive decorations, flowers, music, ice sculptures, and, of course, great cuisine to the club's members.

CANARD AUX ANANAS REVE DE BALMAIN
(Balmain's Duckling and Pineapple Dream)

1 onion, chopped
2 carrots, chopped
3 celery ribs, chopped
Dash thyme
2 bay leaves
1 (2-pound) duck
1 (16-ounce) can sliced pineapple or 2 fresh pineapples
2 tablespoons Cognac, whiskey, or kirsh
2 tablespoons sugar
1 tablespoon vinegar

Combine onion, carrots, celery, thyme, and bay leaf and put in a roasting pan. Place duck on vegetables and roast at 350 degrees F. for 45 minutes.

Cook the sliced pineapple in a sauce pan over medium heat, with the liqueur for 3 minutes. Cover and simmer for approximately 10 minutes if using fresh pineapple.

Melt sugar in a skillet stirring until blond. Add vinegar and pineapple sauce; cook over low heat for 15 minutes.

Cut the duck in half, slice the breast. Place on a platter and garnish with the pineapple. Pour the sauce over duck and serve.

MAKES 2 SERVINGS

Photograph, Page 21

THE LANDING OF LAFAYETTE
1601 Pinhook Rd., Lafayette, LA 70805; (318) 233-8640.

The Landing is a unique restaurant with unique surroundings. The main dining room offers a breathtaking view of the Vermillion River below. The room is stunning, in bright pastel shades and natural wood tones, greenery hangs and grows in profusion. The specialties are duckling, steak, veal, and fresh Maine lobster. The Landing also features an excellent Sunday brunch. It is a lively, fun restaurant, a great place to spend an entire evening.

DUCKLING BALLOTINE WITH FRESH TOMATO SAUCE

Stuffing
1 pound pork
1/2 pound veal
1/2 pound chicken
Thyme to taste
Salt to taste
White and black pepper to taste
4 tablespoons fresh garlic, minced
2 eggs
1/2 cup chopped green onions
Parsley

Ducks
2 (2-4 pound) duck
Salt and pepper to taste
1/4 pound julienned smoked ham (see Glossary)

Tomato Sauce:
12 large tomatoes
1 tablespoon butter
1 small onion, minced
1 bay leaf
Salt and pepper to taste
Chopped garlic to taste

Garnish: 1 tablespoon chopped fresh parsley.

To make stuffing: Grind pork, veal, and chicken twice. Add spices and herbs to taste. Add eggs, green onions, and parsley. Mix well and chill. Cook a small bite and taste; correct seasoning as necessary.

To prepare ducks: bone the ducks leaving the skin intact and spread out in a rectangle skin side down (see Notes). Season the inside with salt and pepper. Divide the meat stuffing in half using half for each duck. Spread two thirds of each meat half on the inside of each duck. Lay strips of julienned ham on top of meat, dividing ham between ducks. Roll with your hands remaining one third of each meat half into a hot dog shape and lay it down the center of duck. Repeat for other duck. Roll up ballotines into a log shape and tie into place with string.

Season ballotine and roast on a rack 1 1/2 hours at 325 degrees F. Remove from oven. Let stand 1/2 hour, then cut off string.

Slice ballotine into six equal slices, slicing off rough ends, and serve on top of tomato sauce. Sprinkle with parsley for garnish.

To make Tomato Sauce: remove stem and score bottom of each tomato with knife. Blanch (see Glossary) 60 seconds, then plunge in a pan of cold water. Peel, halve, and seed tomatoes; then finely chop.

DUCKLING BALLOTINE WITH FRESH TOMATO SAUCE
(Continued)

Melt butter, saute onion until translucent, add tomatoes and bay leaf. Season with salt, pepper, and garlic to taste. Simmer covered for 15 minutes. Let cool 20 minutes; then puree tomato mixture in processor or blender. If sauce is too thick, a little chicken stock may be added.

Note: Boning the Duck: with a very sharp knife split the skin down the back bone. Gradually cut the skin and meat away from the body and rib cage. The legs and wings break away from the main carcass by cutting between the last joint and the bones to which it is attached. These appendages remain attached to the skin and unbend for the moment after the skin and meat are removed from the main body and rib cage, scrape any excess meat from the body. These pieces may be added to the stuffing. It is important to leave as much meat as is possible attached to the skin.

To remove the leg bones, cut the meat away from the bones carefully. Remove one joint at a time. Bone the wings the same way but remove the end tip at the joint since it does not need to be boned.

Turn the boned legs and wings inside out so that the meat lies on the meaty side of the bird. The skin side remains flat with only 4 indentations where the meat was pushed to the inside.

Note: This recipe can be extremely flexible. A boned chicken or pheasant may be substituted for the duck with your favorite stuffing. The addition of fruit, nuts, liver, not to mention madeira or sherry, will result in a variety of dishes from one recipe.

The sauce is also flexible. The bones may be used to make a stock from which a variety of sauces may be made for the ballotine.

MAKES 4 TO 6 SERVINGS

Photograph, Page 20

MENEFEE'S

1101 North Rampart St., New Orleans, LA 70116; (504) 566-0464.

Orleanians who plan an evening of dinner followed by a concert at the New Orleans Theatre of the Performing Arts have found the new Menefee's a welcome addition to the dining scene. Just two blocks from the theater, Menefee's is sensitive to the needs of its theater-going diners and expedites their service without any sacrifice in the imaginative quality of the food. There is a Champagne Sunday brunch, as well as poolside dining and cocktails. A unique feature of Menefee's is its health and swim club on the premises.

ROAST DUCK WITH PLUM SAUCE

Ducks
2 (4½-to 5-pound) ducks
Salt and pepper to taste

Fresh Plum Sauce
2 pounds plums
3 cups water
1¼ cups brown sugar
2 tablespoons cornstarch
1 cup plum brandy
4 cups cooked wild rice

To prepare ducks: Cover ducks with salt and pepper and roast at 350 degrees F. for 2½ hours, draining fat as it accumulates.

To make plum sauce: Chop plums and place in a saucepan with water and brown sugar. Simmer for 1½ hours, then strain. Return to heat and bring to a boil.

Dissolve the cornstarch in the brandy.

Stir into plums and cook until thick.

Serve ducks halved, on a bed of wild rice. Cover with the hot plum sauce.

MAKES 4 SERVINGS

MAYER'S OLD EUROPE

2998 Pontchartrain Dr., Slidell, LA 70458; (504) 649-1426.

Slidell is one of the fastest-growing cities in Louisiana, so it is no surprise that it should be the venue of sophisticated restaurants. One of Slidell's best is Mayer's Old Europe, housed in a forty-year-old residence on Slidell's main street. Inside the surroundings are pure elegance, with white linens, antique appointments, candlelight, fresh flowers, and soft music. The menu emphasis is Eastern European, but you will also find French and Creole specialties.

ROASTED DUCKLING

4 ducks
Seasoned salt to taste
Pepper to taste
2 ribs celery, cut in half
2 large onions, quartered
1 turnip, quartered
4 1/2 cups beef bouillon
4 tablespoons Worcestershire sauce
6 tablespoons soy sauce
3 tablespoons Picapeppa sauce
1 1/2 cups red wine, divided
1 teaspoon marjoram
1 teaspoon garlic powder
Dash Tabasco sauce
5 chopped green onions
1/2 cup triple sec or other orange-flavored liqueur

Rub ducks inside and out with seasoned salt and pepper. Stuff each carcass with one half rib of celery, one quarter of onion and one quarter of turnip. Place ducks in Dutch oven or baking pan and don't worry about crowding them. Cover with hot water until only the upper one third of ducks is exposed. Add bouillon, Worcestershire, soy sauce, Picapeppa, 1 cup of the wine, the other quartered onion, marjoram, garlic powder, and Tabasco.

Place pan, uncovered, in a 550 degrees F. oven and bake until sauce is bubbling vigorously. Reduce temperature gradually to approximately 400 degrees F., but sufficient to maintain the sauce bubbling. Turn the ducks every half hour and baste every 15 minutes. When sauce has been reduced to about half (approximately 2 hours) add the remaining 1/2 cup of wine and the green onions. Pour 1 tablespoon triple sec over each duck. Continue cooking until the ducks are thoroughly tender and sauce has reduced a little more.

Remove ducks from sauce. Remove as much fat as possible from sauce with a spoon and then skim the top with a paper towel. Cut ducks in half and place under broiler until skin is crisp and dark brown. Top with sauce and serve.

MAKES 8 SERVINGS

MR. B'S

201 Royal St., New Orleans, LA 70130; (504) 523-2078.

One of the best advertisements for Mr. B's is the aroma which wafts around a three-block radius of the restaurant — the distinctive, delicious smell of hickory, pecan, and mesquite logs burning on an open grill. Over these woods Mr. B's chefs grill fresh Louisiana redfish, prime strip sirloins, duckling, and platters of sausage and poultry. Another specialty is pasta, made on the premises and assembled into an interesting assortment of cheesy, creamy dishes, al dente and delicious.

HICKORY GRILLED WISCONSIN DUCKLING

1 (4-pound) duck, boned (see Note)
Creole meat seasoning (see page 79)
4 garlic cloves, peeled
5 fresh rosemary sprigs
1/2 cup glace du canard (see Note)
3 tablespoons brandy
1/4 cup butter, chilled

Season duck with creole meat seasoning on skin. Place garlic cloves and 3 springs fresh rosemary in cavity. Roast duck on a hot hickory grill on spit until meat is still moderately pink.

While roasting make a sauce by heating the glace du canard with 2 sprigs of rosemary for fragrance.

When the duck comes off the grill, place it in an ovenproof pan, and roast it at 450 degrees F. for approximately 8 minutes. Remove from pan and keep on a warm serving platter. Pour brandy into the pan, add the glace du canard and stir and scrape the pan. Place over moderate heat and whisk in the butter, one tablespoon at a time. Remove rosemary.

Remove garlic and rosemary from duck and cut in half. Place on a platter and pour sauce over.

The duckling is served crisp, yet the meat is still slightly pink.

Note: Instructions for boning duck may be found on page 103.

Note: To make glace du canard, make a duck stock by substituting duck bones for chicken bones in chicken stock (see Basic Stocks). Reduce the stock to 1 to 1/2 cup, or a glace du canard.

MAKES 4 SERVINGS

Photograph, Page 22

SAFFRON

Sheraton New Orleans Hotel, 500 Canal St., New Orleans, LA 70130; (504) 525-2500.

When this new luxury hotel opened up in 1982 on New Orleans' famed Canal Street, it was decided that nothing would be too good for its principal restaurant. So Saffron has its own kitchen, separate from other hotel food operations, lead crystal and silvery cutlery on fine linen tablecloths, and marble and etched glass appointments. The food is no less impressive; each dish is a surprising work of art both in presentation and taste.

QUAIL WITH WILD MUSHROOMS AND THYME BUTTER

4 cups wild mushrooms (see Glossary)
2 cups butter, divided
Salt and pepper to taste
8 tablespoons fresh thyme, divided (see Note)
4 tablespoons olive oil
4 quail

Saute mushrooms with $1/2$ cup of the butter for 3 to 4 minutes. Add salt and pepper to taste; add 4 tablespoons of the fresh thyme and set aside.

In a hot skillet, place 4 tablespoons of olive oil and cook quail for about 3 to 4 minutes on each side.

Arrange the mushrooms in the top portion of the plate; below the mushrooms place quail.

In a separate pan melt the remaining $1 1/2$ cups of butter and add the remaining 4 tablespoons of fresh thyme. Pour the butter mixture over the quail and serve.

Note: Fresh basil or tarragon may be substituted for fresh thyme.

MAKES 4 SERVINGS

Photograph, Page 24

MAURICE'S BISTRO

1763 Stumpf Blvd., Gretna, LA 70053; (504) 361-9000.

Two of the dishes most talked about at Maurice's Bistro come free with dinner. They are a pair of tidbits served at the beginning of the meal, French-fried parsley and Bistro bread. The latter is coated with a spicy, tomato mixture and toasted. Together, the parsley and bread make a fine match with cocktails at the Bistro's romantic tables. The tables are set on three levels, with a mezzanine overlooking the entire rustic, exposed-wood-beam dining room.

QUAIL A LA BISTRO

1/2 cup blanched almonds
1/2 cup hickory smoked almonds
1/4 cup bread crumbs
1/2 cup chopped mushrooms
1 whole egg, beaten
1 tablespoon sugar
1/4 cup chicken bouillon
4 quail
Paprika
4 teaspoons butter

Orange Almond Sauce
2 tablespoons butter
2 tablespoons blanched almonds
1 1/2 teaspoons brown sugar
2 teaspoons cornstarch
1 cup orange juice
1 1/2 tablespoons grated orange peel
1/4 tablespoon powdered cloves
1/2 teaspoon seasoned salt

Pulverize almonds in food processor. Add bread crumbs, mushrooms, egg, sugar, and bouillon and mix.

Wash and dry quail, stuff, sprinkle with paprika, and dot with butter. Bake at 375 degrees F. for 5 to 7 minutes, uncovered. Serve with orange almond sauce.

To make orange almond sauce: Melt butter in skillet. Saute almonds until golden brown. Remove almonds. In the same skillet, combine sugar, cornstarch, and orange juice. Cook on medium heat stirring constantly until clear and thickened. Add orange peel, cloves, seasoned salt, and almonds.

Serve with croquette potatoes and broccoli with hollandaise.

MAKES 4 SERVINGS

ANTOINE'S

713 St. Louis St., New Orleans, LA 70130; (504) 581-4422.

You have not really arrived in New Orleans until you have your personal waiter at Antoine's. "Your" waiter is the person you call to make a reservation, he lets you in the back door, thereby avoiding the line in front and, he's the professional who creates special dishes to suit your gustatory whims. It is not unheard of for a son to "inherit" his father's waiter, who often becomes a personal friend as well as a server. It's a fine old system which has great benefits for both waiter and customer.

PIGEONNEAUX PARADIS (Squabs with Paradise Sauce)

6 squabs
Salt and white pepper to taste
1/4 cup butter, softened

Paradise Sauce
1/3 pound bacon, julienned (see Glossary)
1/4 cup julienned green onions
3/4 cup julienned celery
3 tablespoons butter
3 tablespoons currant jelly
1 cup canned seedless white grapes, 1/2 cup juice reserved
1 cup thick chicken velouté (see Basic Sauces)

Wash and dry the squabs. Rub inside and out with salt, pepper, and butter. Place in a shallow baking pan and cook at 325 degrees F. for about 45 minutes or until done. While squabs are cooking, prepare paradise sauce.

To make paradise sauce: Fry bacon, discard grease, and set aside. Saute onions and celery in the butter until limp. Add bacon, currant jelly, and juice from the grapes. Bring to a boil, add velouté sauce and grapes.

Simmer for 15 minutes. Makes 3 cups of paradise sauce.

Place squab in a deep casserole, pour the paradise sauce over squabs, and bake for 20 minutes.

MAKES 6 SERVINGS

"Fish dinners will make a man spring like a flea."
THOMAS JORDAN

SEAFOOD

MASSON'S

7200 Pontchartrain Blvd., New Orleans, LA 70124; (504) 283-2525.

Masson's success as a major restaurant in New Orleans is well documented by the many awards and testimonials which line the walls near the dining room entrance. The cuisine which has won these accolades is French Provincial, seasoned with the Creole seasonings that make it unique. At dinner, the menu has a table d'hote format; the price includes hors d'oeuvre, soup, salad, entree, vegetable, dessert, and coffee. The restaurant's reasonable prices combined with good food make it a favorite among Orleanians.

SOFT SHELL CRAB & CRAWFISH ROBERT

6 large soft shell crabs, cleaned
Salt and pepper to taste
Paprika
1 cup unsalted butter, divided
1/2 stalk fresh fennel, chopped
1/2 cup sliced green onions
1/2 bunch fresh dill chopped
1 cup sliced mushrooms
1 pinch crushed red pepper
2 pounds peeled crawfish tails
1/4 cup dry white wine
1/4 cup Herbsaint or Pernod (see Glossary)
6 cups cooked rice

Season crabs with salt, pepper, and paprika. In a large skillet, saute crabs in one half of the butter for 5 minutes on each side.

Remove crabs. To the skillet add the remaining butter, fennel, green onions, dill, mushrooms, and red pepper. Saute until the green onions are tender, about 4 to 5 minutes. Add crawfish, white wine, and Herbsaint and saute for another 3 minutes.

Place crab on a mound of cooked rice and pour crawfish mixture around plate.

MAKES 6 SERVINGS

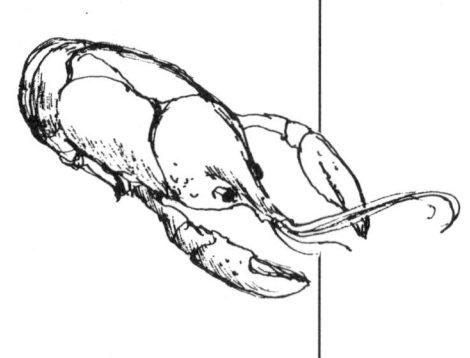

GALATOIRE'S

209 Bourbon St., New Orleans, LA 70112; (504) 525-2021.

The dining room of Galatoire's is unmistakeably that of the turn-of-the-century Creole restaurant which it epitomizes. The one long room has tables with starched white tablecloths, water decanters on every table, two-bladed antique ceiling fans hanging from high above, and rows of large mirrors surmounted with bare light bulbs. The waiters serve their many regular customers with an old-style friendliness that is rarely seen outside the oldline grand Creole restaurant. Even the menus reflect another era; they are thick catalogs of the Creole classics.

CRABMEAT YVONNE

6 artichokes
1 pound mushrooms, sliced
1/2 cup clarified butter (see Glossary)
2 pounds fresh backfin lump crabmeat
Salt and white pepper to taste
1/4 cup finely chopped parsley
Toast points

Garnish: 6 lemon wedges

To cook artichokes bring a large pot of water to boil. Cut off stem of artichoke flush with base and place artichokes in water. Cover with a fabric towel placed directly on top of the boiling artichokes to keep them below the surface of the water. Boil about 45 minutes or until a leaf pulls off easily from the base of an artichoke. Remove from pot and allow to cool.

Pull off leaves (set aside to enjoy later). Remove small cap of leaves and expose the fuzzy choke. Remove choke by scraping with a spoon to release it from the artichoke bottom. Discard choke, slice artichoke bottoms, and reserve.

In a large skillet saute the mushrooms in the butter; add the artichoke bottoms and crabmeat. Saute gently until heated thoroughly. Season with salt and white pepper. Sprinkle with finely chopped parsley. Serve over toast points with a lemon wedge on the side.

MAKES 6 SERVINGS

THE ROYAL RESTAURANT & PUB

Travelodge, 2502 Port Dr., Jennings, LA 70546; (318) 824-6550.

Besides the main dining room in this good motel restaurant there is a smaller, more elegant room complete with white tablecloths for private parties. In the main dining room, there is a liberal buffet which is highly active and bountiful at lunch. The evening menu consists of steaks and seafood, with fresh fried Louisiana catfish and a variety of seafood with sauce piquante among the house specialties. Prices are modest and the atmosphere is suitable for family meals.

CRAB SAUCE PIQUANTE

12 small crabs
Salt and pepper to taste
6 eggs
2/3 cup flour
2/3 cup Bisquick mix
1/3 cup oil

Sauce Piquante
2 tablespoons cooking oil
1/2 cup chopped onions
2 cloves garlic, chopped
1/2 cup chopped parsley
6 tablespoons hot sauce (preferably Bayou Bengal sauce)
1 pound lump crabmeat
1 quart water
Salt to taste
6 cups cooked rice or cream potatoes

Remove top shell and lungs from crab. Cut legs off close to body and break crab in half. Season with salt and pepper.

In mixing bowl prepare batter of eggs, flour, and Bisquick mix. Roll crabs in batter and fry in hot cooking oil until brown.

To make sauce: In a large skillet heat oil and saute onions and garlic until transparent. Add parsley, hot sauce, and Bayou Bengal sauce. Cook all ingredients over low heat another 10 minutes. Add crabmeat, crabs and water to sauce.

Cook 8 minutes over medium heat. Salt to taste. Serve over white rice or cream potatoes.

MAKES 6 SERVINGS

THE RESTAURANT ANGELLE'S

Rt. 2, Hwy. 167, Frontage Rd., Lafayette, LA 70505; (318) 896-8416.

Few restaurants in Louisiana were ever built specifically to reflect Louisiana's heritage. Angelle's is the successful exception. Constructed in December of 1973, it incorporates that special feeling of "joie de vivre" that is unmistakeably Acadiana. From the wooden gables to the stately foyer, from the sunken dining rooms with exposed beams to the beautiful oil paintings by local artists, a sense of hospitality prevails.

CRABMEAT AU GRATIN

1/2 cup chopped onions
1/2 cup chopped green peppers
1/2 cup margarine
1/4 pound Cheddar cheese, grated
1 (10-ounce) can mushroom soup
Salt and pepper to taste
1 tablespoon chopped parsley
1/4 cup flour
1/4 cup water
1 large can evaporated milk
1 pound lump crabmeat

Saute onions and green peppers in margarine until tender.

Add cheese, mushroom soup, salt, pepper, and parsley. Cook until cheese is melted.

Mix flour and water until smooth. Add milk. Add to cheese and cook for 15 minutes on low heat or until it makes a thick cheese sauce.

Add crabmeat and cook for 10 to 15 minutes. Try not to break crabmeat. Blend, do not stir. May be refrigerated and re-heated.

MAKES 4 TO 6 SERVINGS

Photograph, Page 18

MASSON'S

7200 Pontchartrain Blvd., New Orleans, LA 70124; (504) 283-2525.

Albert Masson, who manages the day-to-day operation of the restaurant bearing his family's name, has built a reputation for his expertise in the art of wine appreciation. This is reflected in the honors he has received from international organizations such as the Guild of Sommeliers and the Compagnon de Bordeaux. Executive chef Robert Finley, a cousin of the Massons, has also won his share of coveted awards, including a gold medal at the Pan American Culinary Olympics.

CRABMEAT AND ARTICHOKE BOTTOMS

1/2 bunch green onions, thinly sliced
1 pinch cayenne pepper
1 pinch thyme
2 bay leaves
1/2 cup margarine
2 ounces white wine
1 pound lump crabmeat
1 egg, beaten
1/2 cup bread crumbs
Salt to taste
6 artichoke bottoms
1 cup grated Swiss cheese
Hollandaise Sauce (see Basic Sauces)

Saute green onions, cayenne, thyme, and bay leaves in the margarine about 3 minutes. Add wine and crabmeat.

Fold in the egg and bread crumbs and add salt to taste. Roll crab mixture into 6 balls and place on top of artichoke bottoms. Sprinkle with Swiss cheese and bake in a 350 degrees F. oven for 10 minutes.

Top with Hollandaise Sauce and serve.

MAKES 6 SERVINGS

CHRISTIAN'S

3835 Iberville St., New Orleans, LA 70119; (504) 482-4924.

By far the most popular restaurant in the settled Mid-City section of New Orleans, Christian's small church-converted-into-dining-room is so busy that reservations well in advance are a must. So confident in its success is this restaurant that it enforces a policy of disallowing restaurant critics from reviewing its offerings. These are primarily in the seafood category, including grilled, fried, and broiled local fish. Sweetbreads, veal, and beef are other specialties.

CRABMEAT WITH GRAPEFRUIT

3 pink grapefruit
4 shallots, finely chopped
3 tablespoons butter
1 quart cream
2½ pounds crabmeat
2 green onions, sliced
Salt and pepper to taste

Remove the grapefruit peel and cut the peel in narrow strips. Blanche them until tender and set aside to chill.

Carefully remove the sections of grapefruit. Save all the small pieces of meat and juice. Reserve 24 whole sections for the final garnish in a separate dish.

Saute the shallots in the butter until clear. Add the cream and reduce until it starts to thicken. Add the crabmeat, the grapefruit juice, and extra pieces of the grapefruit. Add the green onions and season to taste with salt and pepper. Warm slowly, being careful not to break up the crabmeat.

Serve in individual casseroles and arrange three grapefruit sections in a star on top of each portion. In the middle of the stars sprinkle some of the blanched grapefruit peel. Serve immediately.

MAKES 8 SERVINGS

EMERY'S

501 N. Adams, Welsh, LA 70591; (318) 734-3715.

One block from I-10, Emery's does a hearty business not only from the town of Welsh, but also from the heavy New Orleans-to-Houston traffic. Breakfast, lunch, and dinner are served seven days a week. At lunch and dinner the specialties are seafood, fresh and prepared in a host of different ways, steaks, accurately broiled to order, and Cajun specialties in season. There is also a salad bar and a private dining room. Emery's does catering both on and off the premises.

CRABMEAT AU GRATIN

3 ribs celery, chopped
1 cup chopped onions
1/2 cup butter-flavored oil
1 teaspoon salt
1/2 teaspoon red pepper
1/4 teaspoon black pepper
1/2 cup heavy cream
1/2 pound Cheddar cheese, grated
1 pound lump crabmeat
Additional grated Cheddar cheese

Saute celery and onion in oil. Add salt, red pepper, black pepper, cream, and Cheddar cheese and cook for 5 minutes.

Add the crabmeat and heat gently. Transfer to a lightly greased baking dish. Sprinkle with the additional grated Cheddar cheese. Bake in 375 degree F. oven or in a microwave oven until cheese is melted.

MAKES 4 SERVINGS

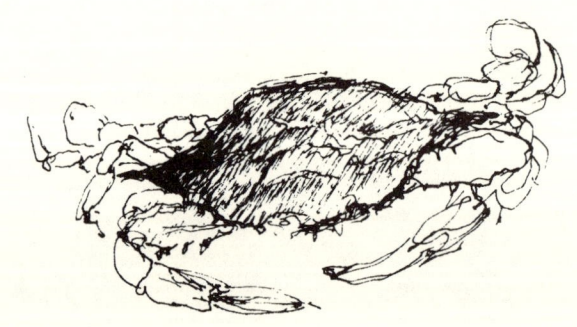

L. R. A.

All shellfish are adulated in Louisiana. Crabs, shrimp, and crawfish are honored in outdoor eating celebrations, cooked over an open fire as friends share conversations and camaraderie. The Louisiana Restaurant Association offers this crab recipe as opportunity to gather a group of friends, boil up a hamper of live crabs, cover your tables with newspapers, and spend a warm Louisiana evening picking and savoring this succulent spicy treat.

HOT BOILED CRABS

1 hamper live crabs (6 to 7 dozen depending on size)
12 lemons, quartered
3 to 4 boxes table salt
12 ounces cayenne pepper
8 ounces liquid crab boil

Fill large pot with crabs and enough cold water to cover crabs. Place on fire.

When crabs stop moving, add all seasonings and ingredients. When water comes to a boil, let boil for about 2 minutes.

Remove from fire. Add about 2 gallons cold water or 4 trays ice cubes. Stir and let soak for about 20 to 30 minutes, then pull out crabs and start eating.

MAKES 30 TO 40 SERVINGS

THE GUMBO SHOP

630 St. Peter St., New Orleans, LA 70116; (504) 525-1486.

There are large murals on all four walls of the Gumbo Shop's dining room. All depict scenes from New Orleans' early history. The first shows the Place D'Armes, now Jackson Square, with troops. The second depicts the old French Market. The third shows a riverfront scene, and the fourth a fine Vieux Carré courtyard. The Gumbo Shop has a small courtyard itself, and alfresco dining is featured in hospitable weather. There is also a good Sunday brunch.

CRAWFISH ETOUFFEE

6 tablespoons butter, divided
1/4 cup flour
1 cup chopped onions
1/2 cup chopped green pepper
1/2 cup chopped celery
1 tablespoon minced garlic
1 teaspoon salt
1/4 teaspoon ground black pepper
1/4 teaspoon cayenne
1 teaspoon lemon juice
1/2 cup sliced green onion tops
1 tablespoon chopped parsley
1/2 cup crawfish fat (see Glossary)
3 cups crawfish stock (see Note)
1 1/2 cups peeled crawfish tails
1 tablespoon paprika
4 cups cooked rice

Melt 4 tablespoons butter, add flour, and cook over a medium heat stirring constantly to make a golden brown roux.

Saute in remaining 2 tablespoons of butter, the onions, green peppers, and celery until tender. Add garlic, salt, black pepper, cayenne, lemon juice, green onions, and parsley. Stir in crawfish fat and cook for 5 minutes.

Stir in the roux, then add the stock, and bring to a boil. Cook for about 15 minutes. Add crawfish tails and paprika. Simmer for about 15 minutes. Serve over rice.

Note: Stock may be made by boiling crawfish shells in 4 cups water with a bay leaf, some peppercorns, 2 stalks celery, and 1 onion, halved. Cook 20 minutes and strain or use seafood stock (see Basic Stocks).

MAKES 4 SERVINGS

THE VERSAILLES

2100 St. Charles Ave., New Orleans, LA 70140; (504) 524-2535.

Chef Gunter Preuss brings culinary prowess to the total menu of offering of The Versailles, from soups, to fresh seafoods and meat entrees, to desserts. This lovely restaurant in the French Quarter enchants diners who are seeking French and Creole cuisine in tasteful surroundings.

CRAWFISH VERSAILLES

2 tablespoons sliced green onions
2 tablespoons minced garlic
1 tablespoon minced shallots
2 tablespoons butter
1/2 cup white wine
Juice of 1/4 lemon
1 3/4 cup medium béchamel sauce
   (see Basic Sauces)
1 1/2 tablespoons fresh dill
   (1 tablespoon dried)
1 1/2 pounds boiled crawfish tails
Salt to taste
Pinch cayenne pepper
Grated Parmesan cheese

Garnish: 6 boiled crawfish tails

Saute onions, garlic, and shallots in butter for 2 minutes without browning. Add white wine and lemon juice and reduce by half. Add béchamel sauce and dill and reduce by another third.

Add crawfish tails and simmer 10 minutes. Season to taste with salt and a pinch of cayenne pepper.

To serve, put in individual ramekins or small sea shells. Sprinkle with freshly grated Parmesan cheese and bake in 350 degree F. oven until cheese is golden.

Garnish each serving with a crawfish and serve.

MAKES 6 SERVINGS

MISTER JAY'S

1604 Hwy. 90 W., Vinton, LA 70668; (318) 589-7300.

One of the distinctive aspects of this restaurant is its Memorabilia Room, honoring the achievements of local people. Momentos include those celebrating Ted Lyons, who is in the Baseball Hall of Fame; Bobbie Kimball, a member of the rock band Toto; Joe Bonsall, who is in the Cajun Music Hall of Fame; and four Vinton men who participated in the death march on Bataan during World War II. This exhibit is well worth a pre- or post-dinner look.

ORIGINAL LOUISIANA CAJUN CRAWFISH PIZZA

1/4 cup water
1 teaspoon cornstarch
2 tablespoons melted butter
1 teaspoon garlic powder
Red pepper (if desired)
1 (12-inch) frozen pizza crust, unbaked
1 cup chopped, peeled crawfish tails
1/2 cup chopped green pepper
1/2 cup chopped onions
1/2 cup grated mozzarella cheese

Mix water and cornstarch until smooth. Add melted butter, garlic powder, and red pepper. Brush evenly over pizza crust, leaving 1/2-inch edge. Spread evenly with crawfish, pepper, and onions and top with mozzarella cheese.

Bake at 500 degrees F. for 15 minutes. Cut into 8 pieces and serve.

MAKES 8 SERVINGS

Photograph, Page 22

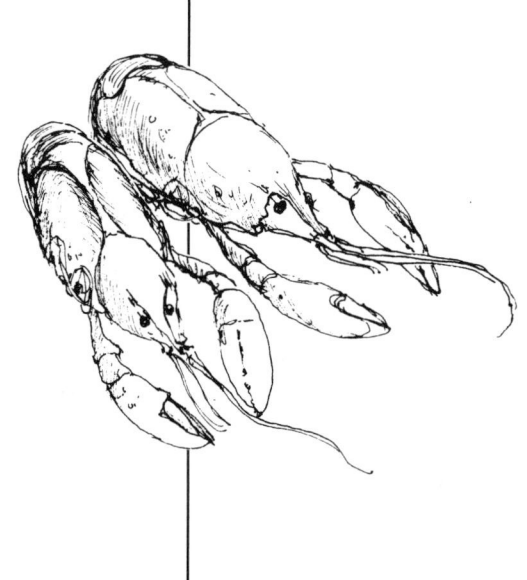

LA COQUILLE

One Shell Square, New Orleans, LA 70139; (504) 523-7259.

One would hardly think that staying in your own office building constitutes "going out to lunch," but for the many who work in One Shell Square, New Orleans' tallest skyscraper, that option is certainly open. On the ground floor of the building is La Coquille, an acclaimed Creole-French restaurant with a lunch menu that would make many restaurants' dinner offerings look unambitious. There are daily specials in the appetizer, soup, and entree courses, and all qualify as delicious creations.

CRAWFISH RAVIOLI WITH NANTUA SAUCE

Pasta
3 cups unbleached all purpose flour
1 pinch salt
3 teaspoons olive oil
1 cup cold water

Filling
2 pounds peeled crawfish tails, finely chopped
1/2 cup béchamel sauce (see Basic Sauces)
1/2 bunch green onions, thinly sliced
1 bunch parsley, chopped
Salt and pepper to taste
Bread crumbs

Sauce
2 pounds peeled crawfish tails
1/4 cup butter
1/2 cup crawfish fat
1 tablespoon tomato paste
1 tablespoon flour
1/4 cup brandy
1 quart heavy cream
1/2 teaspoon tarragon
Salt and pepper to taste

Eggwash
1 egg
1/4 cup water

To make pasta: In food processor with steel blade, combine flour and salt to blend. Combine olive oil and water and gradually pour into bowl, processing until well kneaded, about 1 1/2 minutes. Let dough rest about 20 minutes in refrigerator. Then knead on a floured table with hands to finish kneading process. Roll out dough into sheets about 5 inches by 10 inches by 1/8 inch. Two sheets will be needed for each set of ravioli.

To make filling: Mix all ingredients in bowl, adding only enough bread crumbs to make a dry mixture.

To make sauce: Saute crawfish in butter and fat. Add tomato paste and flour and cook for about 5 minutes. Add brandy and remaining ingredients and let simmer, uncovered, until reduced to the consistency of a medium thick sauce.

To assemble: Place small mounds of filling on first pasta sheet in two rows and brush around them with eggwash. Place second sheet of pasta on top and use hands to seal. Then use crimping wheel to seal and cut out ravioli.

Place in 6-to-8 quart pot of boiling salted water and cook for approximately 8 minutes. Remove from water and cool. Place ravioli in sauce, heat, and serve.

MAKES 6 SERVINGS

L.R.A.

The crawfish boil is a social event of fun-loving proportions, where bright red crawfish, boiled onions, and potatoes are consumed with great quantities of beer. Each guest picks his crawfish, extracting the meat from the tail and sucking the head for the juices. Louisiana is estimated to produce ninety-nine per cent of all the crawfish in the U.S., with eighty-eight per cent eaten in southern Louisiana. The Louisiana Restaurant Association presents this quantity recipe for your enjoyment of a community Cajun tradition.

HOT AND SPICY BOILED CRAWFISH

1 sack crawfish (40 to 50 pounds)
Water
1 bunch celery, chopped
3 whole garlic heads, chopped in half crosswise
12 lemons, quartered
3 to 4 boxes salt
4 medium onions, quartered
12 ounces cayenne pepper
8 ounces liquid crab boil

Purge crawfish in water for about 10 minutes. Drain. Fill large pot with enough water to cover crawfish. Bring water to first boil. Add seasoning and all ingredients, except crawfish and stir. Add live crawfish and stir again.

When water comes to second boil, remove from heat. Add about 2 gallons cold water or 4 to 5 trays ice cubes. Stir and let soak for 20 to 30 minutes.

MAKES 50 SERVINGS

JEFFREY'S RIVERSIDE RESTAURANT

915 River Rd., Norco, LA 70079; (504) 764-9904.

Jeffrey's is a family-style restaurant specializing in Creole cooking and local seafood. Preparations are imaginative; the seafood is fried to order, the poor boy sandwiches are filled with good meats and cheeses, and there are delectable daily luncheon specials. For those looking for lighter fare, Jeffrey's features a full salad bar. The restaurant is located across from the levee on River Road, and offers custom catering as well as full restaurant service.

DEEP-FRIED CATFISH FILLETS

3 pounds fresh Lake DesAllemands catfish fillets
2 eggs, lightly beaten
1 teaspoon ground mustard
1/2 teaspoon salt
1/2 teaspoon white pepper
1/2 teaspoon ground red pepper
1/2 cup corn flour
3/4 cup corn meal
2 quarts light vegetable oil or peanut oil

Thoroughly dry fish fillets. Mix eggs, mustard, salt, white pepper, and red pepper well. Place fish in mixture and chill for 1 to 2 hours.

Mix corn flour and corn meal. Remove fish from egg mixture and dust lightly with flour mixture, shaking off excess. Heat oil to 375 degrees F. Drop fish into oil and fry until fish floats and is light golden brown, 4 to 6 minutes.

MAKES 4 TO 6 SERVINGS

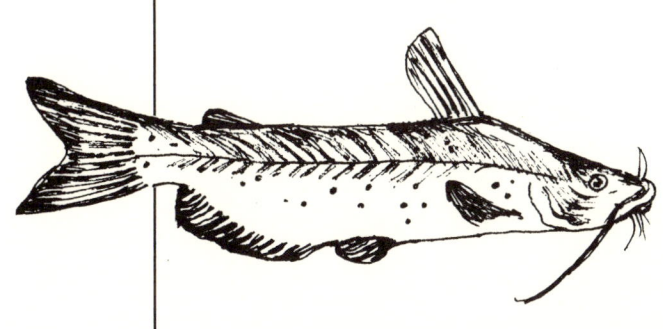

LA SAVOIE

94 Friedrichs Ave., Metairie, LA 70005; (504) 831-1108.

Owner-chef Gerard Thabuis, a native of France and a veteran of many New Orleans restaurants, is a strong believer in the dramatic. One of his performances in the dining room (done only for regular customers and friends, for obvious reasons) involves exploding the neck off a bottle of Champagne with a kitchen knife. Another touch reserved for regulars is the service of "l 'eau de vie," a strong spirit from his hometown, from a bottle with a hand-carved ship in it. His food is equally as adventuresome.

STUFFED FLOUNDER

1 (12-to-16 ounce) flounder
3 ounces crabmeat
3 ounces crawfish tails, chopped
4 tablespoons lemon juice
2 tablespoons grated Parmesan cheese
1 egg
1/4 cup butter
2 tablespoons diced green onions
1 tablespoon chopped celery
2 tablespoons chopped parsley
2 large mushrooms, sliced
Salt and pepper to taste
1/4 teaspoon thyme
1/4 teaspoon basil
Bay leaf
1/2 cup half and half
1/2 tablespoon chopped garlic
2 ounces white wine

Garnish: Lemon wedge and drawn butter

Bone flounder by making incision down the middle of dark side with a knife. Separate flesh from bone by cutting between the fish and bone only to the fin. Fold skin back and remove bones (or buy a whole boned flounder).

In a mixing bowl combine other ingredients and mix well. Put in baking dish. Bake at 450 degrees F. for 30 minutes.

Stuff flounder. Bake 10 minutes more. Garnish with lemon wedge and drawn butter.

MAKES 1 SERVING

ANTOINE'S

713 St. Louis St., New Orleans, LA 70130; (504) 581-4422.

The menu at Antoine's is a highly eclectic one, not a word of English on it, all in French, and often requires deciphering by the waiter. It lists many more dishes than one sees in most restaurants now. This is an old-fashioned practice, but in fact you can find among the non-specialty items many interesting sleepers, particularly in the appetizer section. If you want to brush up on your menu French for your next visit, you can take the menu with you.

POMPANO EN PAPILLOTE *(Pompano in Paper Bag)*

Fish Velouté Sauce
2 tablespoons butter
2 tablespoons flour
1 1/2 cups warm fish or chicken stock (see Basic Stocks)
Salt and white pepper to taste
Additional butter

3 tablespoons butter
1 cup chopped green onions
1 cup raw peeled shrimp
1 1/2 cups white wine, divided
1 cup lump crabmeat
Salt, white pepper, and cayenne to taste
6 (16-ounce) skinned pompano fillets
1 onion, sliced
2 teaspoons salt
5 whole black peppercorns
2 bay leaves
Juice of 1 lemon
Water
Parchment paper

To make veloute sauce: Melt the butter and stir in the flour. Stir and cook until the mixture becomes foamy. Add the warm stock and bring to a boil. Turn heat down to simmer while adding salt and pepper to taste. Remove from heat and dot top of sauce with a few pieces of butter to prevent a film from forming. Makes 1 1/2 cups of velouté sauce.

Melt the butter and saute the green onions until they become limp. Add the shrimp, 1 cup of the wine, and bring to a boil. Blend in the veloute sauce and the crabmeat. Season to taste with salt, pepper, and cayenne. Simmer gently for 10 minutes, then let cool.

Poach the pompano fillets for 3 minutes in a shallow pan with the sliced onion, 2 teaspoons salt, peppercorns, the remaining 1/2 cup wine, bay leaves, lemon juice, and enough water to cover. Remove the fillets from the poaching liquid and keep warm.

Cut parchment paper into 6 heart-shaped pieces, about 10 inches long and 14 inches wide. Spoon some of the sauce onto the center of one half of the heart-shaped paper and top with a pompano fillet. Fold the other half of the paper over the top and seal the edges by folding edges tightly together.

Place these on an oiled baking pan, and bake at 400 degrees F. for 15 minutes or until the paper begins to brown. Bring to the table and cut the top of the paper open.

MAKES 6 SERVINGS

DELMONICO

1300 St. Charles Ave., New Orleans, LA 70130; (504) 525-4937.

The food at Delmonico is a perfect match for the lovely, old-fashioned New Orleans decor; it is traditional Creole. You will find all the most famous classics of New Orleans cooking here, prepared consistently well—gumbos, a vast array of local seafood in every imaginable Creole-style form, great fresh salads, and traditional local desserts. The service style is simple and friendly.

FILLET OF SNAPPER ROME

1/2 cup butter
1/4 cup lemon juice
Dash Worcestershire sauce
4 red snapper fillets
1 cup crabmeat
1/4 cup melted butter
1 1/2 teaspoons butter
1 1/2 teaspoons all purpose flour
1/2 cup half and half
1/2 teaspoon salt
Dash white pepper
1/2 cup dry bread crumbs
8 green pepper strips

Combine the 1/2 cup butter, lemon juice, and Worcestershire sauce in a small saucepan; cook over medium heat, stirring often, until heated thoroughly. Place fillets in a 13-inch by 9-inch by 2-inch baking pan; broil 10 to 15 minutes, basting often with the lemon butter.

Saute crabmeat in the 1/4 cup butter about 3 minutes; set aside.

Melt remaining 1 1/2 teaspoons butter in a heavy saucepan over low heat; add flour, stirring until smooth. Cook 1 minute, stirring constantly. Gradually stir in the half and half; cook over medium heat, stirring constantly until thickened and bubbly. Stir in salt and pepper; add crabmeat, stirring well.

Spoon crabmeat mixture on top of each fillet. Sprinkle bread crumbs over crabmeat mixture; garnish each fillet with 2 strips of green pepper. Bake at 350 degrees F. for 10 minutes. Broil fillets just until bread crumbs are browned.

MAKES 4 SERVINGS

Photograph, Page 17

CHEZ PASTOR

1211 Pinhook Rd., Lafayette, LA 70501; (318) 234-5189.

In Lafayette, where eight months of the year crawfish is king, you can hardly find a restaurant which raises the beloved crustacean to greater heights than Chez Pastor. Operated by the convivial Pat and Maugie Pastor, this restaurant has developed creative and complex creations with crawfish that have become instant classics. The menu also encompasses the breadth of Cajun seafood cookery, but with more of a gilded edge than you are likely to find elsewhere.

SNAPPER FONTENOT

Pan-Broiled Snapper
8 (8-ounce) snapper fillets
Salt to taste
Black and cayenne pepper to taste
1/2 cup cooking oil

Fontenot Sauce
2 cups butter
1 teaspoon salt
1 teaspoon seasoned pepper
1 pound lump crabmeat
1/2 pound shrimp, peeled and deveined
1/2 cup white wine
1/4 cup chopped green onions
1/4 cup chopped parsley

To prepare snapper: Season snapper generously with salt, cayenne pepper, and black pepper. Heat oil in skillet, add fish, and cook over medium heat turning once until fish are done. Set aside.

To make Fontenot Sauce: Melt butter over low heat, add seasonings, crabmeat, shrimp, and wine. Simmer till shrimp are tender. Add green onions and parsley. Serve over broiled red snapper.

MAKES 8 SERVINGS

Photograph, Page 20

RIVERVIEW RESTAURANT

Marriott Hotel, 555 Canal St., New Orleans, LA 70140; (504) 581-1000.

The top floor of New Orleans' tallest hotel, is given over to a large restaurant and lounge with giant windows. Through them one has a breathtaking view of the curves of the Mississippi River as it comes downstream and heads toward the Gulf of Mexico. In another direction there is Lake Pontchartrain; on a clear day, you can see all the way across the lake to Slidell and the North Shore. The food is oriented mainly toward seafood, New Orleans style, with a full selection of other foods.

RED SNAPPER "DORE"

1 (6-ounce) boneless red snapper fillet
1/4 cup buttermilk
Salt and white pepper to taste
1/4 cup flour
1/4 cup salted butter
1/4 cup sliced mushrooms
2 ounces small shrimp, peeled and deveined
2 ounces lump crabmeat
Juice of 1/2 lemon
2 teaspoons chopped parsley

Garnish: *Lemon crown and parsley sprig*

Soak red snapper in buttermilk for 30 minutes. Drain well; season with salt and white pepper and coat with flour. In a skillet melt butter over medium heat. Saute fish fillet on each side for about 4 minutes or until golden brown. Place sauteed fish in center of warm plate.

In remaining butter, saute the mushrooms and shrimp for 2 to 3 minutes. Add crabmeat, lemon juice, and chopped parsley. Let simmer for another minute and spoon over fish. Garnish plate with lemon crown and parsley sprig.

Note: Handle lump crabmeat very carefully to avoid breaking up the lumps.

MAKES 1 SERVING

DON'S SEAFOOD HUT

4309 Johnston St., Lafayette, LA 70503; (318) 981-1141.

For over ten years, Don's has meant the best seafood and Cajun specialties to the gourmets of Acadiana. The menu is extensive and features the best of the local catch in season, prepared in imaginative and authentic ways. Friends meet over oysters and cocktails in the oyster bar and lounge, with its silver coins inlaid in the top of the bar, and then they retire to the main dining room, with its picturesque windows, lofty ceilings, antique stone fireplace, and intimate booths.

SNAPPER A LA KING

1/2 cup finely chopped onions
1/2 cup finely chopped green peppers
1/2 cup finely chopped celery
1/2 cup margarine
1/2 cup flour
4 cans evaporated milk
1/2 teaspoon red pepper
1/2 teaspoon salt
2 chicken bouillon cubes
1/2 cup sliced mushrooms
1 cup peeled, deveined, chopped shrimp
2 teaspoons paprika
2 pounds red snapper fillets
Additional salt and red pepper to taste

Saute vegetables with margarine for 15 minutes over medium heat.

Stir in flour and cook 1 to 2 minutes. Add evaporated milk, one can at a time. Add seasonings, chicken bouillon cubes, and mushrooms. Cook 5 minutes, then add shrimp and paprika. Let cook for 15 or 20 minutes until thick.

Season fish with salt and red pepper and place in a baking pan. Pour sauce over fish. Bake at 350 degrees F. for approximately 25 to 30 minutes.

MAKES 6 SERVINGS

COVINGTON DEPOT

503 N. New Hampshire, Covington, LA 70433; (504) 892-3337.

The seating is comfortable, the atmosphere casual and friendly, and the food very Creole in this renovated train station on the North Shore of Lake Pontchartrain. The Depot is in the center of Covington, one of the state's fastest growing cities. On any given day you can find all the great New Orleans dishes, some in unusual forms, such as red bean soup. There is fresh seafood, steaks, and chicken dishes on a menu quite suitable for pleasing the whole family.

BROILED REDFISH FILLETS ON STEAMED VEGETABLES WITH HOLLANDAISE

4 (6-to 8-ounce) redfish fillets
4 tablespoons butter
4 teaspoons lemon juice
Salt and white pepper to taste
1 tablespoon paprika
1 bunch broccoli
1 head cauliflower
2 medium carrots
2 ribs celery
Hollandaise Sauce (see Basic Sauces)

Try to select redfish fillets that are thick in size. Place in baking pan with butter, lemon juice, salt, and pepper. Sprinkle fish with paprika. Add water to partially cover fish. Broil at 350 degrees F. until fish is tender and flakes.

Cut broccoli and cauliflower into florettes. Cut carrots and celery at a 45-degree angle into pieces about 1-inch long. Place in a steamer and steam until crunchy, about 5 to 7 minutes.

Arrange vegetables on plate, place fish over vegetables, top with Hollandaise.

MAKES 4 SERVINGS

Photograph, Page 18

BON TON CAFE

401 Magazine St., New Orleans, LA 70130; (504) 524-3386.

One of the most engaging restaurants in New Orleans' Central Business District, the Bon Ton Café has a national reputation for its exciting Creole and Cajun cooking. Now operated by Wayne Pierce—a former dentist who took over the restaurant in 1977—the Bon Ton continues to maintain the excitement of its authentic creations of Wayne's uncle, Alvin Pierce. The small dining room fills up early with its many regular customers at both lunch and dinner.

REDFISH BON TON

6 (8-ounce) redfish fillets
Salt and pepper to taste
Paprika to taste
1 1/2 cups butter, divided
Juice of 3 lemons
1/4 cup water
3/4 pound lump crabmeat (approximately 2 cups)
1/2 cup white wine
1/8 cup finely chopped parsley

Sprinkle both sides of the redfish fillets with salt, pepper and paprika lightly.

Melt 1 cup of the butter in a large skillet. Slightly brown the butter. Place the seasoned redfish in the skillet, and cook for 2 minutes over medium heat. Add the lemon juice. Turn the fish over, and add the water. Lightly sprinkle the fish again with paprika.

Cover the fish and cook 8 to 10 minutes. Remove the cover, and simmer for 2 to 3 minutes more until the fish is done.

Remove the fish from the skillet, and place the fillets on heated plates. Stir the sauce that remains in the skillet. If the butter separates, add a little more water to achieve a sauce.

Meanwhile, place the remaining 1/2 cup butter and the white wine and the crabmeat in another pan. Cook it over low heat until warm.

Serve the redfish topped with crabmeat and chopped parsley. Spoon some of the butter sauce over each serving.

MAKES 6 SERVINGS

MENEFEE'S

1101 N. Rampart, New Orleans, LA 70116; (504) 566-0464.

The development of Armstrong Park, New Orleans' tribute to Satchmo, has brought with it a renaissance of nightlife on North Rampart Street. One of the premier establishments in this regard is Menefee's, which occupies an old mansion. It has been completely redecorated into a striking Art Deco design, with fascinating neon art here and there. Cuisine is a creative medley of Continental and Creole dishes. The lounge features live music every night, and the scene is a lively one until well into the wee hours.

REDFISH DE LA MAISON

2 pounds redfish fillets
Salt and pepper to taste
2 cups butter, divided
2 cups sliced leeks
2 tablespoons chopped garlic
4 cups diced tomatoes
3 cups sliced mushrooms
1 cup heavy cream
1 tablespoon crushed red pepper
$1/2$ cup white wine
1 pound lump crabmeat

Salt and pepper redfish. Bake in a greased pan, uncovered at 350 degrees F. for 10 to 15 minutes, depending on the thickness.

In a saute pan heat 3 tablespoons of the butter. Add leeks, garlic, tomatoes, and mushrooms. Saute for 3 to 5 minutes stirring occasionally. Add cream and red pepper and reduce mixture by one-half. Add remaining butter, white wine, and crabmeat. Bring back to boil and remove from stove.

Place the baked fish on heated platter and cover with sauce.

MAKES 6 SERVINGS

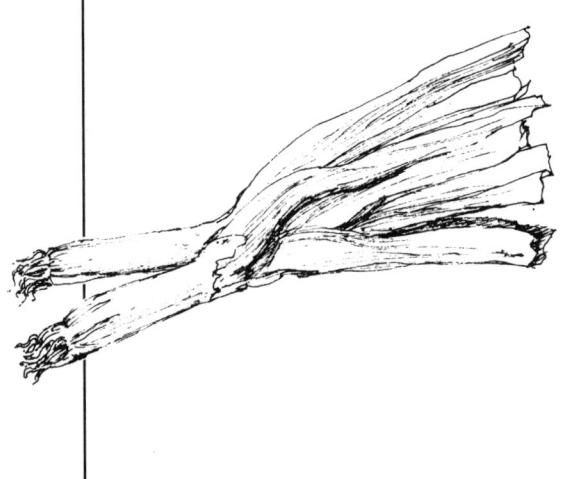

VALENTINE'S

Sheraton Inn Airport, 2150 Veterans Blvd., Kenner, LA 70062; (504) 467-3111.

Although the proximity to the New Orleans International Airport attracts many visitors to this highrise hotel, the Sheraton restaurants have generated a great deal of interest from the residents of Metairie and Kenner. Valentine's, whose trademark is a pair of ruby, wet lips seen on billboards around town, is a handsome, casual, fun restaurant and lounge. The menu includes a collection of international specialties as well as local favorites.

REDFISH VALENTINE'S

Creole Sauce
2 tablespoons butter
1 cup chopped green pepper
1 1/2 cups chopped onion
3 cups chopped tomatoes
1 bay leaf
3 cloves garlic, minced
1 tablespoon minced parsley
Salt and cayenne pepper to taste
1 tablespoon cornstarch mixed with small amount of water

2 tablespoons Hollandaise Sauce (see Basic Sauces)
1/4 cup butter
1 (6- to 8-ounce) redfish fillet
2 tablespoons lemon juice
2 ounces lump crabmeat

To make creole sauce: Saute in butter the green pepper and onions until they become limp. Add remaining ingredients, except cornstarch, and simmer 20 minutes. Stir in the cornstarch until sauce thickens. Makes 3 cups.

Prepare Hollandaise Sauce

Heat butter in a small skillet and add lemon juice. Place redfish into pan with butter and lemon juice. Saute redfish in the mixture for 5 minutes. Top first with creole sauce, then crabmeat, and finally Hollandaise sauce.

MAKES 1 SERVING

LES CHEFS DE CUISINE DE LA LOUISIANNE

One of the most advanced and successful training programs for chefs is administered by this association of Louisiana chefs. Students learn preparation, seasoning, and cooking according to recipes. They work with various national cuisines: France, Germany, Italy, England, Japan, and others. They learn production of baked goods, selecting cuts of meat, and making desserts. Menu and recipe development, requisitioning and purchasing, food cost management, ice carving, and every other skill needed by the professional chef are part of their extensive program. Chef Kurt Wolf presents the following recipe for trout.

TROUT WITH MUSHROOM SAUCE

1 1/2 pounds trout fillets
Water to cover
Bay leaf
1 teaspoon salt
6 peppercorns

Mushroom Sauce
1/2 cup chopped mushrooms
2 tablespoons chopped green onion
2 tablespoons butter, divided
1 tablespoon flour
1 cup light cream
3 drops Tabasco sauce
1 1/2 teaspoons Dijon-type mustard
1 1/2 tablespoons catsup
Salt and pepper to taste

1 1/2 to 2 cups cooked rice

Garnish: parsley sprigs and fresh dill

Place trout in boiling water to cover with bay leaf, salt, and peppercorns. Simmer for 10 to 12 minutes. Remove from the liquid, drain, cool slightly, and remove skin. Place on pieces of greased aluminum foil in a warm oven while making sauce.

To make mushroom sauce: Saute mushrooms and green onion in 1 tablespoon of the butter until cooked and slightly brown, about 7 minutes. Remove from pan and reserve.

Add remaining 1 tablespoon of the butter to pan, heat, and add flour, blending with a wooden spoon. Slowly add cream, stirring and heating until it is thick. Add Tabasco, mustard, catsup, a little salt and pepper, and heat until bubbly. Blend mushrooms and onions into sauce.

Place trout on a bed of cooked rice, spoon sauce over the trout, and serve garnished with parsley and dill.

MAKES 4 SERVINGS

GALATOIRE'S

209 Bourbon St., New Orleans, LA 70112; (504) 525-2021.

The great specialty of Galatoire's, one of New Orleans' essential restaurants, is seafood. You will discover the definitive (and in some cases original) versions of such dishes as trout amandine, trout Marguery, shrimp remoulade, crabmeat maison, and oysters en brochette. The list of seafood variants is long, and there is also an impressive collection of essays in beef, lamb, and poultry. Galatoire's takes no reservations and the line gets long early; however, it can be avoided by going in the afternoon. The restaurant stays open all day.

TROUT MEUNIERE AMANDINE

4 (6- to 8-ounce) speckled trout fillets
Salt and pepper to taste
1 cup milk
1/2 cup flour
Oil for frying
1 cup butter
1 cup sliced toasted almonds
Juice of 1 lemon
1/2 tablespoon chopped parsley

Salt and pepper fillets; dip in milk, then roll in flour. Fry in 3/4 inch hot oil in shallow pan until golden on both sides.

In a separate pan, melt and continuously whip butter until brown and frothy.

Add sliced almonds and lemon juice. Pour butter sauce over trout and sprinkle with chopped parsley.

MAKES 4 SERVINGS

BEGUE'S

Royal Sonesta Hotel, 300 Bourbon St., New Orleans, LA 70130; (504) 586-0300.

Begue's is a lovely, classic dining room in the Royal Sonesta Hotel on New Orleans' famous Bourbon Street. It is named in honor of Madame Begue, who ran one of the city's most popular market cafés in the late 1800s. While the better part of Begue's menu is classic French, it does also include a good selection of Creole dishes, including trout, crawfish bisque, pompano en papillote, and turtle soup. Seafood lovers find a bounty at Begue's popular lunch buffets.

LA TRUITE DE MER AUX CHAMPIGNONS ET ECREVISSES AU BEURRE BLANC *(Speckled Trout with Mushrooms and Crawfish Sauce)*

6 (8-ounce) speckled trout fillets
1 1/2 pounds fresh mushrooms, 6 whole caps, remainder chopped
1 cup white wine
1 piece dry bread or French bread, crumbled
1 cup milk
1 pound crawfish tails, peeled
2 cups butter
6 shallots, chopped
1/2 cup red wine vinegar
1 cup cream

Poach trout fillets and the 6 whole mushroom caps in white wine about 15 minutes or until fish flakes when tested with a fork. Place one fillet and one mushroom cap on individual plates.

In a skillet combine chopped mushrooms, bread, and milk and cook over low heat for 15 minutes. Spread over fillets.

Saute crawfish tails in 6 tablespoons of the butter. Place over mushrooms on trout. Top with mushroom cap.

Simmer shallots in red wine vinegar until barely limp. Add remaining butter and blend with wire whisk. Mix in cream. Pour over trout and serve.

MAKES 6 SERVINGS

SAZERAC

Fairmont Hotel, University Place, New Orleans, LA 70140; (504) 529-7111.

There are some special Creole dishes on the menu at the Sazerac, which utilize the excellent fresh local seafood, although the menu reads classic French in design and execution. No expense is spared in obtaining the best ingredients possible, and you are likely to be surprised by exotic foodstuffs you would not have believed were available. The preparations are gilt-edged, with groomed ceremony at the tableside gueridons. There, waiters and captains do wonders with flames and sauces.

FILLET OF TROUT BAYOU STYLE

8 trout fillets
3 cups heavy cream, divided
2 tablespoons creole mustard (see Glossary)
Juice of 1 lemon
Salt and pepper to taste
4 shallots
1 carrot
2 ribs celery
2 pounds cooked crawfish tails, peeled, reserve shells
Brandy
1 teaspoon tarragon
1 tablespoon tomato paste
1/2 cup butter
Salt and pepper to taste
2 tablespoons butter

Pound trout fillets until they are 1/4-inch thick. Put 1 cup of the cream in a bowl and whip until firm. Add creole mustard, lemon juice, salt, and pepper.

Dice shallots, carrots, and celery into 1/4-inch cubes. Melt 1/4 cup of the butter in a 10- to 12-inch sauce pan, add diced vegetables and saute, very slowly. Add the crawfish shells and flambé brandy over. Stir in remaining 2 cups cream, the tarragon, and tomato paste. Cook 20 minutes, strain, and whisk in remaining butter. Season to taste. Mix with the reserved 1 cup of whipped cream mixture.

Butter a broiler tray, place fish fillets on tray, and pour cream sauce over fish. Place under broiler for 3 minutes (or more, if needed). Fish will cook and cream will turn golden brown.

In separate pan saute crawfish tails in the 2 tablespoons butter.

Place fillets on a serving platter, pour the sauce around fillets, and place sauteed crawfish tails over fillets.

MAKES 4 SERVINGS

RALPH & KACOO'S

215 Bourbon St., New Orleans, LA 70130; (504) 523-0449.

Ralph & Kacoo's restaurant on Bourbon Street in the old French Quarter of New Orleans is a mecca for both tourists and locals, who gather nightly in dining-room-filling numbers to enjoy the crackly goodness of pan-fried Louisiana seafood, served with the luscious corny tidbits of hush puppies. The selection of seafood includes all the great Creole and Cajun specialties, as well as crawfish in season.

TROUT MEUNIERE

1 cup buttermilk
Salt to taste
2 teaspoons black pepper
1 1/2 teaspoons garlic powder
4 (5- to 6-ounce) fresh trout fillets
Flour to coat
5 tablespoons butter
Juice of 1 lemon
1 1/2 tablespoon butter
2 tablespoons fresh parsley

Season the buttermilk with salt, pepper, and garlic powder. Soak the fillets in buttermilk for 10 to 20 minutes. Remove and place fish in a wide pan with flour in it. Roll fish fillets in flour on both sides. Shake excess flour from fish.

Melt the butter in a large skillet and saute fillets until golden brown. Remove fish. Place on warm serving plates and keep hot.

In the same skillet, add the lemon and the 1 1/2 tablespoons butter. Saute for 1 minute until hot. Pour over fish, sprinkle with parsley and serve.

MAKES 4 SERVINGS

Photograph, Page 20

DELMONICO

1300 St. Charles Ave., New Orleans, LA 70130; (504) 525-4937.

Delmonico, founded on St. Charles Avenue near Lee Circle in 1903, has been operated by the LaFranca family since 1911. The building in which the restaurant is housed is even older; it is known to have been there in 1888, and is suspected to be older. The restaurant is esteemed for its unpretentious and consistent serving of New Orleans' greatest Creole classics, particularly seafood.

TROUT DELMONICO

6 large trout fillets
18 large shrimp, peeled
¼ cup butter, melted
1 tablespoon lemon juice
18 oysters
Chopped fresh parsley

Optional garnish: *fresh parsley sprigs, lemon wedges, tomato wedges*

Arrange trout fillets and shrimp in a 15-inch by 10-inch by 1-inch jelly-roll pan.

Combine butter and lemon juice; baste fillets and shrimp lightly with some of butter mixture. Bake at 350 degrees F. for 10 minutes, basting occasionally with butter mixture.

Arrange oysters over fillets. Baste with remaining butter mixture; sprinkle with chopped parsley. Broil for 3 to 4 minutes or until edges of oysters begin to curl.

Garnish with parsley sprigs, lemon wedges, and tomato wedges, if desired.

MAKES 6 SERVINGS

Photograph, Page 23

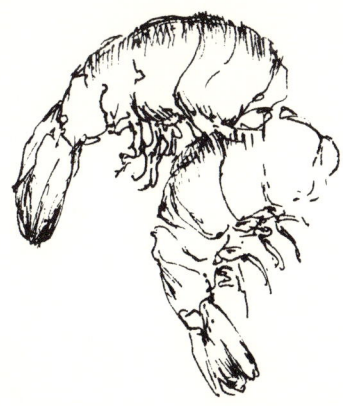

SEAFOOD/Fish

LES CHEFS DE CUISINE DE LA LOUISIANNE

This organization of Louisiana chefs is known for its extremely successful Chef's Apprenticeship Program. Young people who are interested in the restaurant business as a career spend three years and six thousand hours of paid, on-the-job training under the supervision of an executive chef of a hotel or restaurant, along with a further nine hundred hours of related classroom instruction given by a chef. Instructor and Chef Kurt Wolf presents Trout Lisa.

TROUT LISA

4 (11-to-12-inch) trout
Flour, salt, and pepper to coat
1 egg, beaten
1 cup dry bread crumbs
1/4 cup butter
1/4 cup cooking oil
2 tablespoons chopped parsley

Clean trout, remove heads, and dry thoroughly on paper towels.

Mix flour with salt and pepper. Roll the trout in the flour, then dip each in the beaten egg and roll in the bread crumbs. Allow fish to rest for a few minutes on wax paper.

Heat the butter and oil in a large skillet. When the pan is hot, add the trout. Brown for 4 minutes on one side. Turn and brown for 3 minutes.

Cover the pan, reduce the heat to medium, and continue cooking for 3 more minutes. Check fish at the thickest place with a fork. When the flesh flakes, it is done. Sprinkle with parsley and serve.

MAKES 4 SERVINGS

SAZERAC

Fairmont Hotel, University Place, New Orleans, LA 70140; (504) 529-7111.

The Sazerac is the flagship dining room of the luxury Fairmont Hotel and a New Orleans institution. It is a consistent source of copy for national restaurant writers, who extol the elegance of its classic surroundings. The walls are deep red velvet; the paintings are old-school masterpieces. There are gold accents and grand red banquettes, surmounted with banks of flowers, in the center of the room. Tables are set with candles, fresh flowers, and lace napery.

GRENOUILLE ST. MICHAEL

12 pairs frog legs
1 cup milk
Salt and pepper to taste
Flour to coat
1/3 cup olive oil
1 1/2 cups butter, divided
1/4 cup flour
1/2 pound peeled crawfish tails (see Glossary)
1 bay leaf
1/4 cup brandy or Cognac
1 tablespoon chopped shallots
1 cup julienned (see Glossary) leeks
1 tablespoon chopped green onions
1 cup julienned artichoke bottoms
1 cup sliced mushrooms
1 cup white wine
1 cup heavy cream
1 tablespoon chopped fresh dill
1 tablespoon creole mustard (see Glossary)

Place frog legs in milk with salt and pepper to soak for 30 minutes, or more, if desired. Remove from milk and dredge with flour.

In a large saute pan, heat the oil with 1/2 cup of the butter until very hot. Add frog legs to skillet and saute over high heat for about 2 minutes, then lower heat and continue to cook for 5 minutes, turning once until cooked. They should be golden brown in color. Place frog legs on large platter and keep warm in 160 degrees F. oven.

Meanwhile make a roux with 1/2 cup butter and 1/4 cup flour. Do not brown roux (see Glossary). Set aside roux.

Pour off all oil in pan in which frog legs were sauteed, and add remaining 1/2 cup of the butter to pan and heat. Add crawfish tails and bay leaf then saute for 1 minute. Add brandy, then shallots, leeks, green onions, artichoke bottoms, and mushrooms. Continue to cook for 2 minutes. Add white wine to pan and cook for 3 to 4 minutes. Add cream. Bring mixture to a boil, add roux to thicken, stirring constantly to make a smooth sauce. Correct seasonings, if needed. Add dill and stir in creole mustard.

Serve sauce over frog legs with steamed rice or boiled potato and green vegetables.

MAKES 4 SERVINGS

TIVOLI

The Brent House, 1516 Jefferson Hwy., Jefferson, LA 70121; (504) 835-5411.

The Brent House offers hotel accommodations for patients and guests at the adjacent Ochsner Medical Institutions. Of its three dining facilities, the most substantial is the Main Cafeteria, which serves lunch and dinner daily. The menu of this green-hued, pleasant room includes soups, salads, desserts, and five entrees. There is also a daily luncheon special. The Brent House is located a scant block away from the Mississippi River levee, which makes a fine place to walk.

OYSTERS HEBERT

48 oysters, in their liquor
2 eggs, lightly beaten
6 tablespoons milk
1 cup flour, or fine crumbs, or cornmeal
2 tablespoons butter
4 tablespoons shortening

Hebert Sauce
1 cup mushroom stems, chopped
1 cup dry white wine
3 cups oyster liquor or fish stock, divided
6 tablespoons butter, divided
3 tablespoons flour
4 egg yolks
$2/3$ cup heavy cream, divided
2 teaspoons lemon juice
$1/2$ cup cooked, peeled, and deveined shrimp
Salt and white pepper to taste

Garnish: 6 mushroom caps

Drain oysters reserving liquor. Beat eggs with milk and dip drained oysters into mixture, then roll in flour, crumbs, or cornmeal.

Heat butter and shortening in a large frying pan and saute oysters over moderate heat, turning until both sides are brown. Place 8 oysters each in individual casseroles and keep warm.

To make Hebert Sauce: Combine mushrooms, wine, and 1 cup of the stock in a sauce pan. Cook over moderate heat until mixture has reduced to one half the original amount. Strain and set aside.

Melt 2 tablespoons of the butter in a sauce pan and remove from heat. Blend in flour, return to heat and cook, stirring constantly, 1 to 2 minutes or until frothy. Add the remaining stock and the reduced wine and stock. Stir and cook slowly 10 minutes or until sauce is thick enough to coat a metal spoon.

Blend the egg yolks with 4 tablespoons of the cream and $1/4$ cup of the sauce; add mixture back to sauce while stirring and bring to boiling point. Stir in lemon juice and remaining cream and shrimp and heat $1/2$ minute. Season with salt and pepper to taste. Swirl in remaining butter and pour over oysters. Garnish with mushroom caps, and serve.

MAKES 6 SERVINGS

Photograph, Page 23

COMMANDER'S PALACE

1403 Washington Ave., New Orleans, LA 70130; (504) 899-8221.

Among the hardest-to-get tables in a New Orleans' restaurant are those for the Saturday and Sunday jazz brunch at Commander's Palace. Featuring the first-generation jazz sounds of Alvin Alcorn and his trio, the brunch serves up an assortment of famous New Orleans gourmet egg dishes. But there is much more to the brunch menu: great seafood, veal, shellfish dishes, and the restaurant's marvelous flaming desserts.

OYSTERS TRUFANT

1 quart heavy cream
60 freshly shucked oysters, liquor reserved
1 teaspoon seafood seasoning

Garnish: Chopped green onions or caviar

Place cream and reserved oyster liquor in saucepan. Gently simmer until reduced to $1^{1}/_{2}$ cups.

Add 24 oysters and cook for 5 minutes. Strain out oysters for future use (see Note), leaving the sauce.

Take remaining 36 oysters and place in a hot skillet with seasoning (no oil) and toss gently to warm oysters. DO NOT over cook. When oysters are warmed, drain on towel; place on serving dish and cover with sauce. Garnish with green onions or caviar.

Note: Unused oysters may be reserved for use in stews, soups or stuffing. Refrigerate and use up in a few days.

MAKES 6 SERVINGS

Photograph, Page 22

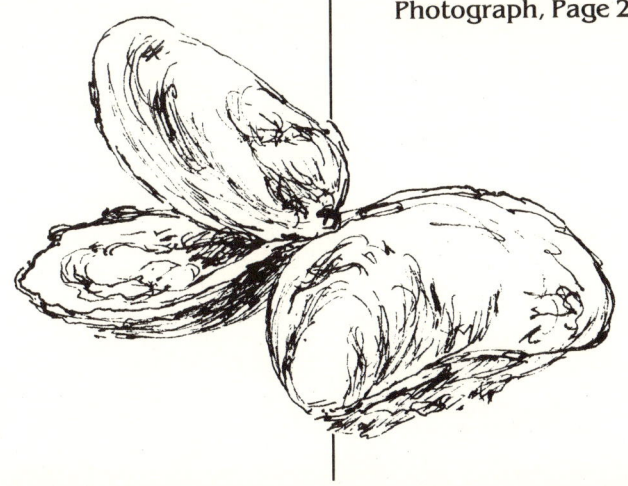

STEPHEN AND MARTIN

1613 Milan St., New Orleans, LA 70115; (504) 897-0781.

One of Uptown New Orleans' most engaging and popular restaurants, Stephen and Martin has expanded on its reputation as a culinary innovator in recent years. The constantly-changing menu and the daily chef's specials make it an always-interesting place to have lunch or dinner. Among the offerings one finds a panoply of New Orleans Creole classics, as well as a soupçon of Italian and Nouvelle American creations.

OYSTER ARTICHOKE CASSEROLE

4 cups oysters, in their liquor
2 cups artichoke hearts
1 cup chopped green onion
1 tablespoon chopped parsley
2 tablespoons chopped garlic
1 1/2 cups butter
1 1/2 cups flour
1 teaspoon salt
2 teaspoons black pepper
1 teaspoon garlic powder
1 teaspoon monosodium glutamate
1 teaspoon lemon juice
2 teaspoons grated Parmesan cheese, or more, to taste
2 teaspoons Worcestershire sauce
1/2 cup bread crumbs
6 lemon slices
Paprika

Simmer oysters in their liquor until edges curl. Remove and save liquor.

Cook artichoke hearts in 1 quart boiling water to cover for 1/2 hour, remove, and reserve stock.

Saute green onion, parsley, and chopped garlic in butter. Add flour and stir for 3 minutes. Add 3 cups oyster liquor. Add 3 cups artichoke stock. Stir well and cook to thicken. Add oysters, artichoke hearts, salt, pepper, garlic powder, monosodium glutamate, lemon juice, grated cheese, and Worcestershire sauce. Cook over medium heat for 10 minutes.

Spoon into 6 individual casserole dishes and top with bread crumbs, lemon slices, and sprinkle with paprika. Bake at 350 degrees F. for about 15 minutes.

MAKES 6 SERVINGS

MR. B'S

201 Royal St., New Orleans, LA 70130; (504) 523-2078.

Ella, Adelaide, Dick, Dottie and John Brennan—the proprietors of the highly-regarded Commander's Palace—opened this modern restaurant as a counterpart to their stunning Garden District antique. You will find Creole food, to be sure, at Mr. B's. But the sauces are reductions, not thickened with a roux. You are likely to find cuts of meat, kinds of poultry, and vegetables you have never tried before. All of it is fresh, with an emphasis on locally-grown ingredients, served with a kind of casual élan that is delightful.

OYSTERS MARAS

12 large oysters, shucked
2 tablespoons white wine
2 tablespoons chopped shallots
2 cloves garlic, minced
2 tablespoons diced, fresh tomatoes
1 pinch each, seafood seasoning, tarragon, basil, crushed red pepper, thyme
1 teaspoon Dijon mustard
2 teaspoons chopped green onions
5 tablespoons cold butter

Place oysters, wine, shallots, garlic, tomatoes, and seasonings in a medium sauce pan. Bring to a quick boil and remove oysters.

Add mustard and green onions. Reduce liquid by half. Swirl in cold butter and bring to a boil.

Add oysters and adjust seasoning.

Serve at once.

MAKES 2 SERVINGS

Photograph, Page 19

TIVOLI

The Brent House, 1516 Jefferson Hwy., Jefferson, LA 70121; (504) 835-5411.

Many of the thousands of patients who travel long distances to come to the Ochsner Medical Institutions, one of the most famous hospitals in the country, spend time before and after their hospital stays in the Brent House. Of the three dining rooms, the main cafeteria serves the greatest number of people, accommodating 200. Breakfast, lunch, and dinner are served daily, with breakfasts and lunches in the smaller Tivoli Room.

COQUILLES SAINT-RAMON

1 quart bay scallops
1 pound lump crabmeat
1 white onion, chopped
2 teaspoons chopped parsley
Dry white wine
1/4 pound mushrooms, sliced
1 shallot, chopped
7 tablespoons butter, divided
2 tablespoons hot water
2 tablespoons flour
2 tablespoons heavy cream
Salt and pepper to taste
1 tablespoon chopped truffle (optional)
1/2 cup grated Gruyere cheese, divided
1/2 cup soft bread crumbs

Cook scallops, crabmeat, onion, and parsley in only enough wine to barely cover for about 5 minutes. Strain, reserving stock.

Simmer the mushrooms and shallots in 1 tablespoon of the butter and water 8 to 10 minutes. Drain liquid and add to stock. Boil until quantity is reduced to one half the original amount. Set aside.

Melt 3 tablespoons of the butter in a 1-quart sauce pan. Remove from heat and blend in flour. Measure 1 cup of the stock, heat it, and add it gradually to the butter and flour mixture, beating with a wire whisk until smooth. Return pan to heat and cook over moderate to low heat until the sauce is medium thick, stirring frequently. Remove from heat and add the cream, 1 tablespoon of butter, salt and pepper to taste and the optional truffle. Add the scallops, crabs, and mushroom to sauce and heat about 2 minutes. Stir in 1/4 cup of the cheese. Add additional seasonings to taste.

Spoon the mixture into 6 buttered scallop shells or ramekins. Sprinkle tops with the remaining cheese. Melt the remaining butter, mix with bread crumbs, and sprinkle on top of the cheese. Place under broiler; heat until the tops have glazed and browned.

MAKES 6 SERVINGS

Photograph, Page 17

CHRISTIAN'S

3835 Iberville St., New Orleans, LA 70119; (504) 482-4924.

Christian's proprietor Christian Ansel started out in the engineering business. But his family ties were too strong for him to stay out of restauranting; his family owns Galatoire's, one of the great old-line classics. Try the many highly original creations served to a devoted clientele here by chef Roland Huet. The restaurant's location in an old, small church is striking; the food is superior.

BOUILLABAISSE

1/3 cup olive oil
1 onion, thinly sliced
3 cloves garlic, chopped
1/2 bay leaf
1/4 teaspoon thyme
1/8 teaspoon powdered anise
1 tomato, peeled, seeds removed, and crushed
1/2 cup white wine
1 1/2 quarts fish stock (see Basic Stocks)
16 shrimp, peeled
12 oysters
1/4 pound crabmeat or blue crabs
8 fish fillets (trout, redfish, etc.)
1/4 teaspoon powdered saffron

Garlic Bread Rounds
French bread
Olive oil
Finely chopped garlic

Rouille
1 quart mayonnaise (preferably home-made)
1 heaping teaspoon chopped garlic
3/4 teaspoon cayenne pepper

To make Bouillabaisse: Heat the olive oil in a very large skillet and add the onion. Saute onion slices for a few minutes on medium heat until transparent. Then add the garlic, seasonings, tomato, wine, and fish stock.

Simmer uncovered until onions are tender, about 15 to 20 minutes. Then add the seafood and continue to simmer until the fish fillets are tender. Do not overcook the fish fillets. Add powdered saffron.

Serve the bouillabaisse immediately, very hot, in large soup plates with toasted garlic bread rounds and rouille in separate plates. Add some rouille to enhance the flavor of the bouillabaisse.

To make garlic bread rounds: Cut French bread into 1/2-inch rounds (about 6 pieces per person), brush with the olive oil and finely chopped garlic, and toast on a tray under broiler until light brown.

To make Rouille: Combine mayonnaise, garlic, and pepper. Allow to sit several hours to develop flavors.

MAKES 4 TO 6 SERVINGS

DON'S SEAFOOD HUT

4309 Johnston St., Lafayette, LA 70503; (318) 981-1141.

Don's recently marked its tenth anniversary, and has an incredible growth record to celebrate. From a small take-out restaurant it has become one of Lafayette's largest restaurants, with seating for 240. The surroundings are warm and friendly; there are wooden booths with stained-glass lamps, and the bar is inlaid with silver coins. Sixteen-foot ceilings tower above the diners in the main dining room, where the large stone fireplace is the centerpiece of a fine rustic design.

CABBAGE ROLLS

1 head cabbage
1 cup butter
1 cup finely chopped onions
1 cup finely chopped celery
1 cup finely chopped green pepper
1 tablespoon tomato paste
$1/2$ teaspoon red pepper
$1^{1}/2$ teaspoons salt, divided
1 pound lump crabmeat
$1/2$ pound shrimp, coarsely chopped
1 cup cooked rice
2 tablespoons chopped green onion tops

Creole Sauce
1 cup tomato sauce
1 10-ounce can whole tomatoes, chopped
1 teaspoon tomato paste
Salt and pepper to taste

To make cabbage rolls remove outer tough leaves if still on cabbage head.

Break off twelve whole leaves and set aside. Chop remaining leaves in 1-inch pieces.

In a skillet melt butter and saute until tender chopped cabbage, onions, celery, green pepper, and tomato paste, red pepper, and $1/2$ teaspoon salt.

Meanwhile boil the 12 whole cabbage leaves with one teaspoon of salt in water for 5 to 10 minutes. Drain and set aside.

Add crab and shrimp to vegetables and cook over medium heat for 10 minutes. Stir in rice and onion tops.

Place stuffing and roll up in cabbage leaves. Place in a greased baking pan and pour creole sauce over top. Bake at 350 degrees F. for 15 minutes.

To make Creole Sauce: Combine ingredients in a sauce pan and cook for 20 minutes over medium heat.

MAKES 6 SERVINGS

Photograph, Page 21

CORRAL STEAKS AND SEAFOOD

2307 N. Parkerson Rd., Crowley, LA 70526; (318) 788-3663

One block from Interstate 10, this restaurant provides the consistently good beef and seafood that Southwestern Louisianans demand. The casual dining room is decorated in rustic cedar and seats up to 200 people. Outside, the grounds are handsomely landscaped and are shaded by large oak trees. Inside, the atmosphere is friendly and the steaks are char-broiled to order. There is a wide assortment of fresh Louisiana seafood.

SEAFOOD SAUCE PIQUANTE

1 cup chopped green onions
2 large yellow onions, finely chopped
2 large green peppers, finely chopped
2 cups margarine
4 cans tomatoes and green chilies
3 pounds small shrimp, peeled and deveined
1 pound white crabmeat
2 pounds catfish fillets
Salt and red pepper to taste
8 cups cooked rice

Garnish: *1/2 cup chopped green onions*

In an ovenproof skillet saute the onions and green peppers for 10 minutes in the margarine. Add tomatoes and bake at 300 degrees F. for 1 hour.

Add shrimp, crabmeat, and catfish and simmer for 30 minutes on low temperature. Add salt and red pepper to taste.

Serve piping hot over rice and sprinkle with green onions.

MAKES 8 SERVINGS

THE GUMBO SHOP

630 St. Peter St., New Orleans, LA 70116; (504) 525-1486.

The Gumbo Shop is not only the place to come for gumbo; it is also the purveyor of another original Louisiana dish—jambalaya. This is a hearty stew of sausage, pork, seafood, and vegetables, all married together with slow cooking by knowledgeable cooks.

JAMBALAYA

$1/2$ cup salad oil
$1/2$ pound smoked sausage, sliced
$1/2$ pound smoked ham, cubed
1 cup chopped onion
1 cup chopped green pepper
1 cup chopped celery
1 cup chopped green onion
2 cloves garlic, minced
1 (16-ounce) can tomatoes, drained, reserving liquid
1 teaspoon thyme
1 teaspoon black pepper
$1/4$ teaspoon cayenne pepper
1 teaspoon salt
1 cup converted rice
$1 1/2$ cups shrimp, ham, or chicken stock, or water
$1 1/2$ tablespoons Worcestershire sauce
2 pounds shrimp, peeled

In a large heavy kettle heat oil, saute sausage and ham until lightly browned. Remove from pot and set aside.

Saute onions, peppers, celery, green onion, and garlic in meat drippings until tender. Add tomatoes, thyme, pepper, and salt. Cook 5 minutes. Stir in rice. Mix together liquid from tomatoes, stock, and Worcestershire sauce to equal $2 1/2$ cups. Bring to a boil, reduce to a simmer.

Add shrimp, ham, and sausage and cook, uncovered, stirring occasionally for about 30 minutes or until rice and shrimp are done.

MAKES 4 SERVINGS

LES CHEFS DE CUISINE DE LA LOUISIANNE

The chefs' association provides a fertile training ground for the next generation of Louisiana's great culinary geniuses. In a sense this association is acting like many of the fine families of Creole and Cajun fame, who have passed on their skills, secrets, and enthusiasm to their immediate heirs. The following recipe brings together the Italian respect for pasta with the larder of fresh Louisiana shellfish.

HOMEMADE PASTA WITH LOUISIANA SHELLFISH

Homemade Pasta
1 pound all purpose flour
1 teaspoon salt
3 eggs
1/4 teaspoon salt
1 gallon boiling salted water

Shellfish Mixture
1/4 cup cold water
1 tablespoon arrowroot (see Glossary)
1/4 cup butter
2 small green onions, sliced
2 medium cloves garlic, minced
8 oysters, drained, liquor reserved
1/2 pound shrimp, peeled and deveined
1/2 pound peeled crawfish tails
1/4 pound lump crabmeat
1/4 cup dry white wine
2 teaspoons lemon juice
1 cup heavy cream
1 teaspoon salt
1/8 teaspoon white pepper
1 tablespoon chopped parsley

To make homemade pasta: Mix flour and salt on board; make a well in center of flour. Whisk the eggs in a small bowl; gradually pour into flour well while mixing with fingertips to form a dough.

Gently knead dough until smooth, about 5 minutes. Cover dough with a clean towel and let rest about 1 hour. Cut dough into strips about 2 to 3 inches long by 1 inch wide and pass through a pasta machine. Place strips on clean surface to dry, about 1/2 hour. Cut strips into desired pasta shape.

Cook pasta al dente (see Glossary) in the boiling salted water, drain, and rinse with hot water.

Toss hot pasta with the warm shellfish mixture and serve immediately.

To make shellfish: Mix 1/4 cup cold water and arrowroot in a cup until smooth, and reserve. Melt butter in a large skillet; add green onions and saute until golden. Add garlic and saute until soft. Add seafood and saute briefly. Add wine, oyster liquor, and lemon juice; simmer 1 minute. Add cream; simmer for 5 minutes. Reduce heat and add arrowroot mixture stirring constantly. Heat gently 3 minutes. Add salt and pepper. Keep sauce over very low heat until ready for use.

MAKES 4 SERVINGS

BENEDICT HOUSE

1381 W. Tunnel Blvd., Houma, LA 70361; (504) 851-3170.

Unique Italian food is a specialty at this restaurant, whose range elsewhere on the menu encompasses prime steaks and some of the freshest seafood in the bayou country. The dress and atmosphere are casual and friendly at Benedict House, where the food begins coming from the kitchen at six in the morning and does not stop until ten at night. The level of cooking, whether it be a basic breakfast or a perfect omelette, a lunch special or something light from the buffet, or a gourmet dinner with a good wine, is consistently high.

SHRIMP AND OYSTER FETTUCINI

$1/2$ cup butter, divided
$1/2$ cup green onion tops, finely chopped
1 garlic clove, minced
1 quart heavy cream
12 medium to large shrimp, peeled
12 oysters
1 pound cooked pasta (fettucini)
1 tablespoon grated Romano cheese
$1/4$ cup grated Parmesan cheese

In a large skillet melt $1/4$ cup of the butter over medium heat. Add green onions and garlic and cook for 5 minutes. Add cream and remaining $1/4$ cup of butter. Stir well.

Add shrimp and oysters and lower heat. Simmer for about five minutes.

Add cooked fettucini and cheeses. Toss or stir until pasta is coated with cheeses throughout, a few minutes. Separate into 4 equal portions.

Spoon sauce over each serving.

MAKES 4 SERVINGS

Photograph, Page 20

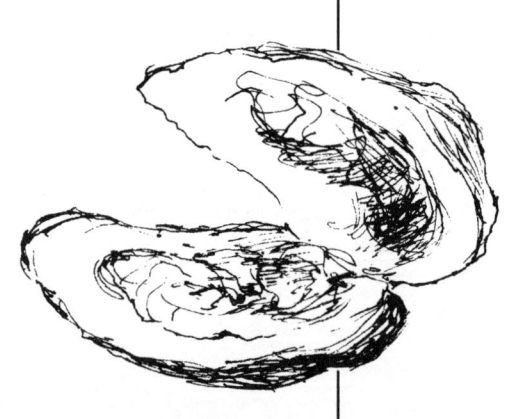

CAFE RANI

315 N. Vermont, Covington, LA 70433; (504) 893-4383.

An unusual aspect of this chef-owned, small gourmet restaurant in downtown Covington is its wine list. It contains nothing but California bottles, and the prices are the same for all of them. The purpose is to remove the intimidation which many people feel when ordering wine. However, anyone who knows wine well will find some incredible vintages on the list, an incentive to study your oenology. Every day the menu reflects fresh meats, seafood, and vegetables available from the local markets.

FISH AND CRAB BOUDIN

2 pounds redfish, boned and skinned
1 cup butter
1 pound crabmeat
1 cup chopped green onion
1/2 cup chopped parsley
1 tablespoon chopped garlic
3 eggs, lightly beaten
1 cup bread, soaked in water and squeezed dry
2 tablespoons lemon juice
1 tablespoon salt
1/2 tablespoon cayenne pepper
1/2 tablespoon white pepper
Sausage casings (available in gourmet stores)

In a food processor with steel knife, blend redfish and butter until a smooth paste is formed, about 2 minutes. Gently fold in remainder of ingredients. Stuff into sausage casings, tying off ends.

Poach in boiling water for 7 to 10 minutes. Serve over fresh pasta.

MAKES 6 SERVINGS

MASSON'S

7200 Pontchartrain Blvd., New Orleans, LA 70124; (504) 283-2525.

Hard by the southern shore of Lake Pontchartrain lies Masson's Restaurant Francais, a favorite for generations in New Orleans. The large classic dining room is the venue for the creations of Ernest Masson Jr., a graduate of the Cordon Bleu in France, where he worked with some of the most famous chefs of that country. The atmosphere is relaxed and enjoyable, and the food is the simple elegant fare of provincial France with the spark of the Creole.

LES MERVEILLES DE LA MER EN CREPES

1/2 cup chopped green onions
1/2 cup sliced mushrooms
1 cup butter, divided
3 teaspoons flour
1/2 cup white wine
1 quart light cream
3 egg yolks, beaten
1/2 pound cooked lobster meat
1/2 pound cooked shrimp
1/2 pound crabmeat
2 teaspoons Cognac
8 crêpes

Saute green onions and mushrooms in half of the butter. Add flour. Cook 2 to 3 minutes. Add wine and cream and simmer 8 to 10 minutes. Remove from heat and stir in beaten yolks.

Saute seafood in remainder of butter for 4 to 5 minutes. Add Cognac and 1/2 of the sauce. Divide this between 8 crêpes and roll up. Place, seam down, on serving platter and pour remainder of the sauce over the crêpes.

MAKES 4 SERVINGS

THE LION'S SHARE

Southland Mall, Houma, LA 70360; (318) 868-3494.

The Lion's Share is a casual family-style restaurant located in the bayou country's biggest shopping mall. The restaurant has the atmosphere of an old-fashioned pub, with low lighting, ceiling fans, and exposed wood exterior. The kitchen follows the time-honored traditions of Southeast Louisiana lunching, which dictate that red beans and rice are served on Mondays, spaghetti on Wednesdays, and gumbo on Fridays. All of these are popular daily specials at the Lion's Share.

SHRIMP A-LA-POOKEY

5 pounds (31-35 count) shrimp, peeled
Salt and black pepper to taste
2 cups peanut oil
1 head garlic, finely chopped
2 bunches celery, cut in 4-inch lengths
1 bunch green onions, finely chopped
4 large onions, finely chopped
2 green peppers, chopped
3 cans small peeled potatoes
2 loaves garlic bread, cut into slices

Wash shrimp in salted water, then season with salt and black pepper.

In a large kettle, heat oil, add shrimp and chopped garlic. Stir continually just until shrimp are pink. Do not overcook shrimp. Add celery, green onions, onions, green peppers, and potatoes. Mix thoroughly, cover, and cook on high heat for 5 minutes. Stir again and cook on medium heat, stirring occasionally until done, about 30 minutes.

Serve shrimp, about 16 per person, on dinner plates with pieces of celery and potatoes.

Place the sauce in a cup and serve along with the shrimp and vegetables.

Serve hot garlic bread. Eat shrimp with celery and garlic bread dunked in sauce.

MAKES 10 SERVINGS

MAURICE'S BISTRO

1763 Stumpf Blvd., Gretna, LA 70053; (504) 361-9000.

The chef, owner, and major domo of this charming multi-level restaurant in suburban New Orleans is Maurice Bitoun, a skilled restaurateur of French-Moroccan extraction. He has worked in New Orleans' best restaurants and hotels for many years, and now in his own restaurant combines the best of his heritage with the excitement and fresh products of the local Creole cuisine. Maurice's menu specializes both in first-class steaks and fresh seafood.

SHRIMP NEOPOLITAN

1/4 cup butter
1/2 cup olive oil
2 bay leaves
3 whole garlic cloves
Pinch each, salt, pepper, oregano, thyme, cayenne, red pepper, and tumeric
1 teaspoon Italian seasoning
6 whole black peppercorns
2 whole cloves
36 large shrimp, unpeeled
1/2 cup white wine

Heat butter and oil in a skillet over high heat. Add seasonings and shrimp; saute 1 to 2 minutes.

Add wine and bring to a boil. Serve on a large platter immediately.

Rice and asparagus make good side dishes. Everyone peels his own shrimp.

MAKES 6 SERVINGS

THE COURT OF TWO SISTERS

613 Royal St., New Orleans, LA 70130; (504) 522-7261.

The Court of Two Sisters is named for Emma and Bertha Camors, two widows who opened a shop in 1886 on the present site of the restaurant. They sold carnival costumes, lace, gowns, and finery, and served tea and refreshments in their courtyard. The restaurant began in the twenties, and came together in its present form in 1963, when Joe Fein Jr. acquired the Court. Now operated by sons Joe and Jerry Fein, the Court of Two Sisters continues as one of New Orleans' premier tourist destinations.

SHRIMP TOULOUSE

1/2 cup butter, clarified (see Glossary)
1/2 cup chopped green onions
1/2 cup diced green pepper
1/4 cup diced pimiento
1/4 cup finely chopped celery
1 cup sliced mushrooms
3 pounds raw shrimp, peeled and deveined
1 cup white wine
1 teaspoon salt
1/2 teaspoon white pepper
1/4 cup chopped parsley
1/4 teaspoon dill
6 cups cooked rice

Heat the clarified butter in a sauce pan. Add the green onions, green pepper, pimiento, celery, mushrooms, and shrimp. Simmer the mixture for 10 minutes.

Add the wine, salt, and pepper, and simmer the mixture an additional 5 minutes. Add the parsley and dill.

Serve over warm rice.

MAKES 6 SERVINGS

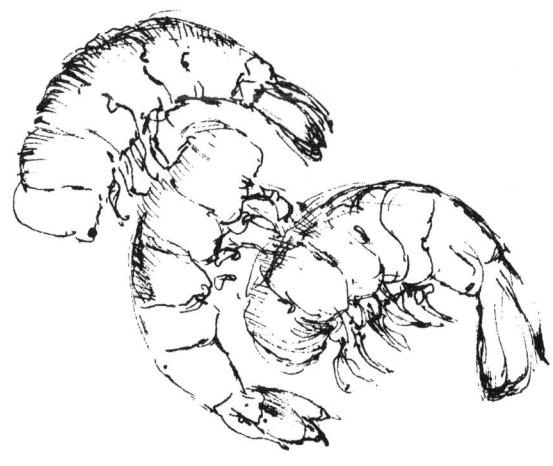

TREY YUEN

600 N. Causeway Approach, Mandeville, LA 70448; (504) 626-4476.

Trey Yuen is an extraordinary Chinese restaurant, inside and out, an architectural masterpiece. Its lengthy menu includes a host of specialties rarely seen. One of the grandest possible dinners here is the gourmet feast for eight or more. On a few days' notice, the Wong brothers, who own the restaurant and develop the food, prepare a repast of wondrous proportions, both in quality and quantity, and serve it in the stunning private dining room.

KUNG MING SHRIMP

1 1/2 pounds shrimp, peeled and deveined
1 tablespoon sesame oil
2 egg whites, one beaten
1/4 cup cornstarch, divided
Oil for deep-frying
1 package rice noodles
1/4 cup peanut oil
1/4 cup straw mushrooms (or substitute sliced domestic mushrooms)
Salt and white pepper to taste
1/4 cup minced green onions
1 teaspoon minced garlic
1 teaspoon minced ginger
3 tablespoons rice wine or sherry
1/4 cup chicken stock
1 teaspoon sugar

Mix shrimp with sesame oil, unbeaten egg white, and half the cornstarch. Let stand for 30 minutes or longer.

Heat deep-frying oil almost to smoking and add rice noodles. When noodles puff, remove and drain.

Heat peanut oil in a wok and stir-fry the shrimp briefly. Add mushrooms. Cook and toss, then season to taste with salt and white pepper. Add beaten egg white, toss.

Remove shrimp and mushrooms. Add green onions, garlic, ginger, wine, stock, sugar, and remaining cornstarch. Toss and cook for 30 seconds. Add shrimp and mushrooms and heat through. Serve on the noodles.

MAKES 6 SERVINGS

ANTOINE'S

713 St. Louis St., New Orleans, LA 70130; (504) 581-4422.

The service style at Antoine's is disarming to some first-time diners. The waiters take a much more direct, personal approach than you might expect, and don't stand on ceremony if they find it gets in the way of a good meal. After all, most of the waiters are good friends of their regulars, for whom they create special dishes—sometimes cooking them themselves. The waiters are assisted by busboys who work in that position for years until they are promoted to waiter.

CREVETTES A LA CREOLE *(Shrimp Creole)*

Creole Sauce
4 tablespoons butter
2 cups chopped green pepper
2 cups chopped onion
6 cups chopped tomatoes
1/2 teaspoon thyme
4 bay leaves
8 cloves garlic, minced
4 tablespoons minced parsley
2 teaspoons paprika
Salt and cayenne pepper to taste
2 tablespoons cornstarch mixed with a small amount of water

1/2 cup butter
3 pounds raw shrimp, peeled
Salt and cayenne pepper to taste
6 cups creole sauce
6 cups cooked rice

To make Creole Sauce: Melt the butter and saute the green pepper and onion until they become limp. Add all the remaining ingredients, except the cornstarch. Simmer for 20 minutes. Blend the cornstarch mixture into the sauce. Cook for a few minutes more to thicken. Makes 6 cups creole sauce.

Heat the butter and saute the shrimp with a little salt and cayenne pepper until the shrimp become pink. Add the creole sauce and simmer together for 20 minutes.

Serve the shrimp and sauce over 1 cup hot cooked rice per serving.

MAKES 6 SERVINGS

JACKSON STREET PIZZA & SPAGHETTI HOUSE

917 Jackson St., Thibodaux, LA 70301; (504) 446-3280.

Located sixty miles from New Orleans, the Jackson St. Pizza & Spaghetti House is in the heart of Cajunland, Thibodaux, Louisiana. The restaurant was once the home of the well known Braud family. The building is now restored to the original Victorian elegance of 1889. Chef and owner Darrell Guidry has maintained the charm of this handsome setting and offers a medly of Cajun seafood dishes and Italian specialties.

SHRIMP ITALIAN

1 pound tiny shrimp (150-200 count), peeled
1/2 bunch green onions, chopped
Salt and pepper to taste
Garlic powder to taste
1/2 cup margarine
1/4 cup plus 3 tablespoons grated Parmesan cheese, divided
1/4 cup grated Swiss cheese
1/4 cup Italian bread crumbs
1 (12-ounce) package egg noodles
1 (3-ounce) can evaporated milk
1 tablespoon chopped parsley

Saute the shrimp and green onions with salt, pepper, and garlic powder to taste in the margarine for about 10 minutes or until cooked. Add 1/4 cup of the Parmesan cheese, the Swiss cheese, and Italian bread crumbs.

Cook egg noodles until tender, drain, and rinse with cold water. Season lightly with salt and garlic powder. Add evaporated milk and the remaining 3 tablespoons of Parmesan cheese.

Pour shrimp mixture over egg noodles and sprinkle with parsley.

MAKES 3 SERVINGS

Photograph, Page 18

THE MAGNOLIA PLANTATION

818 Wholesalers Parkway, New Orleans, LA 70123; (504) 733-5020.

This restaurant and catering operation serves the fast-growing Elmwood Village section of Jefferson Parish. At lunchtime, the Magnolia Plantation's comfortable dining room attracts a strong following from the many people who work in the area. The restaurant features daily specials familiar to most Orleanians, beginning with savory red beans and rice on Mondays. But there is also lots of seafood, a salad bar, and steaks. After hours, this is the site of many successful private parties.

SHRIMP MAGNOLIA

2 pounds medium shrimp, unpeeled
6 large mushrooms, sliced
2 cups butter
2 teaspoons salt, or to taste
1 tablespoon black pepper
1 tablespoon Worcestershire sauce
2 bunches green onions, chopped
1 tablespoon celery salt
2 cloves garlic, finely chopped
$1/2$ cup white wine

Saute shrimp and mushrooms in butter for 15 minutes.

Add remaining ingredients, except wine, and cook another 15 minutes. Remove from heat and add wine.

Serve unpeeled in 6-inch bowls with French bread on the side for dipping in sauce.

MAKES 8 SERVINGS

COVINGTON DEPOT

503 N. New Hampshire, Covington, LA 70433; (504) 892-3337.

The suggestion in the name of the halcyon days of passenger railroading is no affectation. This charming restaurant actually does occupy the former passenger depot of the Illinois Central Railroad in Covington, across the lake from New Orleans. In the days before convenient travel to the North Shore, those Orleanians who kept weekend homes in Covington traveled there by way of the railroad. Many pictures and timetables from that epoch are framed on the walls of the restaurant, and there is a room of train memorabilia.

FETTUCCINI AND SHRIMP

1 (8-ounce) package fettuccini pasta
1/4 cup vegetable oil
6 tablespoons butter
1 1/2 cups heavy cream
1/2 pound (50-60 count), raw shrimp, peeled and deveined
6 tablespoons grated Romano cheese
Salt and white pepper to taste
3 tablespoons chopped parsley

Cook fettuccini in boiling salted water according to package instructions. Do not over cook. Drain, rinse with cold water, and toss with vegetable oil.

In a medium pan, melt butter and add cream. Add shrimp and cook over low heat until pink. Add fettuccini, cheese, salt, and white pepper, and parsley. Toss to coat well; remove from heat. Serve immediately.

MAKES 4 SERVINGS

EMERY'S

501 N. Adams, Welsh, LA 70591; (318) 734-3715.

Welsh is in the center of Louisiana's rice-growing country. In this small town, Emery's performs with an élan that would put it in good stead in a large city. This restaurant draws from its Cajun roots to produce an appetizing menu of seafood and steaks and a delightful array of authentically-prepared Cajun classics. The salad bar is bountiful; and if you are in the mood for wonderful spicy or fried seafood, you have come to the right place at Emery's.

SAUTEED SHRIMP

1 1/2 tablespoons butter-flavored oil
1 tablespoon chopped onion
1 tablespoon chopped green pepper
1 tablespoon diced pimiento
1 teaspoon minced garlic
6 fresh mushrooms, sliced
1 pinch crushed red pepper
1 pinch basil
12 large shrimp
Juice of 1/2 lemon
1 ounce white wine
1/4 cup heavy cream
1 teaspoon butter
1 teaspoon parsley

Garnish: *4 Lemon wedges and 4 sprigs fresh parsley*

In a large skillet, heat oil and cook onions, green pepper, pimiento, minced garlic, mushrooms, red pepper, and basil for 45 seconds. Cook shrimp in mixture for 30 seconds, turn, and cook on other side for 30 seconds. Add lemon juice and wine and heat.

Remove shrimp and place on a hot platter. Add cream, butter, and parsley to sauce and stir until butter melts. Pour over shrimp.

Garnish with lemon wedge and parsley.

Variation: Crab Meat à la Julia: Use same recipe for the sauteed shrimp substituting 1 pound lump crabmeat for the shrimp.

MAKES 2 SERVINGS

Photograph, Page 17

SAFFRON

Sheraton New Orleans Hotel, 500 Canal St., New Orleans, LA 70130; (504) 525-2500.

The Saffron Restaurant is named for the most expensive herb in the world—saffron, harvested from the crocus flower. The flower is used as a visual theme, as well; you will see it in etched glass dividing the large, spacious, elegant room, in the tissue-like paper enclosing the menu, and even in the shape of the candle-holders. The spice itself appears in a number of the restaurant's elaborately-presented creations.

SPANISH SHRIMP

Saffron Sauce
4 cups dry white wine
1 cup champagne vinegar (white vinegar may be substituted)
6 whole shallots, peeled
1 cup heavy cream
2 cups unsalted butter
Salt and white pepper to taste
1 teaspoon saffron

Lobster Sauce
1 pound lobster shells (shrimp or crawfish shells may be substituted)
2 quarts water
1 onion, halved and sauteed until black
1 cup heavy cream
1 1/2 cups butter

Parsley Puree
1 cup chicken stock (see Basic Stocks, chicken bouillon may be substituted)
2 bunches fresh parsley, finely chopped
1 cup heavy cream
Salt and pepper to taste
1 tablespoon Pernod (see Glossary)

Shrimp
16 jumbo fresh shrimp, unpeeled (Spanish if available)
8 tablespoons olive oil

To make Saffron Sauce: Combine wine, vinegar, and shallots and cook over high heat until liquid is reduced to about 1 cup or until thickened. Add cream and cook until sauce is thickened. Remove from heat, add butter, 1 tablespoon at a time. Add salt and white pepper to taste, then add the saffron, and mix until evenly colored. Set aside.

To make Lobster Sauce: Combine lobster shells, water, and cooked onion. Cook over medium heat until liquid is reduced to about 2 cups, about 45 minutes. Strain stock and pour into a large deep skillet. Cook over high heat until mixture is reduced to about 1 cup, or until thickened. Add cream, and cook 4 to 5 minutes until thick, stirring occasionally with whisk. Remove from heat. Whisk in butter 1 tablespoon at a time until incorporated into sauce. Set aside.

To make Parsley Puree: Over medium heat, combine stock and parsley; reduce until almost dry. Add cream and cook until thickened. Add salt and pepper to taste and stir in the Pernod. Set aside.

To prepare the shrimp: Leaving the shrimp in their shells, split them open cutting from the front but not all the way through. Spread into a butterfly shape—bending shells open. Leave tails intact. Saute in hot oil cut side down for about 3 minutes. Turn to saute shell side for 3 additional minutes.

SPANISH SHRIMP *(Continued)*

To serve: In the center of each plate, place about 4 tablespoons of parsley puree, arrange 4 of the shrimp around the puree so that they are standing.

In the 4 corners of each plate (alternating with the Lobster Sauce and the Saffron), pour about 2 tablespoons of each sauce so that the sauces meet to make an attractive presentation.

MAKES 4 SERVINGS

Photograph, Page 17

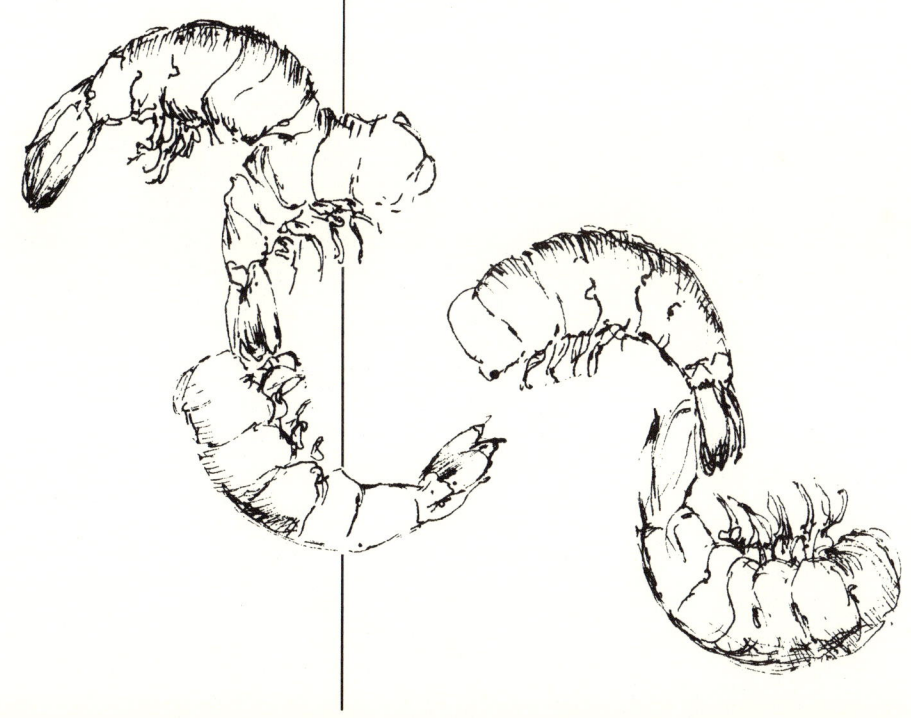

L.R.A.

The shrimping season in Louisiana opens each year at the end of May. The shrimps fill the estuaries and bays in their migrations to and from the spawning grounds of the Gulf of Mexico. The original method of shrimping was seining; motorized trawlers, especially the Lafitte skiffs, are now used. When the catch is in, neighbors and friends gather for a joint celebration. In this recipe the Louisiana Restaurant Association welcomes you and your friends to try a Louisiana hot shrimp boil.

HOT AND JUICY BOILED SHRIMP

20 to 35 pounds fresh shrimp
12 lemons, quartered
3 whole garlic heads, chopped in half crosswise
3 to 4 boxes salt
1 bunch celery, finely chopped
3 medium onions, chopped
8 ounces cayenne pepper
6 ounces liquid crab boil
2 tablespoons cooking oil

Boil water in a large pot, enough to cover shrimp. When water comes to first boil add shrimp and all ingredients, except salt. Reduce heat just a little.

When water comes to second boil, let boil for 1 to 2 minutes. Remove from heat.

Then add salt and about 2 gallons cold water or 4 to 5 trays of ice. Stir and let soak for 3 to 6 minutes depending on size of shrimp. Sample shrimp while soaking for seasoning and doneness. They are ready when meat begins to separate from shell.

MAKES 50 SERVINGS

MR. B'S

201 Royal St., New Orleans, LA 70130; (504) 523-2078.

Mr. B's is the avant-garde restaurant of the Brennan family of New Orleans fame. Operated on a day-to-day basis by the second generation of Brennans, the restaurant is a large mahogany room with a cool, dark elegance reflected in the art deco frosted mirrors. Several banquettes in bay windows give diners a curbside view of the French Quarter outside. The bar, which is the longest in the Quarter, specializes in delicious ice cream drinks.

SHRIMP CHIPPEWA

Chippewa Butter Sauce
2 cups fish velouté (see Basic Sauces)
3/4 teaspoon seafood seasoning
Pinch red pepper
1/2 cup white wine
1 teaspoon Louisiana hot sauce
1 1/2 cups salted butter

10 raw shrimp, butterflied (see Glossary)
1/3 cup quartered mushrooms
1 tablespoon chopped green onions
1/3 cup fish stock (see Basic Stocks)
Pinch seafood seasoning

To make Cheppewa butter sauce: In a large pot heat everything except butter and bring to a boil. Put on low heat and beat in butter, 1 tablespoon at a time. Remove from heat and keep in a warm place.

In a small pan, poach shrimp, green onions, mushrooms, and seasoning in fish stock until shrimp are cooked. Add Chippewa butter sauce and bring to a boil. Serve in bowl. Garnish with French bread.

MAKES 1 SERVING

Photograph, Page 24

THE ROYAL RESTAURANT

Travelodge, 2502 Port Dr., Jennings, LA 70546; (318) 824-6550

Travelers who spend the night in this comfortable little Southwestern Louisiana town will be happy to find that there is food fine enough to awaken their weary palates in the Royal Restaurant and Pub at the Travelodge, right off the I-10 at Exit 65. The lounge is a congenial place to loosen up and build an appetite; the dining room does its part by offering up a cornucopia of fresh seafood delights.

TURTLE SAUCE PIQUANTE

3 pounds turtle meat (no fat, no skin)
4 tablespoons salad oil
1 quart water
2 cloves garlic, chopped
1/2 cup chopped green onions
1/2 cup chopped parsley
2 tablespoons cornstarch
6 tablespoons hot sauce (preferably Bayou Bengal Sauce)
Salt and pepper to taste

In a large kettle, cook turtle meat in salad oil over low heat until brown. Add 1 quart water and remaining ingredients. Cook until tender, adding water if necessary. Remove turtle meat and mince.

Return to kettle and add salt and pepper to taste.

Serve over white rice or cream potatoes.

MAKES 6 TO 8 SERVINGS

VEGETABLES · BREADS

CAROUSEL CAFETERIA

3110 Louisville Ave., Monroe, LA 71201; (318) 325-7794.

One of the largest and most popular restaurants in Monroe, the Carousel Cafeteria has two dining rooms. The main room seats over 300 diners; the private Briarwood Room has capacity for up to 100 and handles private parties. The service at the Carousel is standard cafeteria self-service, but the assortment of food is uncommonly broad. Every day there are 14 entrees, 18 salads, 14 vegetables, and 18 desserts from which to choose. They range from cafeteria favorites to daily specials of the chef.

SAUTEED MUSHROOMS

1/4 cup margarine
1/4 cup onions, finely chopped
1 tablespoon Worcestershire sauce
2 teaspoons A-1 sauce
1 teaspoon garlic powder
1 teaspoon salt
2 pounds fresh whole mushrooms

Melt margarine in a skillet and add onions, Worcestershire sauce, A-1 sauce, garlic powder, and salt. Cook until onions are soft. Add mushrooms to sauce and simmer mixture until mushrooms are done.

Excellent served with grilled steak.

MAKES 8 TO 10 SERVINGS

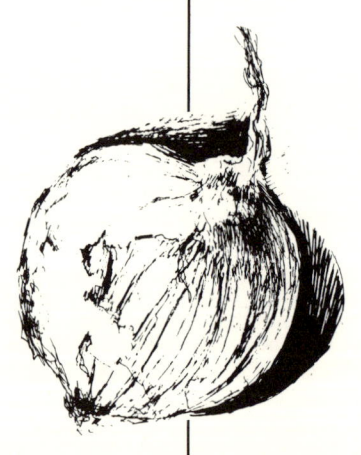

K-PAUL'S LOUISIANA KITCHEN
406 Chartres, New Orleans, LA. 70130; (504) 522-3818.

K-Paul's is without question the most phenomenal restaurant to open in New Orleans in many a year. Before the renovated French Quarter barroom was two years old, it had diners from all over the country standing in line (since there are no reservations) to sit with strangers (since a "community seating" policy is in force) and enjoy a distinctive brand of Cajun cooking by chef Paul Prudhomme. Everything is fresh and prepared to order; much of the food is raised on the restaurant's own farm.

CALAS *(Rice Cakes)*

Basic Rice
1/2 cup chicken or beef stock (see Basic Stocks)
1/3 heaping cup uncooked converted rice
1/2 tablespoon finely chopped onions
1/2 tablespoon finely chopped celery
1/2 tablespoon finely chopped green peppers

Rice Cakes
1 egg
2 1/2 tablespoons sugar
1 1/2 teaspoons baking powder
1/2 teaspoon salt
1 tablespoon vanilla
1/2 cup all purpose flour
Cooking oil for deep-frying
Sifted confectioners' sugar

To make basic cooked rice: Combine all ingredients in a 1-quart saucepan. Cover and bring to a rapid boil. Simmer over very low heat for 8 minutes. Turn off the heat and let sit, covered, for 20 minutes. Remove and cool 5 to 10 minutes. Makes 1 cup of rice.

To make rice cakes: In a medium size bowl beat the egg vigorously with a metal whisk until frothy and bubbles are the size of pinheads, about 1 to 2 minutes. Add the sugar, baking powder (break up any lumps), and salt and whisk until well blended. Whisk in the vanilla, then the flour. With a spoon fold in the rice. Cover bowl with a towel and let stand 20 minutes at room temperature.

In a deep skillet or deep fryer, heat the oil to 350 degrees F. Drop batter by rounded tablespoonfuls into the hot oil, slipping it into the oil so it maintains a relatively flat shape. Fry, turning at least once, until both sides are golden brown and centers are cooked, about 3 to 4 minutes.

Drain on paper towels. Keep calas warm in a 275 degrees F. oven while frying the rest. Sprinkle with confectioners' sugar and serve immediately.

Note: Hot calas were sold on the streets of the French Quarter during the 1800s. Now these cakes may be used as a side dish for an authentic Creole meal as a bread or vegetable.

MAKES ABOUT 16 CALAS

THE EMBERS STEAK HOUSE

700 Bourbon St., New Orleans, LA 70116; (504) 523-1485.

Now in its third decade of serving some of the best quality steaks to be found anywhere, The Embers is well-known as the premier house in the French Quarter. Six different cuts of beef are char-broiled to order over open flames. Lamb chops are also a specialty, and for lost seafarers there is a soupçon of seafood on the menu. The full array of favorite steakhouse side dishes get careful attention from the Embers' cooks, from salads to baked stuffed potatoes, to hot French rolls.

SPECIAL STUFFED POTATO

1 large, 12-ounce Idaho baking potato per person
2 teaspoons butter
Salt and pepper to taste
4 teaspoons sour cream
1 teaspoon chopped chives
3 teaspoons coarsely grated sharp Cheddar cheese (Wisconsin Black Rind Midget cheese recommended)
Additional grated Cheddar cheese

Bake potato(es) at 450 degrees F. for one hour or until done. Make lengthwise slit in each potato, 3 to 4 inches long. Carefully insert fork into slit and break potato away from skin, so that potato is left inside skin but is broken up. While doing this, add butter, salt, and pepper. Add sour cream, chives, and grated cheese. Mix into potato being careful not to break skin.

Sprinkle each potato with additional cheese. Bake for 7 minutes or until cheese melts and begins to brown at edges.

MAKES 1 SERVING

ANTOINE'S

713 St. Louis St., New Orleans, LA 70130; (504) 581-4422.

A long book could be written of the stories behind some of Antoine's most famous dishes. Soufflee potatoes, for instance, were created by a French chef who started out frying some potatoes for the king. When his majesty showed up late, the chef fried them lightly a second time, and found to his amazement that they puffed up like balloons. The dish is a favorite now at Antoine's and was first served there to a visiting balloonist early in the century.

POMMES DE TERRE SOUFFLEES *(Puffed Potatoes)*

2 pounds large potatoes
Oil for frying
Salt to taste

Wash and peel the potatoes and cut lengthwise into slices $1^{1}/_{4}$ inches wide and $^{1}/_{8}$ inch thick. Soak the potato slices in cold water to remove excess starch.

Have two pots filled with oil, one at a moderately hot temperature, 275 degrees F. and the other at a very hot temperature, 400 degrees F. Drain the potatoes and dry them carefully. Put a single layer of potatoes into a frying basket and lower the basket into the moderately hot oil. Keep moving the potatoes around, dipping the basket in and out of the oil until the potatoes begin to brown and to puff. The partially cooked potatoes may be set aside for awhile before the second stage, or may be finished immediately.

Put the partially cooked potatoes in a basket and dip the basket into the pot of very hot oil. Again be careful to cover only the bottom of the basket with potatoes and to keep them moving around in the oil until they are golden brown, well-puffed and crispy.

Remove from the oil, drain on absorbent paper and sprinkle with salt for seasoning.

MAKES 6 SERVINGS

THE RED ONION

2700 Edenborn, Metairie, LA 70002; (504) 455-6677.

The Red Onion was the first of the big, elaborate suburban restaurants to open in Metairie, and it has set the standard for good service and food ever since. The menu is a Creole approach to Italian food, or vice-versa. There is much fresh seafood, and a long list of specialties involving baby white veal. The restaurant is also respected for its skill in preparing prime steaks, prime rib, and Maine lobster. The large dining rooms and many private rooms offer options for all sorts of affairs.

BAYOU EGGPLANT

3 whole eggplants
1 cup milk
2 eggs, beaten
1 cup flour for dredging
1 cup bread crumbs
Oil for deep-frying
2 pounds medium-sized shrimp
1 1/2 tablespoons salt
6 dashes Tabasco sauce
2 1/2 tablespoons monosodium glutamate
1 1/2 tablespoons garlic powder
2 cups butter
1/2 cup flour
1 pound fresh lump crabmeat
3 shallots, finely chopped
6 large mushrooms, sliced
1/2 cup white wine

Peel eggplants, cut in half lengthwise, and hollow out insides leaving a 3/4-inch thick wall.

Combine milk with eggs to make eggwash. Dust eggplant shells with flour, dip in eggwash, roll in bread crumbs, and deep-fry at 375 degrees F. until golden brown.

Boil shrimp with salt, Tabasco, monosodium glutamate, and garlic powder until tender. Drain shrimp, peel, and devein. Reserve stock.

Cook oysters on medium heat in their liquor until edges curl. Drain.

In a saute pan melt butter and add 1/2 cup flour to make roux (see Glossary).

Boil reserved shrimp stock, stir in roux and cook, stirring until smooth. Add shrimp, oysters, shallots, and mushrooms. Cook 5 minutes.

Remove from heat, add white wine, spoon into eggplant, and serve immediately.

MAKES 6 SERVINGS

Photograph, Page 18

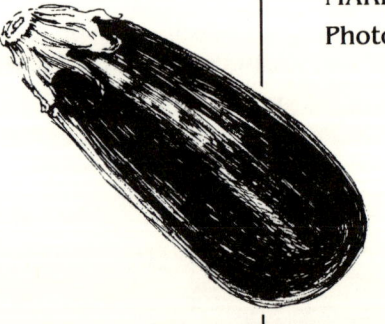

BENEDICT HOUSE

1381 W. Tunnel Blvd., Houma, LA 70361; (504) 851-3170.

Situated in the heart of the Bayou Country in Houma, the Benedict House, serves breakfast, lunch, and dinner in a casual and friendly atmosphere. The range of the kitchen is broad, from the fine crab and shrimp dishes to filé and seafood gumbo, from Italian specialties to Creole-French creations like trout Louie. Evenings find a relaxed company of diners, interesting food, and a fine wine list at the Benedict House.

PLANTATION EGGPLANT

2 medium to large eggplants
1/2 cup bacon drippings
1 large onion, finely chopped
1/2 bunch green onions, finely chopped
1/2 cup finely chopped celery
1 garlic clove, minced
2 tablespoons minced parsley
3 to 4 slices bread (French preferred) soaked in seafood stock (see Note)
1 egg, beaten
1/2 teaspoon sugar
Salt and pepper to taste
1/4 teaspoon oregano
1/4 teaspoon thyme
1 pound shrimp, peeled
1/2 pound white crabmeat
Parmesan cheese

Cut eggplants lengthwise, place in a 2-quart sauce pan and cover with hot water. Cover and boil until eggplants are fork tender. Allow eggplants to become cool enough to handle. Remove the meat from the eggplants using a spoon, being careful to leave the skin intact. Reserve skin and meat.

To make stuffing, in a 2-quart sauce pan melt bacon drippings over medium heat. Add onion, green onions, celery, and garlic and saute for 10 minutes. Do not brown. Add the eggplant and simmer 30 minutes, stirring and scraping the bottom of the pan often. Add parsley and simmer 5 minutes.

Squeeze seafood stock from bread and mix bread into stuffing. Remove from heat. Blend in egg, sugar, salt and pepper, oregano, and thyme. Add shrimp and gently fold in crabmeat.

Stuff the eggplant; sprinkle with Parmesan cheese and dot with butter. Bake at 350 degrees F. for 20 to 30 minutes.

Note: A seafood stock may be made by simmering shrimp shells, fish bones, and crab shells in a pot of water for 30 minutes.

MAKES 4 SERVINGS

BILL'S SEAFOOD RESTAURANT

5252 Veterans Blvd., Metairie, LA 70002; (504) 887-9635.

The specialty at Bill's, a small family-style restaurant in the New Orleans suburb of Metairie, is seafood; but that is not the end of the menu. You will also find a variety of reasonably priced non-seafood dishes and a children's menu. Seafood is offered, both broiled and fried New Orleans-style, along with a fresh oyster bar serving good cold bivalves on the half shell. There are daily lunch specials.

STUFFED BELL PEPPER WITH SHRIMP

1 1/2 pounds medium size yellow squash
1 loaf stale French bread
1/2 cup margarine
1/4 pound onions, chopped
1/4 pound green peppers, chopped
3 ribs celery, chopped
5 cloves garlic, chopped
2 1/2 pounds uncooked shrimp, peeled, chopped
2 1/4 teaspoons salt
1 1/2 teaspoons pepper
6 green onion tops, chopped
1/4 cup chopped parsley
3 eggs, beaten
2 cups Italian bread crumbs
8 large green peppers, halved, leaving stems for attractive look
Additional Italian bread crumbs
9 teaspoons butter

Cook squash in water to cover until tender, approximately 20 to 30 minutes. Allow to cool, cut in halves, and scoop out centers. Discard skins.

Break bread into pieces and place in water to cover. Soak until soft; then squeeze out the water from the bread, being sure to remove as much water as possible.

In large sauce pan melt margarine and saute onions, chopped green peppers, celery, and garlic. Add squash centers and shrimp. Cook until shrimp turn pink, mixing well. Add squeezed dry bread, salt, and pepper. Mix very well and cook for 10 minutes, stirring periodically. Allow to cool. Add green onion tops, parsley, beaten eggs. Add bread crumbs slowly until stuffing has a stiff consistency.

Remove seeds and membranes (not stems) on pepper halves. Stuff the peppers with the stuffing mixture and place them in a baking pan with 1/2 inch of water in the pan. Sprinkle Italian bread crumbs over top of peppers and then top each half with 1/2 teaspoon butter. Cover with foil and cook at 350 degrees F. for approximately 20 to 30 minutes. When peppers soften remove foil and brown top.

Note: Peppers will freeze well. Wrap individually and omit browning until ready to serve. For main course serve 2 pepper halves.

MAKES 16 SERVINGS

LA SAVOIE

94 Friedrichs Ave., Metairie, LA 70005; (504) 831-1108.

This small gourmet restaurant, owned by Chef Gerard Thabuis, specializes in French food with a nod toward the Creole way of seasoning. The chef scours the markets looking for fresh fish, and especially delights in showing up back in his kitchen with something unusual. He creates an interesting selection of homemade pâté, terrines, and smoked fish every day, displaying them on a table in the dining room. He also does wonders with veal, beef, and lamb, and serves fresh vegetables with entrees.

ARLEQUIN DE COURGETTES

2 large zucchini
2 carrots
1/2 bunch spinach
1/2 bunch broccoli
1/4 cup butter
Salt and pepper to taste
Nutmeg to taste
1 to 2 cups instant potatoes (do not prepare)

Cut zucchinis in long slices 1/2 inch thick. Poach 1 minute in boiling water. Set aside. Separately cook the carrots, broccoli, and spinach in boiling water until very tender. Puree the carrots in a blender or food processor. Add butter, seasoning, and a portion of the dry potatoes to thicken. Puree broccoli and spinach together and add dry potatoes to thicken to the consistency of whipped cream.

Using a pastry bag, pipe a row of carrot puree and a row of broccoli puree side by side on each zucchini slice.

Bake 5 minutes at 350 degrees F.

Note: Instant potatoes are used here as a thickening agent.

MAKES APPROXIMATELY 8 PIECES

CAROUSEL CAFETERIA

3110 Louisville Ave., Monroe, LA 71201; (318) 325-7794.

The Carousel proves that cafeteria dining can be first class. The selection of fresh foods is staggering; for instance, there are 20 different pies baked daily. A specialty of the house is spinach, which goes into salads and unusual side dishes. At lunch and dinner, there is live organ music to complement your gustatory pleasures. Non-smokers will be glad to see a separate section reserved for their use. The prices are inexpensive and the Carousel's family fare is accessible to all Monroe hotels and I-20.

ARTICHOKE AND GREEN BEAN CASSEROLE

1 large onion, finely chopped
1/2 cup olive oil
3 cloves garlic, minced
2 (16-ounce) cans French-style green beans, drained
2 (14-ounce) cans artichoke hearts, drained
1 cup grated Parmesan cheese
1 3/4 cups Italian bread crumbs, divided
1 teaspoon salt, or to taste
1/2 teaspoon pepper, or to taste

Saute onion in oil; add garlic. Remove from heat. Chop beans and artichokes and mix together with onions and garlic. Add remaining ingredients, reserving 1/4 cup bread crumbs. If mixture is dry, add more olive oil. Place in casserole and sprinkle with the reserved bread crumbs. Bake at 350 degrees F. for 30 minutes.

MAKES 8 TO 10 SERVINGS

FLAMINGOS CAFE

1625 St. Charles Ave., New Orleans, LA 70130; (504) 523-6141.

Don't let the nutty decor of this restaurant fool you; they know how to cook expertly at Flamingos. The specialty is quiche, available in at least a dozen different ways at any time, rich with eggs and heavy cream and cheese. Omelettes are also an emphasis, big fluffy three-egg jobs. There are crêpes with many different fillings, smoked meats, and seafoods, and salads of gargantuan size and imaginative composition. The breads are baked on the premises and every platter comes with a variety of fresh fruit.

ARTICHOKE HEART QUICHE

1 (10-inch) deep dish pie shell, homemade or frozen
4 eggs
1½ cups heavy cream
Dash each Tabasco sauce, salt, pepper, and nutmeg
3 ounces Cheddar cheese, shredded
1 cup diced artichoke hearts, frozen or canned
⅓ cup chopped onions
1 red pimiento, chopped
6 ounces Swiss cheese, coarsely grated

Prebake the pie shell at 375 degrees F. until light brown about 10-15 minutes. To keep the pie dough from bubbling, either line shell with wax paper and weight with pie shell weights or prick with a fork before baking.

Beat the eggs well; add the cream and spices. Blend well, but do not beat.

Cover the bottom of the pie shell with the Cheddar cheese. Add artichoke hearts, onions, pimiento, dividing evenly around shell. Add Swiss cheese. Slowly add custard so that it flows around all the ingredients.

Bake at 375 degrees F. for 45 minutes or until the top is brown and a knife comes out clean when inserted. The quiche may puff, but will flatten slightly when it stands. It is recommended that the quiche stand for at least 45 minutes or be refrigerated and re-warmed before serving to let the flavors merge.

The quiche should be served at a warm room temperature to bring out the flavors and make cutting and serving easier.

The quiche may be served chilled for a picnic.

MAKES 6 SERVINGS

MARTI'S

1041 Dumaine St., New Orleans, LA 70116; (504) 524-6060.

When movie producers come to New Orleans in search of a restaurant setting, they often stop looking when they get to Marti's. It is pure New Orleans with red walls, tiny lights around the perimeter, small mirrors through which one can covertly survey other diners, and antique frosted glass. The centerpiece is a mural depicting the entrance to City Park in the early years of this century. The bar is also a great period piece, with tile floor and antique wood and copper fixtures.

PAIN PERDU *(Lost Bread)*

6 eggs
2 cups sugar
1/2 teaspoon cinnamon
1/2 teaspoon nutmeg
3 cups milk
3 teaspoons vanilla extract
1 teaspoon grated orange rind
2 cups oil
Loaf French bread (one day old)
Confectioners' sugar
Cane syrup

Mix eggs, sugar, cinnamon, nutmeg; then add milk, vanilla, and orange rind. Stir until mixed well.

Slice the French bread into 12 slices on angle 1 inch thick. Pour 2 cups oil in a large skillet. When the oil reaches 300 degrees F., dip 6 slices of bread in the mixture then place in the hot oil.

Brown on both sides. As they brown, remove the bread slices to paper towels to drain.

Sprinkle the pain perdu with confectioners' sugar and serve at once, accompanied by a pitcher of cane syrup.

Note: This is the local version of French Toast and originated as a way to use stale bread.

MAKES 6 SERVINGS

K-PAUL'S LOUISIANA KITCHEN

406 Chartres St., New Orleans, LA 70130; (504) 522-3818.

Few chefs have made the kind of national impact that chef Paul Prudhomme of New Orleans has managed in just a few years. When he took the entire restaurant, staff and all, to San Francisco for a month's operations there, curious gourmets stood in line as long as eight hours to sample the highly-seasoned Cajun cooking. A curious man himself, Prudhomme dabbles in Mexican, French, Indian, and any other cuisine that strikes his fancy in his little modest dinner-only French Quarter Café.

SOUTHERN BISCUIT MUFFINS

2½ cups all purpose flour
¼ cup sugar
1½ tablespoons baking powder
¼ teaspoon salt
½ cup plus 2 tablespoons unsalted butter, softened
1 cup cold milk

Combine the flour, sugar, baking powder, and salt; mix well, breaking up any lumps. Work the butter in by hand until the mixture resembles coarse corn meal, making sure no lumps are left.

Gradually stir in the milk, mixing just until dry ingredients are moistened. Do not overbeat.

Spoon the batter into 12 greased muffin cups. Bake at 350 degrees F. until golden brown, about 35 to 40 minutes. The finished muffins should have a thick crust with a cake-like center.

MAKES 1 DOZEN MUFFINS

RALPH & KACOO'S

601 Veterans Blvd., Metairie, LA 70005; (504) 831-3177.

There is a garden in the center of the three large dining rooms at Ralph & Kacoo's Metairie restaurant, and lush green plants also infiltrate the dining rooms themselves, with hanging baskets and unusual china plates hanging on the walls. The lounge has a cozy, comfortable atmosphere. The restaurant is incredibly popular with Metairie residents, who enjoy the famous catfish and hush puppies, the generously-piled seafood platters, and the excellent steaks. A fun atmosphere prevails at all hours.

HUSH PUPPIES

2 1/2 cups cornmeal
1 1/2 cups flour
1 tablespoon sugar
1 teaspoon salt
1/2 teaspoon baking soda
1/8 teaspoon red pepper
2 teaspoons baking powder
1/8 teaspoon garlic powder
1 tablespoon chopped green onions
1 cup evaporated milk
3/4 cup water
1 egg, beaten
1 teaspoon chopped parsley
Oil for deep-frying

Mix all dry ingredients in a large bowl. Add onion, milk, water, eggs and parsley and blend well.

Refrigerate until ready to use.

Heat oil for deep-frying and spoon batter into oil, frying until golden brown.

MAKES 30 TO 40 HUSH PUPPIES

L.R.A.

The Louisiana Restaurant Association offers the special beignet recipe below for those who have never had the pleasure of this delicate sweet bread for breakfast or brunch. Beignets are rectangular doughnuts served as an accompaniment to coffee, especially café au lait, in the New Orleans French Market. They are slim, light pastries, fried quickly in oil, and served hot, sprinkled with the sweet dust of confectioners' sugar.

BEIGNETS *(French Market Doughnuts)*

1/3 cup warm water (103 to 115 degrees F.)
2 1/2 packages active dry yeast
2 cups milk
3/4 cup vegetable shortening
1 cup sugar
1 scant tablespoon salt
2 jumbo eggs, lightly beaten
10 to 12 cups all purpose flour
Oil for deep-frying
Confectioners' sugar

Note: Unused dough may be kept in the refrigerator for up to one week and used as needed.

Put the warm water into a large bowl; add the yeast, stirring to mix. Allow to dissolve 5 to 8 minutes. Meanwhile, in a saucepan, heat the milk and shortening together until shortening is melted. Remove from heat and allow mixture to cool to 115 degrees F. or below.

Add milk mixture, sugar, salt, and eggs to the dissolved yeast. Set 1/2 cup flour aside. Gradually stir in 5 cups of the remaining flour and beat with a wooden spoon until thoroughly blended. Continue to beat in flour about 1/2 cup at a time, beating with a spoon until it becomes too stiff to stir. Begin working flour into dough with your fingers until dough no longer sticks to your hand.

Cover the bowl with dry dish towel and allow to rise in a warm spot at about 85 degrees F. until double. Dough may also be covered with plastic wrap and refrigerated overnight.

Sprinkle a board with the reserved flour. Remove a portion of the dough from the bowl. Place on board and roll to 3/8-inch thickness. Cut into 3-inch squares. Allow to rise about 30 to 45 minutes.

Pull and stretch each piece of dough to about 1/4-inch thickness. Fry in hot oil at 360 degrees F. until puffed and golden, about 2 to 3 minutes, turning so they brown evenly.

Drain on paper towels and place in an oven at 200 degrees F. to keep warm. Sprinkle with confectioners' sugar and serve hot with café au lait.

MAKES ABOUT 7 DOZEN BEIGNETS.

"Man did eat angels' food."
PSALMS LXVI, VERSE 12

DESSERTS · BEVERAGES

THE GUMBO SHOP

630 St. Peter St., New Orleans, LA 70116; (504) 525-1486.

The Gumbo Shop is a short stone's throw from the most historic part of the French Quarter in New Orleans. It is literally behind St. Louis Cathedral, the Cabildo, and the Pontalbas. The restaurant itself has local charm; one enters through a small courtyard into a dining room decorated with large murals depicting scenes of life in old New Orleans. Venerable black ceiling fans rotate slowly overhead, and windows give one a view of the passing parade.

BREAD PUDDING WITH RUM SAUCE

Bread Pudding
1/4 cup butter
2 cups milk
1 quart cubed day-old French bread
1/2 cup cubed pineapple
1/2 cup raisins
1/2 cup sugar
1/4 teaspoon salt
1/2 teaspoon cinnamon
1/2 teaspoon nutmeg
2 eggs, beaten
1 teaspoon vanilla

Rum Sauce
1/4 cup butter, softened
2 cups confectioners' sugar
1/2 cup Meyer's rum

To make bread pudding: Combine butter and milk in a sauce pan and heat until butter is melted. In a large mixing bowl combine bread, pineapple, and raisins. Add the milk and butter. Mix and let stand several minutes to let bread absorb liquid.

Combine sugar, salt, and spices. Add beaten eggs and vanilla and mix well. Pour over bread-milk mixture and stir until well mixed.

Pour into a well greased 1 1/2-quart baking dish or black iron skillet. Bake at 350 degrees F. for 40 minutes. Serve warm with rum sauce.

To make sauce: Cream together butter and powdered sugar. Slowly beat in rum.

MAKES 6 TO 8 SERVINGS

BON TON CAFE

401 Magazine St., New Orleans, LA 70130; (504) 524-3386.

The Bon Ton Café is considered by New Orleans businessmen one of the city's premier places for lunch. The tables are filled by 11:15 am daily, and the restaurant stays busy until it closes much later at night. The specialties in the small, sociable dining room include a broad range of seafood, with crawfish a specialty in season. Crawfish first appear in late November and last until June and those are fine times at the Bon Ton.

BREAD PUDDING AND WHISKEY SAUCE

Bread Pudding
6 ounces stale French bread
2 cups milk
2 eggs
1 cup sugar
1 tablespoon vanilla
$1/2$ cup raisins
$1 1/2$ tablespoons melted butter or margarine

Whiskey Sauce
1 cup sugar
1 egg
$1/2$ cup melted butter
$1/3$ cup whiskey

To make bread pudding: Break the bread into pieces and soak it well in the milk. Add the eggs, sugar, vanilla, and raisins, and stir well.

Pour the melted butter into the bottom of a heavy pan (approximately $4 1/2$-inch by 6-inch by 3-inch). Pour the bread mixture into the pan. Bake at 350 degrees F. for approximately 45 minutes or until the pudding is firm and a knife inserted in the middle comes out clean.

Let the pudding cool. Then cut the pudding into individual portions, and put each in a dessert dish.

To make the whiskey sauce: Cream the sugar and 1 egg. Add the melted butter and stir until the sugar is dissolved. Stir in the whiskey.

When ready to serve, pour sauce over pudding and heat under broiler.

MAKES 8 SERVINGS

COMMANDER'S PALACE

1403 Washington Ave., New Orleans, LA 70130; (504) 899-8221.

In the center of the Garden District in uptown New Orleans stands one of the city's most celebrated restaurants, Commander's Palace. The elaborate Victorian "palace" is situated in a section which was the original Livaudais Plantation, one of many plantations growing sugar cane and indigo west of New Orleans. This area became a part of the city in 1852. Commander's Palace retains the original residential charm with lush gardens and patios.

BREAD PUDDING SOUFFLE WITH WHISKEY SAUCE

Home-style bread pudding
3/4 loaf of stale French bread, cut into 1-inch cubes
3 eggs
9 egg yolks
2 1/4 cups sugar, divided
4 1/2 tablespoons vanilla
1 teaspoon cinnamon
1 teaspoon nutmeg
1/2 cup softened butter
4 cups milk
1/2 cup raisins
6 egg whites
1/2 cup confectioners' sugar

Whiskey Sauce
2 1/4 cups water, divided
1 cup sugar
1 cinnamon stick or dash cinnamon
1 tablespoon butter
1/2 teaspoon cornstarch
1 tablespoon bourbon

To make bread pudding: Spread bread cubes in a 13-inch by 9-inch by 2-inch baking pan and bake at 350 degrees F. for 12 to 15 minutes or until golden brown. Set aside.

In large mixing bowl beat eggs and 3 of the egg yolks on medium speed until frothy. Beat in 1 3/4 cups of sugar, the vanilla, cinnamon, and nutmeg. Beat in soft butter and stir in milk.

Sprinkle raisins over the toasted bread and pour milk mixture over all. Let rest until bread cubes are thoroughly soaked, then bake at 350 degrees F. for 40 minutes. During the baking the pudding will rise 2 or 3 times its original height but, once removed from oven, will decrease and be slightly higher than the uncooled pudding. Cool slightly. Set aside 2 1/2 cups of the pudding for the souffle.

To make the souffle, put the remaining 6 egg yolks and 1/2 cup sugar into top of a double boiler sauce pan. Whisk over simmering water until mixture is frothy and shiny. Whip yolk mixture into the reserved bread pudding.

Beat the 6 egg whites until frothy. Gradually add confectioners' sugar, beating constantly until the resulting meringue stands in stiff peaks. Gently fold egg whites into bread pudding mixture.

Butter and lightly sugar a 1 1/2-quart souffle dish. Turn souffle mixture into the dish, filling it three quarters full. Wipe lip of the souffle dish clean and bake at 375 degrees F. for 35 to 40 minutes.

BREAD PUDDING SOUFFLE WITH WHISKEY SAUCE *(Continued)*

To make the whiskey sauce: In sauce pan combine 2 cups of the water, the cinnamon, and butter. Bring to a boil. Stir in the cornstarch mixed with the remaining 1/4 cup water and cook, stirring, until sauce is clear. Remove from heat and stir in whiskey.

Remove souffle from oven and serve immediately. Serve the whiskey sauce in a separate bowl.

MAKES 8 SERVINGS

Photograph, Page 19.

CHEZ PASTOR

1211 Pinhook Rd., Lafayette, LA 70501; (318) 234-5189.

"Manger en francais, c'est laisser le bon temps rouler" is the motto of Chez Pastor, one of the most elegant and consistent restaurants in Lafayette in the center of the Cajun country. Translated, that means "Eat in French and let the good times roll." A very appropriate credo for this highly skilled kitchen, which combines on its menu the greatest of the Cajun country's culinary specialties with excursions into classical French cuisine.

BREAD PUDDING WITH RUM SAUCE

Bread Pudding
1/2 cup butter
3 egg yolks
1/2 cup sugar
1 teaspoon vanilla
1 cup evaporated milk
1 quart milk
4 hamburger buns

Meringue
3 egg whites
1/4 cup sugar

Rum Sauce
1 quart evaporated milk
1/4 cup sugar
1/4 cup rum
1/4 cup cornstarch dissolved in 3 tablespoons water (more if needed)

To make pudding: Melt butter, mix egg yolks into melted butter, add sugar, vanilla, evaporated milk, and milk. Mix thoroughly. Separate hamburger buns in baking pan. Pour egg-milk mixture over buns. Bake at 350 degrees F. for 30 minutes.

To make meringue: Beat egg whites and sugar together in mixer until meringue starts to peak. Then spread lightly over baked bread pudding. Return to oven and bake at 325 degrees F. until meringue is golden brown.

To make rum sauce: Combine all ingredients in the top of a double boiler and cook over medium heat for 1 hour.

Pour sauce over bread pudding when served.

MAKES 10 SERVINGS

Photograph, Page 18

ARNAUD'S

813 Bienville St., New Orleans, LA 70112; (504) 523-5433.

Founded in 1918, Arnaud's is considered to be one of the essential old-line Creole restaurants in New Orleans. It was the product of the flamboyant Count Arnaud Cazenave, who assembled a classic menu of French food with highly distinctive Creole accents of the count's own devising. After passing into the hands of his daughter, Germaine Wells, who held the restaurant for decades, it was acquired by Archie Casbarian in 1978. He renovated all the many dining rooms into the sparkling, very old New Orleans look they now have.

CREME BRULE

2 cups heavy cream
4 tablespoons sugar
4 egg yolks
1 1/2 to 2 tablespoons vanilla
Sifted brown sugar to cover

In a sauce pan scald the cream.

In a medium bowl beat the sugar with the egg yolks and add the vanilla to mixture. Slowly add scalded cream to mixture, whisking to blend.

Pour in ramekins and bake in a pan of hot water at 350 degrees F. for 50 minutes or until a knife inserted in the center of the custard comes out clean.

When done, sprinkle brown sugar on the top of the custard and place under the broiler for a few seconds until brown sugar melts and browns slightly.

Refrigerate and serve cold.

MAKES 6 TO 8 SERVINGS

DESSERTS

BEGUE'S

Royal Sonesta Hotel, 300 Bourbon St., New Orleans, LA 70130; (504) 586-0300.

Begue's, the elaborate French-Creole dining room of the Royal Sonesta Hotel in New Orleans' French Quarter, is especially popular among the locals for its daily lunch buffets. These feature, besides a cornucopia of salads and desserts, a host of fresh local seafood. On Sundays the buffet serves up one of the city's most popular brunches. Adjacent to the restaurant is a typical, beautiful Quarter patio for post-prandial relaxing.

LE RIZ AU CARAMEL *(Rice Flavored with Caramel)*

3/4 cup rice
3 cups water, divided
Dash vanilla
1/8 teaspoon grated orange rind
1 quart milk
3/4 cup sugar, divided
4 egg yolks

Blanch the rice in 2 cups of the boiling water for 3 minutes. Drain rice and rinse under cool water.

Add vanilla and orange rind to milk in a sauce pan, mixing lightly. Stir in the rice and 1/4 cup of the sugar. Cover and cook over low heat for 25 minutes. Remove from heat and allow to cool.

Blend remaining 1/2 cup sugar and 1 cup of water in sauce pan over medium heat, stirring constantly, until mixture thickens and darkens to a caramel color. Remove from heat.

Beat egg yolks and stir into cooled rice mixture. Slowly add caramelized sugar while stirring. Pour into six individual custard cups. Serve chilled.

MAKES 6 SERVINGS

CAFE RANI

315 N. Vermont, Covington, LA 70433; (504) 893-4383.

This restaurant is the creation of Chef and owner Gary Darling, well-known to his peers as an extremely capable and imaginative kitchen presence. His place is located in a renovated house in downtown Covington. The proximity to the courthouse brings in a great many local businessmen for the daily lunch specials. Many of them return after dark for the thrice-weekly dinners.

KAHLUA PECAN PIE

1 1/2 cups butter
2 cups dark Karo syrup
1 1/2 cups brown sugar
3 ounces semi-sweet chocolate
1 cup cocoa powder
3 tablespoons powdered Sanka
1/2 teaspoon cinnamon
1/3 cup cornstarch
1/2 cup Kahlua
8 eggs, beaten
1/8 teaspoon salt
1 tablespoon vanilla extract
3 1/2 cups pecan pieces
1 pie pastry

In a sauce pan heat the butter, syrup, sugar, chocolate, cocoa powder, Sanka, and cinnamon.

Mix the cornstarch into the Kahlua and add to hot syrup mixture. Add 1 cup of hot syrup mixture to eggs and add back to remainder of syrup. Add salt, vanilla, and pecans. Put into 2-inch by 12-inch pastry-lined springform pan.

Bake at 350 degrees F. for approximately 1 1/2 hours or until filling is almost set.

MAKES 12 SERVINGS

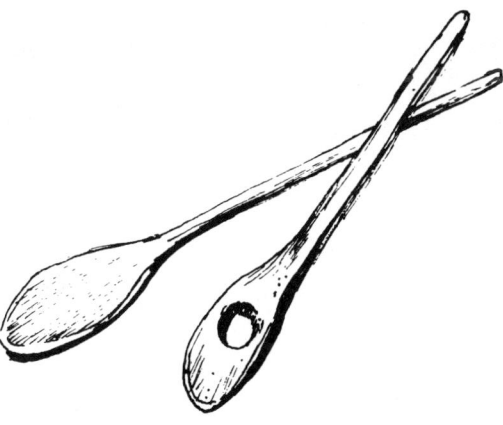

STEPHEN AND MARTIN

1613 Milan St., New Orleans, LA 70115; (504) 897-0781.

Stephen and Martin started out in the mid-forties as a neighborhood restaurant in uptown New Orleans. The reputation as a reliable dining resource was greatly enhanced in 1976, when the restaurant underwent a major rebirth. It emerged as a handsome art-deco dining room with highly creative specialties. In 1981 it became even more impressive with the addition of the patio dining area looking out onto the streetcar tracks.

ALMOND TORTE

1 1/2 cups sliced almonds, divided
1 cup butter, softened
1/2 cup sugar
1 2/3 cups packed brown sugar
1 egg
1 tablespoon almond extract
Whipped cream for topping

Toast almonds at 350 degrees F. until golden brown, about 10 minutes. Set aside to cool.

Cream the butter and sugar in a mixing bowl. Gradually add the brown sugar. Beat in the egg, almond extract, and 1 cup of the roasted almonds. Beat the mixture with a mixer for 15 minutes on high speed. Turn the mixture into a pan lined with plastic wrap, cover, and freeze for 1 hour.

Shape the mixture into a log 2 1/2 inches in diameter. Roll the log in 1/4 cup of the roasted almonds and refreeze it.

To serve, cut the log into 1/2-inch slices, and place each slice onto a serving plate. Garnish each slice with a dollop of whipped cream. Divide the remaining 1/4 cup of almonds among the portions to garnish.

MAKES 6 TO 8 SERVINGS

MAYER'S OLD EUROPE

2998 Pontchartrain Dr., Slidell, LA 70458; (504) 649-1426.

Here is a rare restaurant indeed, one which serves in delectable, beautiful form, the great cuisines of Europe. You will find dishes from Austria, Hungary, Germany, Italy, and France; enjoy as well Louisiana's good local specialties. Mayer's uses the best of local fresh seafood and steaks. Home-baked desserts are also a special delight of dining here. The service is sensitive and attentive.

LINZER TORTE

1¾ cups all purpose flour
1 cup ground almonds
⅓ cup sugar
1 cup unsalted butter, room temperature
3 egg yolks, beaten
¼ teaspoon cinnamon
½ teaspoon vanilla
¼ teaspoon ground mace
1½ cups finest quality raspberry preserves
1 tablespoon Framboise (raspberry brandy)
2 tablespoons confectioners' sugar

In a bowl mix the flour, almonds, sugar, butter, egg yolks, cinnamon, vanilla extract, and mace. Place on a board and smear mixture with the heel of hand to combine well. Set aside until ready to use.

Combine the preserves with the brandy and set aside. Spread dough in the bottom and sides of a removable bottom tart shell or in a 10-inch flan ring leaving some overhang. It should be about ¼ inch thick. Trim excess dough and roll into noodle-like strips.

Spread the jam on the bottom of the dough. Arrange the strips of dough on top of the jam in a lattice, crisscross manner, about 4 strips in each direction. Fold the edge of the overhanging dough gently over the jam and the strips and press gently to seal.

Cook at 375 degrees F. oven for about 35 minutes until nicely browned and crisp. Sprinkle with confectioners' sugar. Let rest at least 2 hours before serving at room temperature.

MAKES 8 SERVINGS

Photograph, Page 17

THE GUMBO SHOP
630 St. Peter St., New Orleans, LA 70116; (504) 525-1486.

The Gumbo Shop, true to its name, offers a host of gumbos and other local fare. Gumbo is an original Louisiana dish, served as a soup, vegetable, or entree over rice. The Gumbo Shop also has delectable desserts to conclude a hearty meal in the French Quarter.

CHOCOLATE CHEESECAKE

Filling
1 1/2 pounds cream cheese
1 cup sour cream
1 1/2 cups sugar
3 eggs
1 teaspoon vanilla
6 ounces unsweetened chocolate, melted

Crust
4 Holland rusks
3/4 cup chopped pecans
2 tablespoons sugar
1/3 cup melted butter

Topping
2 ounces unsweetened chocolate, melted
1/2 cup sugar
1 cup sour cream

To make filling: Soften cream cheese to room temperature. Add sour cream and sugar and beat well. Add eggs one at a time beating well and scraping bowl sides after each addition. Add vanilla. While stirring constantly, pour in melted chocolate. Prepare crust.

To make crust: Put all ingredients except butter in the food processor and process for 30 seconds. Add butter and process until well mixed. Press into a buttered 9-inch spring form pan and chill before filling with batter.

Pour filling into pan prepared with crust. Bake at 350 degrees F. for 1 hour. To cool, turn oven off, leaving the door open and let stand for 45 minutes.

To make topping: Melt chocolate and very quickly beat in sour cream and sugar. Spread on top of cooled cake. Chill cake before serving.

MAKES 10 SERVINGS

WILLY COLN'S CHALET

2505 Whitney Ave., Gretna, LA 70053; (504) 361-3860.

Few restaurants are as distinctive in both appearance and menu as Willy Coln's. The cooking covers a broad range of cuisines, from the chef's native German, to the classic French of his hotel-chef years, to Caribbean cooking styles. To top it off, some distinctly Creole items can be found here, with fine ingredients and polish that only a chef of Coln's skill can give. An accomplished pastry chef, Chef Coln creates a tempting array of desserts nightly.

SCHWARZWALDER KIRSHTORTE *(Black Forest Cake)*

Cake
6 eggs, room temperature
1 cup sugar
1/2 cup sifted flour
6 tablespoons flour
1/2 cup unsweetened cocoa
6 tablespoons clarified butter (see Glossary)
1 teaspoon vanilla

Filling and Topping
1 can dark pitted cherries
3/4 cup sugar
2 tablespoons cornstarch
3 cups heavy cream
1/2 cup confectioners' sugar
1/2 cup Kirschwasser (Cherry Brandy)
1 (8-ounce) bar semisweet chocolate, shaved into curls

Garnish: 12 fresh sweet cherries with stems or maraschino cherries

To make cake: Beat the eggs with the sugar until light and fluffy, about 5 to 8 minutes. Using a spatula fold in the 1/2 cup sifted flour lightly. Sift the 6 tablespoons flour and cocoa together and add to eggs in 3 additions, beating well after each. Sprinkle butter and vanilla over batter and beat in quickly. Pour into a greased and floured 8-inch cake pan. Bake at 350 degrees F. about 35 minutes or until cake springs back when touched in the center.

To make filling and topping: Drain cherry juice from can into a small skillet, add sugar mixed with cornstarch and simmer until slightly thick. Let cool. Put cherries back into juice.

In a large chilled bowl beat the cream until thickened. Then sift confectioners' sugar over cream and whip until firm. Cut cake horizontally into three even slices. Sprinkle each generously with Kirschwasser. Cover bottom layer with the dark cherry mixture and cover with some of the whipped cream. Gently place second layer on top and cover with whipped cream, about 1/2 inch. Then set third layer in place and cover sides and top with remaining cream. Cover sides and top of cake with chocolate curls and decorate with maraschino cherries.

MAKES 8 to 10 SERVINGS

Photograph, Page 23

SAFFRON

Sheraton New Orleans Hotel, 500 Canal St., New Orleans, LA 70130; (504) 525-2500.

Saffron is the flagship restaurant of one of New Orleans' largest and most striking hotels. In a stunningly-appointed room gleaming with mirrors, polished brass, and etched glass is served incomparably beautiful, elegant "cuisine moderne." The particular specialty of Saffron is presentation; every dish is as delightful a visual experience as it is a gustatory one. The chef searches the world, literally, for the foodstuffs of Saffron's creations.

PUFF PASTRY WITH CARAMEL SAUCE

Caramel Sauce
3 cups sugar
4 cups water
Juice of 3 lemons
2 cups butter
1/2 cup Tia Maria liqueur

Pastry Layers
2 sheets of puff pastry, frozen
2 bananas
2 kiwi
1 pint fresh strawberries
1/2 cup confectioners' sugar

To make caramel sauce: In a medium sauce pan combine sugar, water, and lemon juice. Reduce over medium heat until mixture becomes brown in color. Remove from heat. Add butter, stir to melt, and add Tia Maria.

To make pastry layers: Prepare puff pastry according to label directions. Bake until golden brown. Cut sheets into 8 (4 1/2-inch by 2 1/2-inch) pieces. Slice bananas, kiwi, and strawberries. In center of dessert plate place pastry square. Layer kiwi, banana, and strawberries. Set aside.

On a separate plate, dust remaining squares with confectioners' sugar and place atop the squares layered with fruit. Pour caramel sauce around plate, but not on top of square.

MAKES 4 SERVINGS

Photograph, Page 20

ANTOINE'S

713 St. Louis St., New Orleans, LA 70130; (504) 581-4422.

One of the grandest ways to end a meal at Antoine's is with a flaming dessert. The waiters have a dramatic ritual in their preparation of cherries jubilee, crêpes suzette, or café brûlot diabolique. The lights are dimmed in the dining room as the flames are lit. The waiter stirs the potion around a bit, and then alarms all those seated at the table by pouring some of the liquid flames onto the tablecloth. It quickly burns out, causing no harm, and then the treat is ready to be enjoyed.

CREPES SUZETTE *(French Pancakes Suzette)*

Sauce
1/2 cup confectioners' sugar
2 tablespoons grated orange rind
1 tablespoon vanilla
2 tablespoons orange juice
1 tablespoon lemon juice
2 tablespoons brandy
2 tablespoons melted butter

Crêpe Batter
3/4 cup flour
1 teaspoon sugar
1/2 teaspoon salt
2 eggs
1 1/2 cups milk, scalded
1 1/2 tablespoons butter

Additional butter

To make sauce: Combine all ingredients and keep at room temperature.

To make crêpe batter: Sift the flour and sugar into a mixing bowl; add the salt, eggs, and half the milk. Whisk thoroughly, add the remaining milk, and whisk some more. Let it rest. Just before making the crêpes, melt the butter and whisk into the batter.

To make crêpes: Melt butter in a small pan to use in coating the crêpe pan. The crêpe pan should have a base of about 6 inches.

Heat the crêpe pan very well, then spoon some melted butter into the pan to coat the bottom and sides. Pour the excess butter back into the butter pan. Pour three tablespoons batter into the pan. Tilt the pan from side to side to completely coat the bottom. When the batter in the pan all becomes dry, turn the crêpe and cook for about 30 seconds on the other side.

Place the cooked crêpes one on the other on a dish and cover with a damp cloth.

To assemble: Heat sauce in a skillet or flambe pan. Dip crêpes in sauce and fold in half. Fold in half again so the crêpe looks like a triangle. Repeat with remaining crêpes. Ignite crêpes and flambé. When flames die, place 3 crêpes on each plate and spoon remaining sauce over.

MAKES ABOUT 15 CREPES

LES CHEFS DE CUISINE DE LA LOUISIANNE

The chef's school for the State of Louisiana has the good fortune of the internationally famous cuisines of Creole and Cajun cooking within the state and the availability of world-class chefs for faculty positions. Training in this field is rigorous; standards are high. The dessert recipe that follows is from pastry chef Mark Fitch.

ZITRONEN ROLLCHEN *(Lemon Wine Roll)*

Roulade (Cake Roll)
5 eggs, separated
8 tablespoons sugar, divided
1/2 cup flour, sifted
10 tablespoons melted butter

Lemon Wine Filling
6 tablespoons dry white wine
6 tablespoons sugar
4 tablespoons water
Juice and grated rind of 2 lemons
2 egg yolks
2 tablespoons cornstarch
1 cup heavy cream

To make Roulade: In an electric mixer beat the egg yolks and sugar together until light and fluffy, 5 to 8 minutes. Add flour and butter to yolks and mix lightly.

In a separate bowl beat egg whites until they form stiff peaks. Fold yolk mixture into egg whites.

Grease a 10 1/2-inch by 15-inch jelly roll pan and place greased wax paper in pan. Spread rowlade batter in pan and bake at 350 degrees F. 20 to 25 minutes or until light brown. Allow to cool. Then refrigerate.

To prepare Lemon Wine Filling: In a sauce pan combine wine, sugar, water, lemon rind, and juice. Bring to a boil. Combine egg yolks, cornstarch, and cream and stir into filling. Cook until thick.

To assemble: Remove roulade from pan by turning upside down onto a sheet of wax paper sprinkled with confectioners' sugar. Peel off baked wax paper from roulade in small strips. Spread lemon filling over and roll roulade from long edge toward other long edge, using wax paper to facilitate rolling. Chill. Slice to serve.

MAKES 10 TO 12 SERVINGS

GALATOIRE'S

209 Bourbon St., New Orleans, LA 70130; (504) 525-2021.

Galatoire's is considered by many authorities on food, both local and national, to be among the greatest restaurants ever assembled in New Orleans. Founded just after the turn of the century, the restaurant is now in its third generation of family ownership. Perhaps the most convincing testimony to the consistent excellence of Galatoire's cuisine is the line which forms for lunch and dinner daily. Despite the no-reservation policy, Orleanians find it worthwhile to wait in line to enjoy Galatoire's perfect seafood and other specialties.

CREPES MAISON

Crêpe Batter
7/8 cup flour
Pinch salt
1 tablespoon sugar
3 eggs
1 teaspoon vanilla
2 tablespoons Cognac
2 tablespoons melted butter
1 1/2 cups milk
Additional melted butter or oil

8 tablespoons grape or apple jelly
6 tablespoons toasted, sliced almonds
Grated rind of 1 orange and 1 lemon
Confectioners' sugar
4 ounces Grand Marnier

To make crêpe batter: Sift the flour, salt, and sugar together. Add the eggs, one at a time, stirring constantly. Then add vanilla, Cognac, and butter. Add milk, whisking, until mixture has the consistency of light cream.

Heat a crêpe pan and rub it with a towel soaked in butter or oil. Pour about 1 1/2 tablespoons of batter into the pan and spread the batter thinly and evenly over the bottom of the pan. Cook about 45 seconds or until crêpe is light brown. Turn and cook about 30 seconds on the other side. Cooked crêpes may be stacked one on top of the other. Stir the batter occasionally to keep it smooth and rebutter the pan every other crêpe. Makes 8 (6-inch) dessert crêpes.

To assemble crêpes: Roll 1 tablespoon grape or apple jelly in each crêpe. Place 2 crêpes on each of four ovenproof plates. Top with sliced almonds, orange and lemon peel, and sprinkle with confectioners' sugar. Place under broiler until hot. Pour 1 ounce of Grand Marnier over each serving.

MAKES 4 SERVINGS

VERSAILLES

2100 St. Charles Ave., New Orleans, LA 70140; (504) 524-2535.

The Versailles is the creation of owner-chef Gunter Preuss and co-proprietor Evelyn Preuss. Chef Preuss is a New Orleans culinary figure of considerable renown, having headed up other major kitchens before opening The Versailles in the early seventies. The skills of the chef are obvious in the extreme polish of the food. Unlike many restaurants, Chef Preuss and his staff stand ready to prepare almost any classic dish to suit your taste of the moment.

LEMON TEQUILA SOUFFLE

2/3 cup sugar
1 cup water
6 egg yolks
5 tablespoons lemon juice
3 ounces white wine
1 1/2 ounces tequila
1 1/2 cups heavy cream, whipped
6 lemons, hollowed

Garnish: additional whipped cream and 6 mint leaves

Combine sugar with 1 cup water in a sauce pan and boil gently until mixture begins to thicken. Remove and let cool thoroughly.

When mixture is cool, combine with the egg yolks, wine, lemon juice, and tequila. Cook this mixture over low heat, whisking constantly until the foam disappears.

Place in refrigerator and stir occasionally to cool. When cool, fold in the whipped cream and place in freezer.

To serve, place souffle in hollowed out lemons, put on a bed of shaved ice and freeze. Garnish with whipped cream and a mint leaf.

MAKES 6 SERVINGS

BRENNAN'S

417 Royal St., New Orleans, LA 70130; (504) 525-9711.

"Breakfast at Brennan's" is one of America's best-known meals, and with good reason. This lavish Creole repast, for which you best reserve the whole morning, is unlike any breakfast you have ever eaten. After an "eye-opener" cocktail, a Creole appetizer, and a loaf or so of the crusty hot French bread, you are confronted with one of about a dozen original egg dishes which take egg cookery to undreamed-of heights. Another couple of cups of coffee and a flaming dessert later, you know you have reached the height of breakfast dining pleasure.

BANANAS FOSTER

4 tablespoons butter
1 cup brown sugar
1/2 teaspoon cinnamon
4 tablespoons banana liqueur
4 bananas, cut in half lengthwise, then halved
1/4 cup rum
4 scoops vanilla ice cream

Melt the butter over an alcohol burner in a flambé pan or attractive skillet. Add the sugar, cinnamon, and banana liqueur and stir to mix. Heat for a few minutes, then place the halved bananas in the sauce and saute until soft.

Add the rum and allow it to heat well; then tip the pan so that the flame from the burner causes the sauce to ignite. Allow the sauce to flame until it dies out, tipping the pan with a circular motion to prolong the flaming.

Lift the bananas carefully out of the pan and place four pieces over each portion of ice cream, then spoon the hot sauce from the pan over the bananas and ice cream.

Note: This is one of Brennan's most famous and most popular desserts. It's really quite simple to prepare. Wait until the rum gets hot, so that there is a good flame when it is ignited. This can also be prepared over a stove burner, then brought to the dinner table and flamed.

MAKES 4 SERVINGS

DEANO'S PIZZARAMA

305 Bertrand Dr., Lafayette, LA 70501; (318) 233-5446.

The allure of the Cajun country is what brought Dean Metcalf to Lafayette. He had previously owned a pizza parlor in Santa Barbara, California. There he developed a now-patented blend of spices for the sauce, as well as a special recipe for making pizza dough. In addition to the standard varieties of pizza, Deano's prepares special Cajun-style pizzas and dessert pizzas. The restaurant also serves great salads and poor boy sandwiches. The surroundings are suitable for family dining.

APPLE PIZZA

Pie Pastry
2 1/2 cups flour
1/2 teaspoon salt
1/2 cup butter, chilled
4 tablespoons shortening, chilled
6 tablespoons cold water

Apple Topping
3 tablespoons butter, softened
1/2 cup brown sugar
1 teaspoon cinnamon
3 cups thinly sliced, peeled tart apples
1/4 cup chopped pecans
12 maraschino cherry halves

To make pie pastry: Sift four and salt into a bowl. Using a pastry blender or 2 knives cut the butter and shortening into the flour until the mixture resembles small peas.

Stir water into dough only until particles cling together when pressed between finger tips. Form dough into a ball, cover and refrigerate 30 minutes.

Roll dough on a well floured surface to fit 2 10-inch pizza pans. Freeze extra crust for future use.

To make apple topping: Mix in bowl butter, sugar, and cinnamon and spread the mixture on dough. Place apple slices on dough, beginning with the outer edge. Lay apples in overlapping circles until crust is covered. Top with remaining butter, sugar, and cinnamon. Decorate with pecans and cherry halves in a circular pattern. Bake at 400 degrees F. for 35 minutes.

MAKES 8 SERVINGS

THE OAKS PLANTATION

Avenue of Oaks, Old River Rd., Destrehan, LA 70047; (504) 764-1798.

Twenty miles upriver from New Orleans in an alley of ancient live oaks and pecan trees is this lovely restaurant, a memorable stop on your way back from a day of plantation-touring. The Oaks Plantation resembles an antique red barn from the outside, but inside is a warm country-style decor, with antique tables and buffets, lush exotic plants, and gleaming brasswork. Among the specialties are included great weekend chef's specials.

BANANAS CLEMENT

1/2 cup butter
1 1/2 cups brown sugar
1/2 cup coconut concentrate
1/2 cup finely grated coconut (optional)
1 tablespoon rum
4 bananas sliced lengthwise and cut in half
6 scoops vanilla ice cream

Melt butter over low heat. Add brown sugar and cook stirring until dissolved.

Add the coconut concentrate and cook briefly. If using the grated coconut, add and mix well. Add the rum and cook for 2 minutes.

Add bananas and cook over medium heat until bananas are tender.

Serve hot over vanilla ice cream.

MAKES 6 SERVINGS

LA SAVOIE

94 Friedrichs Ave., Metairie, LA 70005; (504) 831-1108.

After working for many years in some of the country's most famous restaurants, including Tavern on the Green in New York and Brennan's and Winston's in New Orleans, Gerard Thabuis decided to open his own restaurant. It is named for the region of France, near Switzerland, where he was born and raised. Thabuis is a genius in the kitchen, and his flair works its way into the dining rooms, as well. A fine pastry chef, he prepares a mouth-watering array of desserts daily.

ANANAS FLAMBES AU POIVRE VERT
(Flamed Pineapple in Green Peppercorn Sauce)

1 fresh pineapple, peeled
6 tablespoons butter
2 tablespoons green peppercorns, crushed
8 strawberries
2 ounces dark rum
1 1/2 cups brown sugar
6 tablespoons orange juice
6 tablespoons heavy cream
4 scoops vanilla ice cream

Garnish: *pineapple leaves*

Slice the pineapple into 8 rings, core, and saute in butter with crushed peppercorns. Add strawberries. Add the rum and ignite to flambé. Remove fruits. Add brown sugar, stirring until it melts and becomes caramelized. Add orange juice and cook to reduce a bit. Then add cream and cook 3 to 5 more minutes.

To serve, use 2 pineapple slices per serving, put a strawberry in each hole, pour pepper sauce over and top with a scoop of ice cream. Garnish with pineapple leaves on the side of the plate.

MAKES 4 SERVINGS

SAZERAC

Fairmont Hotel, University Place, New Orleans, LA 70140; (504) 529-7111.

The Sazerac practices, in its red-velvet classic dining room, the kind of elaborate service which would otherwise be lost locally. The formal staff includes maitre d', captains, waiters, and a sommelier—the last a gentleman whose sole job is to help diners with the restaurant's list of over two hundred and fifty wines. As if that were not enough to keep you well served, enter a strolling accordionist and singer. All service is from a gueridon at tableside, where the captain performs the final steps in your food preparation.

COONASS CABBAGE LEAVES

1 large cabbage
Water
4 eggs
1/4 cup flour
2/3 cup sugar
1/2 cup heavy cream
Butter
3 cups raspberries, blueberries, or bushberries
6 tablespoons butter
Prepared raspberry or blueberry sauce

Blanch cabbage for 10 minutes in lightly salted water.

Mix eggs, flour, sugar, and cream in a bowl. Strain this mixture. Set aside.

Separate cabbage into leaves. Butter a 9-inch square baking pan and place cabbage leaves on bottom of pan. Place berries over cabbage leaves and pour cream mixture over. Cover completely with more cabbage leaves.

Bake at 350 degrees F. for 15 to 20 minutes. The leaves should be golden in color.

Serve from baking pan with a raspberry or blueberry sauce.

MAKES 8 SERVINGS

LEROY'S RESTAURANT AND LOUNGE

1133 MacArthur Dr., Alexandria, LA 71031; (318) 448-9175.

Five nights a week this lively place serves excellent food from a limited menu. The specialty is steaks all the way, with heavy aged Western beef, charcoal grilled before your eyes to your specifications. The steaks are served with baked potatoes with all the trimmings, a good crisp salad, and sweet desserts. For the less hungry there is also a freshly-ground chuckburger. Tables are draped in white cloth with red napkins. Live music, mostly country and western, plays nightly in the lounge.

BLUEBERRY DELIGHT

1 angel food cake
1/2 cup sugar
1/2 cup evaporated milk
1 (8-ounce) package cream cheese
1 can blueberry pie filling
2 cups heavy cream, whipped

Line a 9-inch cake pan with angel food cake broken into bite-size pieces.

Mix sugar, milk, and softened cream cheese together and pour over broken pieces of angel food cake. Spoon blueberry filling over mixture.

Cover blueberry filling with whipped cream and refrigerate for several hours.

MAKES 6 SERVINGS

THE NEW ORLEANS SCHOOL OF COOKING

835 Conti St., New Orleans, LA 70112; (504) 525-2665.

If you have been excited by your culinary experiences in New Orleans, you will probably want to know how to reproduce authentic Creole and Cajun at home. And Joe Cahn, proprietor of the New Orleans Cooking School, would like you to know, too. In the space of three hours, he gives a demonstration of the basics of the cuisine, from gumbo to pralines. And lest there be any doubt about the validity of the instruction, the class gets to eat all the results. There are few complaints.

PRALINES

1 1/2 cups sugar
3/4 cup light brown sugar, packed
1/2 cup milk
6 tablespoons butter
1 1/2 cups pecan halves

Combine all ingredients in a heavy saucepan.

Cook to soft ball stage, 238 to 240 degrees F. Remove from heat and beat until mixture cools and thickens.

Drop by spoonfuls onto buttered wax paper, aluminum foil, or parchment paper.

MAKES 12 PRALINES

VALENTINE'S

Sheraton Inn Airport, 2150 Veterans Blvd., Kenner, LA 70062; (504) 467-3111.

In this good-looking, modern hotel near the New Orleans International Airport are two good restaurants. The larger and more elaborate is Valentine's, a combination of international cuisine dining room and lively lounge. Oysters, Etc. is a more casual place, with fresh local seafood prepared in a host of imaginative ways, served at reasonable prices. With these two the Sheraton proves you don't have to go far in New Orleans to have a great meal.

STREGA SALUTE

1/3 ounce Strega
1/3 ounce green crème de menthe
1/3 ounce grenadine

In a tall fluted glass pour grenadine into bottom. Next carefully and slowly pour the crème de menthe down the side of the glass. Pour very slowly so that the crème de menthe does not combine with the grenadine. Now carefully and slowly pour the Strega on the crème de menthe so as to form a drink that has 3 distinct layers in one glass.

Note: Strega is an Italian Liqueur, first made in the 1860s, in Beneveto, Italy, of 70 different herbs and spices. Strega in Italian means "witch". This drink was the winner of the National Strega Taste-Off, Chicago, Illinois, April 1982.

MAKES 1 DRINK

Photograph, Page 24

ANTOINE'S

713 St. Louis St., New Orleans, LA 70130; (504) 581-4422.

The two public dining rooms most often used at Antoine's are both lovely examples of eighteenth-century restaurant design. The front room is a bright, mirrored parlor with ceiling fans and a row of small lights around the top of the walls. The much larger, and more popular "red room" has a certain Germanic feel to it, with dark wood hues and red walls covered with framed testimonials, newspaper clippings, and photos of the famous who have dined in New Orleans' oldest restaurant.

MILK PUNCH

$1^1/_2$ ounces brandy or bourbon
1 ounce simple syrup (see Glossary)
$1/_2$ teaspoon orange flower water (available in gourmet shops)
$1/_2$ teaspoon vanilla extract
4 ounces light cream
$1/_2$ cup crushed ice
Grated nutmeg to taste

Mix the first five ingredients together in an electric blender with the crushed ice. Pour into a highball glass and top with nutmeg.

MAKES 1 DRINK

MINT JULEP

4 mint leaves
1 tablespoon sugar
$1^1/_2$ ounces bourbon

Garnish: 1 sprig mint

Use a mortar and pestle to crush the mint leaves with the sugar into a paste. Put the mint paste and the bourbon in a mint julep cup or highball glass and fill with crushed ice. Stir vigorously until the glass frosts on the outside. Serve with straws. Garnish with a sprig of mint.

MAKES 1 DRINK

BEVERAGES

MARTI'S

1041 Dumaine St., New Orleans, LA 70116; (504) 524-6060.

When it comes to old-style Creole cooking, there are few chefs anywhere who can match the prowess and experience of Henry Robinson, chef at Marti's since the restaurant opened in 1971. Before that he had a long career as a practitioner of everyday New Orleans cooking and his credentials include being cook for Louis Armstrong in New York. The talents of Robinson are perfectly matched to the old-style Creole thrust of Marti's.

SATCHMO PUNCH

1 ounce dark rum
1 ounce simple syrup (see Glossary)
3 ounces orange juice
3 ounces pineapple juice
3 ounces grenadine

Garnish: *orange slice and maraschino cherry*

Put all ingredients into blender with ice. Blend until frozen.

Garnish with orange slice and cherry.

Note: Satchmo Punch was created by Marti Shambra, owner/proprieter of Marti's for the dedication of Louis Armstrong Park, April 15, 1980. Satchmo Punch was served to the visiting dignitaries during the reception given in the Jazz Complex in Armstrong Park and became the official toast drink to Jazz.

MAKES 1 DRINK

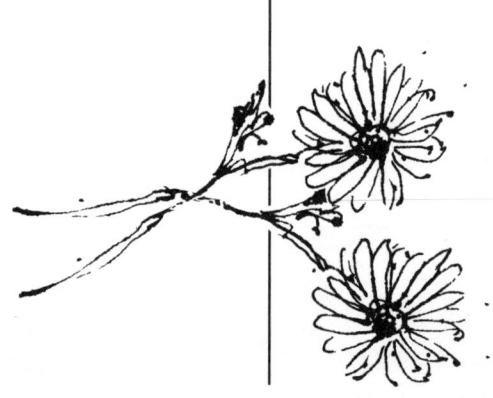

ANTOINE'S

713 St. Louis St., New Orleans, LA 70130; (504) 581-4422.

A few pleasant hours could be spent studying the walls at Antoine's. In the large red room and the small adjoining rooms are hundred of newspaper and magazine clippings, some from the nineteenth century, telling of the past successes of New Orleans' oldest restaurants. Also in frames are such items as napkins on which cartoonists have depicted their satisfaction, old menus from banquets decades ago, and personal cards and letters sent to Antoine's proprietors from the famous.

AMBROSIA

3/4 ounce brandy
3/4 ounce Cointreau
4 ounces chilled champagne

Shake the brandy and Cointreau together with ice and strain into a champagne glass. Add the champagne.

MAKES 1 DRINK

RAMOS GIN FIZZ

1 1/2 ounces gin
1 teaspoon confectioners' sugar
1/2 teaspoon orange flower water
   (available in gourmet shops)
1/2 teaspoon vanilla extract
1 egg white
3 ounces light cream
1/2 cup crushed ice
Soda water

Mix all ingredients, except soda water, with crushed ice in a blender. Pour into a highball glass and fill with soda.

MAKES 1 DRINK

BEVERAGES

THE NEW ORLEANS SCHOOL OF COOKING

835 Conti St., New Orleans, LA 70112; (504) 525-2665.

Among the great food cities of America, New Orleans is set apart by the fact that it has its own regional cuisines, Creole and Cajun. And if you are not sure how to cook Creole and Cajun dishes, the man to see is Joe Cahn at the New Orleans School of Cooking. In a rapid-fire three-hour course, he demonstrates the basic principles of gumbo, jambalaya, red beans and rice, bread pudding, and pecan pralines. His classes are as entertaining as they are informative and his enthusiasm is infectious.

CAFE BRULOT

Thin slice of butter
5 whole cloves
8 curls orange peel
8 curls lemon peel
4 teaspoons dark brown sugar
4 ounces brandy
2 ounces triple sec liqueur
Pinch ground cinnamon
2 cups strong New Orleans coffee

Place butter, cloves, orange peel, lemon peel, brown sugar, brandy, and triple sec in a deep chafing dish or brûlot bowl over flame. Heat and ignite.

Rotate pan to keep flame burning and add a few pinches of ground cinnamon to the flame. Pour hot coffee into bowl, and let flames go out.

Serve in demitasse cups.

MAKES 4 SERVINGS

TOP OF THE MART

International Trade Mart, New Orleans, LA 70130; (504) 522-9795.

The Top of the Mart is well-known among Orleanians as one of the best places in the city to have a cocktail. The Top could not be more atmospheric; as the revolving lounge turns, it offers fine views of the river and French Quarter below, as well as a panorama of the rest of the Crescent City. Every evening there is live Dixieland music in a more-or-less easy listening vein. The drinks are exceptionally well-made; with three of the specialties, you get a souvenir dubloon.

ORIGINAL DUBLOON DRINK

1 ounce rum
1 ounce banana liqueur
1 ounce orange juice

Combine ingredients and blend well. Pour over ice into a tall 8-ounce glass.

Note: Dubloon's in New Orleans are the highly prized coins that are tossed to the crowds during Mardi Gras.

MAKES 1 DRINK

"The appetite grows by eating."
FRANCOIS RABELAIS

CULINARY COMPLEMENTS

WINES

LOUISIANA WINES

Wine history in Louisiana can be traced to altar wines made by Jesuit priests about 1750. Before Prohibition many wineries made fruit wines, and some orange wine was made after Prohibition, but there are no commercial wineries in the state now. Two companies, one in Alexandria and one in Church Point, buy grape concentrate or wine from California and bottle it as high alcohol dessert wines.

Currently, Louisiana's per capita consumption of wine is about 1.6 gallons per year, below the national average of 2.2 gallons. Sherry, Port, and Champagne are still traditional for celebrations and special occasions.

Distilled spirits and beer have proven much more popular than table wine partly because of the hot climate and the spicy regional foods. "Cocktails" were actually invented in New Orleans in the early 1800s by a pharmacist named Peychaud. Potent concoctions such as Sazerac Cocktails and Gin Fizzes are now part of the New Orleans mystique.

Brunches are the heart of New Orleans social life, and the traditional beverages include Brandy Milk Punch, Café au Lait, or Champagne.

MATCHING FOOD AND WINE

This guide offers a host of suggestions for basic food categories. As helpful and time-proven as these traditional accompaniments are, they are not shackles. Use them as springboards for launching new ideas of your own.

In the following guide groups of food are matched predominately with groups of wine that are from California, Italy, and France, since those are the leading producers of wines consumed in the U.S.A., followed by Germany and others. If you cook with wine always use good quality wine and serve it with that food.

HORS D'OEUVRES, OYSTERS, ESCARGOTS, PATE, MUSHROOMS. Traditionally served with dry white wines or Brut Champagne; often lightly sweet wines such as Riesling or Chenin Blanc are better choices, especially in hot weather.

California—Brut Champagne, Sauvignon Blanc, Chardonnay, French Colombard, Riesling, Chenin Blanc.
Italy—Frascati, Corvo Bianco, Soave, Trebbiano.
France—Brut Champagne, Sancerre (especially with raw oysters), white Graves, jug white Bordeaux, Pouilly-Fumé, St. Veran.
Other—Johannisberg Riesling from Washington State, Vinho Verde from Portugal, Qualitatswein or Kabinett quality wines from Germany's Mosel or Rhine or Franken regions.

DUCK, QUAIL, GAME BIRDS, TURKEY. Good with light red dry wines.

California—Pinot Noir Burgundy, jug red table wine, Cabernet Sauvignon, Merlot.
Italy—Valpolicella, Chianti, Nebbiolo, Merlot.

France—Medoc red Graves, St. Emillion, Cote de Beaune Villages, red Burgundy Note, simple Rose' or Beaujolais-Village are best with Thanksgiving feasts which are more vegetable than turkey dinners.

BEEF, LAMB, HEARTY, SPICY VEAL OR CHICKEN OR PASTA, BARBECUE, STRONG CHEESE. Dry red table wines.

California—Cabernet Sauvignon, Merlot, Zinfandel, Barbera, Charbonc, Petite Syrah, Pinot Noir, Burgundy, jug reds.

Italy—Chianti Riserva, Nebbiolo Barolo, Brunello de Montalcino, Gattinara, Bardolino Grignolino, Merlot, Montepulciano de Abruzzo.

France—St. Julien Pauillac, St. Emmon Pomerol, Gevrey-Chambertin, Nuits St. George, Côte de Nuits Villages, Hermitage, Châteauneuf-du-Pape jug red Bordeaux or red Burgundy.

Other—Cabernet Sauvignon from Romania, Bulgaria, South Africa, Australia; South African Pinotage, Australian Shiraz, red Rioja or Catalan from Spain; Marechal Foch, Leon Millot, New York State Burgundy from U.S.A.

LIGHT VEAL, CHICKEN, PORK ROAST, LIGHT SEAFOOD GUMBO— Generally light white wines, either dry or off-dry, or some light reds.

California—Chardonnay, Chablis, Sauvignon Blanc, brut Champagne, Gamay Beaujolais (light red).

Italy—Pinot Bianco, Pinot Grigio, Frascati, Soave.

France—white Bordeaux, Muscadet, Vouvray, Pouilly-Fumé, Chablis, St. Veran.

Other—Qualitatswein or Kabinett quality wines from Germany; Vinho Verde from Portugal; Riesling from Alsace or Romania; white table wine from South Africa.

HEARTY VEAL, CHICKEN, PASTA, MILD CHEESE—Red or white wines with more body and robust flavors.

California—Merlot, Napa Gamay, Barbera, jug reds, Gewurztraminer, Fume Blanc, Chardonnay, jug whites.

Italy—Orvieto Secco, Corvo Blanco, Verdicchio (whites); Valpolicella, Chianti, Bardolino (reds).

France—Beaune, Beaujolais, jug red Bordeaux or Burgundy.

Other—dry white from Rioja or Catalan regions of Spain; Gewurztraminer from Alsace; Seyval Blanc, Vidal Blanc from U.S.A.

CRAB, LOBSTER, OYSTERS, TROUT, POMPANO, BOILED CRAWFISH—Dry white wines with high acidity or German Mosel wines which are off-dry but have high acidity. For rich fish such as salmon, a light red wine may work well.

California—Dry Riesling, Sauvignon Blanc, Brut Champagne, jug whites.

Italy—Pinot Grigio, Frascati, Corvo Bianco, Soave, Trebbiano.
France—Chablis, Pouilly-Fumé, Sancerre, jug white Bordeaux.
Other—German Mosel or Rhein of Qualitatswein or Kabinett quality or Trocken (dry); white table wines from South Africa; Rieslings from Pacific Northwest, U.S.A.

LIGHT PASTA. Light white or red wines depending on power of sauce.

California—Chardonnay, Pinot Noir Blanc, dry Riesling.
Italy—Corvo Bianco, Orvieto Secco.
France—Chablis, Beaujolais.
Other—Seyval Blanc, Vidal Blanc from U.S.A.

HAM. Generally matched with rosé.

California—Grenache Rosé, Cabernet Rosé, Gamay, Rosé or Blanc of Pinot Noir, Gewurztraminer, jug rosé.
France—Tavel Rose, Anjou Rosé.
Other—Rose from Italy or Portugal.

SPICY FOOD, INCLUDING CHICKEN GUMBO, JAMBALAYA, ETOUFFEE, SPICY CHINESE, MEXICAN, OR PEPPERY BARBECUE. The powerful peppers and very complex flavors in these dishes can smother the taste of wine, often leaving it thin and bitter. Beer is often the best beverage with these foods, but carefully chosen (and well chilled) wines can work very well. These include Gewurztraminer from Alsace or California, Beaujolais from France or U.S.A., Pinotage from South Africa, young California Chardonnay for seafood, French Colombard from California, and hearty young Cabernet Sauvignon or Zinfandel or Merlot from California (especially when chilled to cellar temperature of about 60 degrees F.).

SOUP. No wine is required, but it is delightful to serve a dry sherry with and in creamed soups. In many French country homes there is a custom of pouring about a spoonful of dry red wine into each person's bowl when their soup is nearly gone. The warmth of the bowl releases the wine's bouquet and makes the last spoonful of soup taste even better.

DESSERTS. You may prefer a fine sweet wine either simply alone or with your dessert.

California—Sweet Chenin Blanc; sweet Riesling; late harvest wines from grapes such as Riesling. Gewurztraminer, or Zinfandel; Port; Cream Sherry; sparkling Moscato or Chenin Blanc; fruit wines such as Blackberry.
Italy—Asti Spumante, Marsala.
France—Sauternes, Barsac, sweet Champagne, sparkling Muscat.
Germany—Rieslings from the Spatlese, Auslese, Beerenauslese, or Trockenbeerenauslese categories.
Other—Portugal's Port; sweet Oloroso or Cream Sherry from Spain; Bual or Malmsey Madiera; Concord or Catawba from New York State.

BOLD EXPERIMENTS. There are trendy new flavor combinations springing up, such as light red wine with fish. Chocolate, long shunned as a wine accompaniment now is being seen served with red Burgundy or Pinot Noir. Sweet wines are considered poor food-companions, yet in the Sauternes and Barsac regions of France, the winemakers serve them with melon as an appetizer, with pate instead of the traditional Champagne-and-pate pairing, and with lamb. German wines are sometimes ignored because of their delicacy and light sweetness, but these wines do very well with fish because of their high acidity, and with light meals and snacks because of their crisp fruity flavors. By all means, experiment and search for new pairings.

DIET WINES. Wines labeled "light" list calorie information; most are around 57 calories per 100 milliliters (about 3.8 ounces). Since alcohol is the main source of wine calories, these wines have low alcohol content (8 to 9%). They also have low or no residual sugar, a further culling of calories. German Trocken wines are low in alcohol but they do not list calorie information. To roughly estimate wine calories, take the percent of alcohol listed on the label, double it to determine "proof" and that is the number of calories per ounce. At 12% alcohol, or 24 proof, a wine has 24 calories per ounce, plus calories from any sweetness. (This formula is not accurate enough for people who must strictly measure sugar intake.)

HOW TO READ THE LABEL

The number one question consumers ask is whether the wine is sweet or dry, and yet most labels do not specify it in so many words, although jug wine producers are getting better at providing this information. The truth is, many people talk dry wine and then drink sweet wine, an irony brought about by a lack of wine vocabulary and a false image of prestige accorded dry wines. The largest categories of wine consumed by Americans are American white and rose jug wines, which tend to have a slight sweetness. Truly dry wines are generally too harsh for casual wine drinkers. Further, there is a range from about .05 to 1.0% sugar in wine where a person's ability to detect the slight sweetness influences their perceiving the wine as sweet or dry. Each person should rely on her/his own palate and decide each wine on its own merits and price value.

What a label will tell you is who made the wine, where, when, and from what grapes or in what style (such as American winemakers borrowing the French terms Burgundy, Chablis, or Champagne.) The name by which the wine is ultimately called can be either the name of a grape (Cabernet Sauvignon), a place (Napa Valley), a region (Sonoma County), a vineyard (Sterling Vineyards), or a name the producer made up as a proprietary name (Classic Red.)

Vintage dates do not certify quality, they only mean the grapes were harvested in that year, and any year can produce a poor, good, or fabulous crop.

YOUR WINE CELLAR

A wine cellar might really be in your cellar, but it may be in your closet or in the dining room or anywhere you have space. A wine cellar is first and simply a storage space that is cool, dark, and undisturbed. Second it is a source of convenience, a cache of handy wine. Third it is an attractive investment, not in financial dividends, but in psychic dividends of tasting a properly matured wine.

Lay all bottles, including Port and Champagne, on their sides flat enough to keep the corks wet and swollen, but not enough to let sediment collect in the bottle shoulder or neck. Jug wines should not be cellared; drink them within a few weeks or months while still fresh.

All wine has life curve. It is born in fermentation, endures adolescence in barrels or bottles, and in bottles it matures to its prime, then declines and loses all allure. For some like light, fruity, red Nouveau Beaujolais, this takes only a few months. For others like robust, tannic Cabernet Sauvignon it can take decades. While the best red table wines outlive the best white table wines, age does not benefit all reds, nor destroy all whites.

HOW COLD IS CHILLED?

It is a national crime that we drink our red wines too warm and white wines too cold. The taste of a warm red wine is not at all refreshing and leaves your mouth feeling like flocked wallpaper. What remorse springs from enduring a glass of white wine so cold it makes your teeth recede, only to discover it has warmed and released its bouquet and flavor just as you take the last sip? If you must err, do so in favor of cold and then warm the wine in the glass. In the refrigerator wine drops about 5 degrees per hour, faster in icy water.

DRY RED WINE should be served at 60 to 65 degrees F.
LIGHTER RED WINE AND DRY WHITE WINE: 55 to 60 degrees F.
LIGHTER WHITE WINE, VINTAGE CHAMPAGNE, SWEET SHERRY, SAUTERNES: 50 to 55 degrees F.
OTHER CHAMPAGNES AND SPARKLING WINES, DRY SHERRY: 45 to 50 degrees F.

Thermometers are available in some wine stores, wine-making supply shops, or you can get them through a wine accessories company.

HOW MUCH IS ENOUGH?

Wine is a beverage of moderation. A serving of wine is 3 to 4 ounces (100 milliliters). If you are serving a different wine with each course, one bottle can serve 8 people allowing 3 ounces each. Using the same wine throughout the meal, allow one-half to a full bottle of wine per person, depending on their fondness for wine and the length of the dinner.

LEFTOVER WINE

Yes, there will be leftover wine. Give it a second chance, don't pour it out. Recork the bottle, refrigerate, and serve the next day, or use it within a week in a sauce, stew, casserole, or roast. Take advantage of the economy of jug wines by pouring into clean, smaller bottles with screw tops, such as those for club soda, and use over the next few weeks (especially handy when cooking for only one or two people).

WINE GLASSES

Each style of wine shows its best features of color, bouquet, and taste in specific styles of stemmed glassware. Buy the thinnest, clearest stemware you can, starting with at least a dozen all-purpose glasses which hold about 8 to 10 ounces of wine. Choose a tulip-shaped bowl, or rounder, so you can swirl the wine without sloshing it. These will suffice for red or white wine. In a restaurant, a glass of house wine served from the bar may be 6 to 8 ounces so the glass is quite full. If poured from a bottle at the table, or in your home, a glass should be about one-third full only. This leaves air space for the wine's bouquet to develop and rise.

Dee Stone
Wine Columnist and Editor,
The Arbor Wine Magazine

FLUTE CHAMPAGNE • ALL PURPOSE • RED WINE • SHERRY OR PORT • WHITE WINE

BASIC STOCKS & SAUCES

BASIC STOCKS

BROWN STOCK. Place 6 pounds of marrow bones and two short ribs in pot with 4 quarts water. Add 1 cup drained canned tomatoes, 3 large carrots, 4 ribs celery, 1 large onion, 2 sprigs parsley, 1 bay leaf, 1 leek if available, pepper, and salt to taste. Bring to a boil, reduce heat, and simmer for 2 to 3 hours. Strain and cool uncovered. When cool remove all fat that comes to top. Refrigerate or freeze in small containers for use as needed. *MAKES 3 QUARTS.*

CHICKEN STOCK. Place about 4 pounds of chicken parts (backs, wings, and necks will do) in 4 quarts water. Add 2 medium whole onions, 5 ribs celery, 3 large carrots, 1 leek if available, pepper, 1 teaspoon salt (more if desired). Simmer for 2 to 3 hours. Strain and cool uncovered. When cool remove all fat that comes to top. Refrigerate or freeze in small containers for use as needed. *MAKES 3 QUARTS.*

FISH STOCK. Heat $1/4$ cup olive oil in pot, saute 1 chopped small onion until golden. Add 1 small clove garlic, $1/4$ cup white wine, 2 quarts water, fresh herbs (such as tarragon or thyme), sprig fresh parsley, 1 rib celery, 2 carrots, pinch nutmeg, salt and pepper to taste. Add $1 1/2$ pounds fish heads and bones (these are available in any market from the butcher and usually are complimentary) and cook for 45 minutes to 1 hour. Strain through fine cheesecloth twice to make sure no bones get through. After straining, $1/4$ cup butter may be melted in stock for extra richness. Cool uncovered, place in small containers, and refrigerate or freeze for future use. *MAKES $1 1/2$ QUARTS.*

VEAL STOCK. Place 4 pounds of veal knuckles or other veal bones and 1 pound beef bone with marrow in large pot with 2 quarts of water. Add 1 small onion, 1 bay leaf, 4 cloves, 3 sprigs parsley, 1 teaspoon thyme, 2 ribs celery with leaves, 2 medium carrots, and salt and pepper to taste. Bring to a boil, reduce heat, and simmer for 2 to 3 hours. Strain, cool covered, and refrigerate or freeze. *MAKES $1 1/2$ QUARTS.*

BASIC SAUCES

BEARNAISE SAUCE. *A classic sauce traditionally served with grilled red meat, but sometimes with fish, chicken, or eggs.* Simmer 2 chopped shallots, 1 sprig chervil chopped, 1 sprig tarragon chopped, and 2 peppercorns in 4 tablespoons wine vinegar or white wine until all but 2 teaspoonfuls of vinegar or wine have evaporated. Strain and cool.

Put 2 egg yolks in top of double boiler over simmering water. Whisk wine mixture into them. Slowly whisk in $1/4$ cup butter, cut into little pieces, until mixture resembles mayonnaise. If sauce curdles, remove from heat and vigorously whip in a teaspoon of cold water. *MAKES ABOUT 1 CUP*

BECHAMEL SAUCE. *A liquid seasoning for food, also known as white sauce, and probably the most important sauce of all as it is the basis for countless dishes.*

Medium Béchamel Sauce. Melt 2 tablespoons butter, but do not brown, over moderate heat. Add 2 tablespoons flour and stir until well blended. Use a wooden spoon or wire whisk. Heat 1 cup milk almost to a boil and add all at once to flour and butter, stirring virogously. It will thicken when it comes to a boil. Simmer for about 5 minutes. Add salt and white pepper to taste.

Thin Béchamel Sauce. Use 1 tablespoon each butter and flour for 1 cup milk.

Thick Béchamel Sauce. Use 3 tablespoons each butter and flour for 1 cup milk. *MAKES 1 CUP.*

BORDELAISE SAUCE. *A French sauce for grilled meats.* Melt 2 tablespoons butter in saucepan. Add 2 tablespoons minced shallots and cook until transparent. Add $1/4$ cup dry red wine and continue to cook until reduced by one-half. Then add in 1½ cups brown sauce or canned beef gravy, 2 tablespoons lemon juice, 2 tablespoons minced parsley, salt and freshly ground white pepper to taste, ½ cup sliced mushrooms, sauted in butter optional, and heat through. MAKES ABOUT 2 CUPS.

BROWN SAUCE. *Also called Espagnole Sauce, one of the most versatile of the French basic sauces. May be prepared and frozen.* In a saucepan melt ½ cup clarified butter (see Glossary). Saute in the butter 1 chopped carrot and 1 chopped onion. Add ½ cup flour and stir making a roux. Cook until it turns a deep brown, but do not burn. Add 4 cups boiling beef stock gradually while stirring, 2 cloves garlic, 1 rib of celery, diced, 4 sprigs of parsley, and 2 bay leaves. Cook, stirring often, for about 5 minutes.

Add 2 more cups beef stock. Cook 1½ to 2 hours over low heat until sauce reduces by about one-half. Skim off fat as it is cooking. Add ½ cup tomato puree or ¼ cup tomato paste if desired. MAKES 3 TO 4 CUPS.

CREOLE SAUCE. *A sauce named for the classic cuisine of New Orleans and used with many seafood dishes.* In heavy skillet melt 2 tablespoons bacon grease. Stir in 2 tablespoons flour and make a dark brown roux (see Glossary). Add 1 cup each of finely chopped onions, finely chopped green onions, finely chopped green pepper, and finely chopped celery (with a few leaves), 1 clove garlic minced, 1 bay leaf. Saute 30 minutes. Add ⅓ cup tomato paste, 1 cup canned tomatoes diced, and ½ cup tomato sauce. Stir, partially cover, and simmer gently 1 hour. Stir occasionally to avoid sticking. Remove bay leaf. Add Tabasco sauce and lemon juice to taste before serving. MAKES ABOUT 2 CUPS.

ESPAGNOLE SAUCE. See Brown Sauce.

HOLLANDAISE SAUCE. *A popular sauce, similar to Bearnaise sauce, made from eggs, butter, and lemon juice. A quick version may be made in a blender.* Place 3 egg yolks at room temperature, 2 tablespoons lemon juice at room temperature, ¼ teaspoon salt, and pinch cayenne in blender. Turn on low speed for 2 seconds.

Heat ½ cup butter until bubbling but not brown. Turn blender on low speed and gradually add butter. Blend about 15 seconds or until sauce is thickened and smooth. MAKES ABOUT 1 CUP.

TOMATO SAUCE. Heat 3 tablespoons olive oil in pan, add 1 clove garlic and 1 whole small onion. Lightly brown. Add 2 (10-ounce) cans tomato puree, 1 (6-ounce) can of tomato paste, ½ (tomato paste) can water, and 1 bay leaf. Simmer at least 1 hour. Remove garlic, onion, and bay leaf.

For richer sauce a short rib or other meat may be browned with onion and cooked in tomato sauce.

For seasoned sauce add fresh or dried herbs of choice. MAKES ABOUT 3 CUPS.

VELOUTE SAUCE. *A rich white sauce for either chicken or fish dishes.* Prepare Béchamel Sauce recipe, substituting chicken stock for milk for a Chicken Velouté Sauce, and substituting fish stock for milk for a Fish Velouté Sauce. MAKES ABOUT 1 CUP.

WHITE SAUCE. See Béchamel Sauce.

GLOSSARY

ANDOUILLE. *A thick Cajun pork sausage highly seasoned with garlic, herbs, and spices.*

AL DENTE. *"To the teeth," an adjective describing food, usually pastas or rice, that is firm to the bite, in contrast to food cooked until soft throughout.*

ARROWROOT. *A plant whose tuberous roots yield starch; a thickening agent.*

BASES. *Concentrated powders or cubes to be added to chicken, beef, or seafood dishes or to be reconstituted with water to make broths or stocks. Commercially available.*

BEARNAISE SAUCE. *See Basic Sauces.*

BECHAMEL. *See Basic Sauces.*

BLANCH. *To cook an ingredient about 1 minute in a large amount of boiling water to set color or flavor of a vegetable, to loosen skin of fruit or vegetable, to remove excess salt, or to precook. Depending on vegetable, cook approximately 30 seconds to 2 minutes.*

BORDELAISE SAUCE. *See Basic Sauces.*

BOUDIN. *A Cajun sausage made of pork, chicken, rice, and vegetables, with garlic, herbs, and spices.*

BOUILLON. *A clear soup or broth, made from various kinds of meat, where the fat has been removed from the stock. Also available in cubes to be reconstituted.*

BREAD, SQUEEZED DRY. *A method of soaking bread in a liquid and then pressing the bread manually to eliminate the moisture but retain the flavor. Used to prepare stuffings.*

BROWN ROUX. *See roux.*

BROWN SAUCE. *Also Espagnole sauce. A rich sauce made using trimmings of raw veal and ham, or rabbit, pork or game, seasonings and stock or bouillon. The stock may be made from meat, poultry, and fish, their bones, and from vegetables and seasonings. See Basic Sauces.*

BUTTERFLY. *To cut partially through and spread open to increase the surface area of food, e.g. shrimp.*

CARAMEL COLOR. *A brown substance obtained by heating sugar and used as a coloring and flavoring agent.*

CEPES. *Large mushrooms grown in France and canned for export markets, often in olive oil or some other sauce, and they have a somewhat stronger flavor than the common mushroom. Cap is six inches or more in diameter and yellowish or reddish in color.*

CHANTERELLE. *French name for small edible yellow mushroom.*

CLARIFIED BUTTER. *Butter that has been gently heated and strained so that the whitish deposit is left behind. Available in packages at supermarkets and gourmet stores. Often in seafood section.*

CRAWFISH, CRAYFISH. *"Crawfish" is the local Louisiana pronunciation for this small lobster-like crustacean, generally 3 inches to 6 inches long. The meat comes from the tails; crawfish fat is picked from the heads. Both meat and fat are available in frozen packages at markets and gourmet stores.*

CREOLE MUSTARD. *A local mustard made with spicier and darker mustard seeds which have been marinated. Available in markets and gourmet stores.*

DEGLAZE. *To add liquid to the crusty bits left in a saute pan to dissolve them, usually done over heat. This adds flavor to many dishes.*

DEMI-GLACE. *Sauce made from one cup of glace de viande (see below), added to 2 cups brown sauce, simmered over low* heat until reduced by half. It should be of a consistency to "half glaze" or coat food.

DEVEIN. Commonly refers to cleaning the small black filament from the back of a fish or prawn either before or after cooking.

EGG WASH. A combination of eggs and water, one egg to one tablespoon water, which when brushed on pastry encourages even browning. It can also be used to seal one piece of pastry to another.

ESCARGOTS. Snails.

ETOUFFEE. A cooking technique, with seafood covered with vegetables and cooked over low heat in a covered pot.

FILE. A powder made from sassafras leaves used as a flavoring and thickening agent in gumbos. Available at spice counters of grocery and gourmet stores.

FISH STOCK AND BOUILLON POWDER. See Bases.

FLAME or FLAMBE. To pour warmed alcoholic beverages such as brandy, whiskey, or rum over food to set fire to it for purpose of adding flavor.

FOLD. To gently incorporate one food stuff into another without breaking it, particularly egg white which needs to remain frothy. If beaten, rather than folded, the froth would be broken down.

GLACE DE VIANDE, GLACE DU CANARD. A concentrated stock obtained by reducing beef or duck broth or stock.

GLAZE. A stock that is reduced until it coats the back of a spoon. Also a shiny coating, such as syrup, applied to a food. Also to make a food shiny or glossy by coating it with a glaze or by browning under a broiler in a hot oven.

GUMBO. Gumbo is the African word for okra. Gumbo is an original American dish from Louisiana, a thick soup of okra, vegetables, and meat or seafood.

HERBSAINT. An alcoholic substance similar to Pernod, for which Pernod may be substituted.

HOLLANDAISE SAUCE. See Basic Sauces.

JAMBALAYA. A highly seasoned Cajun rice dish with ham, chicken, and shellfish, similar to a Spanish paella.

JULIENNE. To cut into small, thin strips, about one-eighth by one-eighth by two-and-a-half inches.

KITCHEN BOUQUET. A vegetable-based browning and seasoning sauce.

MARINATE, MARINADE. To marinate food in a marinade is to soak food for a period of time in a highly seasoned liquid to impart flavor as well as to tenderize it. A marinade often includes wine, vinegar, olive oil, lemon peel and juice, salt, pepper, bay leaves, onions, thyme, parsley, cloves, garlic, and so forth.

MEDALLIONS. Small round or ovals of food, particularly of beef or veal, such as tournedos.

MIREPOIX. Cubes of uncooked carrots, onions, ham or pork (optional) barely sauteed in butter with bay leaves and thyme. It is used as a garnish or a flavor enhancer to braised meat or poultry.

MONOSODIUM GLUTAMATE. A flavor enhancer sold under such names as MSG and ACCENT.

MOREL. An edible mushroom found in the springtime.

MUSHROOMS, WILD. See Cepes, Chanterelle, and Morel.

NAP. To coat a food with a rich white sauce, a procedure which is called napping or glazing.

OYSTER LIQUOR. The liquid from the oysters and their shells, used in flavoring.

PERNOD. An aromatic French liqueur, available in liquor stores.

PHYLLO. *A papery-thin pastry used in many Greek and Middle Eastern dishes. Difficult to make, but available in the frozen-food case of many grocery and gourmet stores.*

POACH. *To cook food in water or other liquid that is not actually bubbling at a temperature of 160 to 180 degrees F.*

PRAWNS. *In the United States, large shrimp are often called prawns.*

PUFF PASTRY. *A flaky combination of flour and butter bound with water. A rather tedious and exacting procedure to make at home, it fortunately is generally available in frozen-food cases of most grocery stores, and is very good.*

PUREE. *A paste produced by rubbing cooked food through a sieve or strainer.*

REDUCE. *To simmer or boil liquid until quantity is decreased. Usually for purpose of concentrating flavors.*

ROUX. *A mixture of equal parts butter, or other fats, and flour cooked together for varying periods of time depending on its use. It is the thickening agent in sauces. Brown rouxs are achieved by cooking and stirring the roux for half an hour, until the color of the roux becomes a rich, dark brown.*

SEAR. *To brown surface of food quickly at high temperature.*

SCALD. *To pour boiling water over an ingredient placed in a collander so that the water will immediately drain from it.*

SCALLOPINE. *Italian for small, thin pieces of meat (scallop), usually veal or fish, flattened and fried in butter.*

SHRIMP TO COOK. *Shrimp may be peeled and deveined either before or after cooking. Whichever way, shrimp should be placed in boiling water and cooked until they begin to turn pink, about 3 to 5 minutes, depending on size. Drain immedi-*

ately and run cold water over them to stop cooking process. The cooking water may be seasoned with commercial crab boil, lemon slices, bay leaf, and so forth.

SIMMER. *To cook food in water or other liquid that is bubbling gently, about 185 to 200 degrees F.*

SIMPLE SYRUP. *Combine 1 quart water to 2 cups sugar and boil for 5 minutes. May be bottled and kept in the refrigerator.*

SOFT BALL. *Syrup that has reached 234 degrees F. To test for soft ball stage, drop a small quantity of syrup into chilled water. Soft ball stage has been reached when it forms a ball that does not disintegrate but flattens out of its own accord when picked up with the fingers.*

STOCKS. *See Basic Stocks.*

TOMALLEY. *The liver of lobster and some other shell fish.*

WATER BATH. *To cook food in a container of water (bain marie) to keep it hot and/or prevent it from drying out during cooking. Produces an even heat.*

WHITE SAUCE. *See Basic Sauces under Béchamel Sauce.*

WOK. *A multi-functional cooking pan, traditionally used for Chinese cooking to conserve energy and cook foods quickly. It can be used for steaming, stir frying, deep-fat frying, braising, or stewing.*

EQUIVALENT MEASURES

MEASURE	EQUIVALENT
A few grains, pinch, etc. (dry)	Less than $1/8$ teaspoon
Dash (liquid)	2 or 3 drops
1 tablespoon	3 teaspoons
1 fluid ounce	2 tablespoons or $1/8$ cup
$1/4$ cup	4 tablespoons or 2 fluid ounces
$1/3$ cup	$5 1/3$ tablespoons or $2 2/3$ fluid ounces
$1/2$ cup	8 tablespoons or 4 fluid ounces
$3/4$ cup	12 tablespoons or 6 fluid ounces
1 cup	16 tablespoons or 8 fluid ounces
1 cup (liquid)	$1/2$ pint
1 pint	2 cups (liquid) or 16 fluid ounces
1 quart	2 pints or 32 fluid ounces
1 gallon	4 quarts
1 pound (dry)	16 ounces

INDEX BY FOODS AND RECIPE NAME

A

ALLIGATOR
   Alligator Sauce Piquante . .86
   Barbecued Alligator. 87

ALMONDS
   Almond Torte. 196
   Linzer Torte 197
Ambrosia. 215
Ananas Flambes au
   Poivre Vert 208
Andouille Filé Gumbo. 44

APPETIZERS
   Caponata. 37
   Crab Ravigotte. 32
   Escargot aux
     Champignons 33
   Escargot Roguefort 34
   Flamingos Country Pâté . .36
   Huitres Bienville 27
   Marinated Shrimp 31
   Oysters Rockefeller 29
   Oysters Suzette 28
   Pâté de Poissons
     Marie-France 35
   Spring Rolls 38
   Stuffed Artichoke Bottoms.26
   Stuffed Mushrooms 30

APPLES
   Apple Pizza 206
Arlequin de Courgettes 179

ARTICHOKE
   Artichoke Heart Quiche . .181
   Crabmeat and Artichoke
     Bottoms. 116
   Fonds D'Artichauts
     Bayard. 65
   Green Bean and Artichoke
     Casserole. 180
   Oyster and Artichoke
     Soup 55
   Oyster Artichoke
     Casserole. 146
   Oyster Artichoke Soup 54
   Stuffed Artichoke
     Bottoms. 26

AVOCADO
   Avocado Romanoff. 67

B

BANANAS
   Bananas Clement. 207
   Bananas Foster 205
Barbecued Alligator. 87
Bayou Eggplant 176

BEEF
   Natchitoches Meat Pie 74
   Sauerbraten. 73
   Steak Supreme. 72
Beignets 185

BELL PEPPER
   Stuffed Bell Pepper
     with Shrimp 178

BEVERAGES
   Ambrosia. 215
   Cafe Brulot. 216
   Milk Punch. 213
   Mint Julep 213
   Original Dubloon Drink . .217
   Ramos Gin Fizz. 215
   Satchmo Punch 214
   Strega Salute 212

BISQUES
   Crawfish Bisque. 50

BLACKBERRY
   Chicken Blackberry
     Vinegar 99

BLUEBERRY
   Blueberry Delight. 210
Bongo Bongo. 56
Bouillabaisse. 149
Bread Pudding and
   Whiskey Sauce 189
Bread Pudding Souffle with
   Whiskey Sauce 190
Bread Pudding with
   Rum Sauce. 188,192

BREADS
   Beignets 185
   Hush Puppies. 184
   Pain Perdu 182
   Southern Biscuit Muffins .183

BROCCOLI
   Creamy Broccoli Soup 62
Broiled Redfish Fillets on
   Steamed Vegetables with
   Hollandaise 132

C

CABBAGE
   Cabbage Rolls 150
   Coonass Cabbage Leaves .209
Cafe Brulot 216
Cajun Seafood Gumbo with
   Andouille Smoked Sausage . .41

CAKES
   Calas 173
   Schwarzwalder Kirshtorte .199
Calas 173
Canard aux Ananas Reve
   de Balmain 101
Caponata. 37
Carre D'Agneau a la
   Mongolian 75

CASSEROLES
   Caponata. 37
   Green Bean and Artichoke
     Casserole. 180
   Oyster Artichoke
     Casserole. 146

CATFISH
   Deep-Fried Catfish Fillets .125

CHEESE
   Potato/Cheese/Lobster
     Soup 57

CHEESECAKE
   Chocolate Cheesecake. . .198

CHICKEN
   Chicken and Tasso
     Jambalaya 95
   Chicken Andouille Gumbo .46
   Chicken Bienville. 94
   Chicken Blackberry
     Vinegar 99
   Chicken Breast Maitland . .97
   Chicken Breasts with
     Potato Stuffing. 96
   Chicken Gumbo. 45
   Lemon Chicken 98
   Pollo en Vino Tinto. 100
   Salad Savoyard 66
Chilled Crawfish Curry 52

CHOCOLATE
   Chocolate Cheesecake. . .198
   Schwarzwalder Kirshtorte .199

COFFEE
Cafe Brulot 216
Coonass Cabbage Leaves 209
Coquilles Saint-Ramon 148

CORN
Corn and Shrimp Soup 53

CRAB
Cabbage Rolls. 150
Coquilles Saint-Ramon . . .148
Crabmeat a la Julia. 165
Crabmeat and Artichoke
   Bottoms. 116
Crabmeat au Gratin . .115,118
Crabmeat with Grapefruit .117
Crabmeat Yvonne. 113
Crab Ravigotte 32
Crab Sauce Piquante. 114
Fish and Crab Boudin 155
Hot Boiled Crabs. 119
Soft Shell Crab and
   Crawfish Robert 112

CRAWFISH
Chilled Crawfish Curry 52
Crawfish Bisque 50
Crawfish Etouffee 120
Crawfish Ravioli with
   Nantua Sauce. 123
Crawfish Versailles 121
Hot and Spicy Boiled
   Crawfish. 124
La Truite de Mer aux
   Champignons et
   Ecrevisses au Beurre
   Blanc. 138
Original Louisiana Cajun
   Crawfish Pizza 122
Soft Shell Crab and
   Crawfish Robert 112
Creamy Broccoli Soup. 62
Creme Brule 193
Creme of Leek Chantilly 58,59
Creole Sauce. 227
Creole Seafood Okra
   Gumbo 42

CREPES
Crêpes Maison 203
Crêpes Suzette 201
Les Merveilles de la Mer
   en Crêpes. 156
Crevettes a la Creole 161

CUCUMBER
Flamingos Cold Cucumber
   Soup "Jordan" 61

CURRY
Chilled Crawfish Curry 52

D
Deep-Fried Catfish Fillets 125

DESSERTS
Almond Torte 196
Ananas Flambes au
   Poivre Vert 208
Apple Pizza 206
Bananas Clement 207
Bananas Foster. 205
Blueberry Delight 210
Bread Pudding and
   Whiskey Sauce 189
Bread Pudding with Rum
   Sauce 188,192
Bread Pudding Souffle with
   Whiskey Sauce 190
Chocolate Cheesecake . . .198
Coonass Cabbage Leaves .209
Creme Brule 193
Crêpes Maison 203
Crêpes Suzette 201
Kahlua Pecan Pie 195
Le Riz au Caramel 194
Lemon Tequila Souffle. . . .204
Linzer Torte 197
Pralines 211
Puff Pastry with Caramel
   Sauce. 200
Schwarzwalder Kirshtorte .199
Zitronen Rollchen 202

DOUGHNUTS
Beignets 185

DUCK
Canard aux Ananas
   Reve de Balmain 101
Duckling Ballotine with Fresh
   Tomato Sauce 102
Hickory Grilled Wisconsin
   Duckling 106
Roast Duck with
   Plum Sauce 104
Roasted Duckling. 105
Dutch Oven Venison. 92

E

EGGPLANT
Bayou Eggplant 176
Plantation Eggplant. 177

ESCARGOT
Escargot aux
   Champignons 33
Escargot Roquefort 34
Esquire Salad. 64

F
Fettuccini and Shrimp 164
Fillet of Snapper Rome 128
Fillet of Trout Bayou Style. . . .139
Fish and Crab Boudin. 155
Fish Veloute Sauce 227
Flamingos Cold Cucumber
   Soup "Jordan" 61
Flamingos Country Pâté. 36

FLOUNDER
Stuffed Flounder 126
Fonds D'Artichauts Bayard . . .65

FOX
Fox Stew 88
Fox Stew 88
French Dressing. 68

FROG LEGS
Grenouille St. Michael . . .143

G

GAME
Alligator Sauce Piquante . .86
Barbecued Alligator. 87
Dutch Oven Venison. 91
Fox Stew 88
Le Lapin en Matelote 89
Roast Raccoon. 90
Venison Lasagna 91

GRAPEFRUIT
Crabmeat with Grapefruit .117

GUMBO
Andouille Filé Gumbo 44
Cajun Seafood Gumbo
   with Andouille
   Smoked Sausage 41
Chicken Andouille Gumbo .46
Chicken Gumbo 45
Creole Seafood Okra
   Gumbo. 42
Gumbo Gouter 43
Seafood Gumbo 40

GREEN BEANS
Green Beans and Artichoke
   Casserole. 180
Grenouille St. Michael. 143

H
Hickory Grilled Wisconsin
   Duckling. 106
Homemade Pasta with
   Louisiana Shellfish 153
Hot and Juicy Boiled
   Shrimp 168
Hot and Spicy Boiled
   Crawfish 124
Hot Boiled Crabs. 119
Huitres Bienville. 27
Hush Puppies 184

J
JAMBALAYA
   Chicken and Tasso
      Jambalaya 95
   Jambalaya 152

K
Kahlua Pecan Pie 195
Kaiser Schnitzel 83
Kolb's House Salad 63
Kung Ming Shrimp 160

L
LAMB
   Carre D'Agneau a la
      Mongolian 75
LASAGNA
   Venison Lasagna. 91
La Truite de Mer aux
   Champignons et
   Ecrevisses au Beurre
   Blanc 138
Le Lapin en Matelote. 89
Le Riz au Caramel 194
LEEKS
   Creme of Leek Chantilly .58,59
LEMON
   Lemon Chicken 98
   Lemon Tequila Souffle. . . .204
   Zitronen Rollchen 202
Les Merveilles de la Mer en
   Crêpes. 156
L'Etoile de Melon au
   Jambon Fume 69
Linzer Torte 197
LOBSTER
   Potato/Cheese/Lobster
      Soup 57

M
Marinated Shrimp. 31
MELONS
   L'Etoile de Melon au
      Jambon Fume 69
Milk-Fed Veal Chop Francisco . .80
Milk Punch 213
Mint Julep 213
MUFFINS
   Southern Biscuit Muffins. .183
MUSHROOMS
   Escargot aux
      Champignons. 33

La Truite de Mer
   aux Champignons
   et Ecrevisses au
   Beurre Blanc. 138
Sauteed Mushrooms 172
Stuffed Mushrooms. 30

N
Natchitoches Meat Pie. 74

O
Original Dubloon Drink 217
Original Louisiana Cajun Boudin
   Pizza. 76
Original Louisiana Cajun
   Crawfish Pizza. 122
OYSTERS
   Bongo Bongo. 56
   Huitres Bienville 27
   Oyster and Artichoke
      Soup. 54,55
   Oyster Artichoke
      Casserole. 146
   Oyster Artichoke Soup 54
   Oysters Hebert. 144
   Oysters Maras 147
   Oysters Rockefeller 29
   Oysters Suzette 28
   Oysters Trufant 145
   Shrimp and Oyster
      Fettucini 154

P
Pain Perdu 182
PASTA
   Fettucini and Shrimp 164
   Homemade Pasta with
      Louisiana Shellfish. 153
   Shrimp and Oyster
      Fettucini 154
PATE
   Flamingos Country Pâté. . .36
   Pâté de Poissons
      Marie-France 35
PECANS
   Kahlua Pecan Pie 195
   Pralines 211
PIES
   Kahlua Pecan Pie 195
   Natchitoches Meat Pie 74
Pigeonneaux Paradis 109
PINEAPPLE
   Ananas Flambes au
      Poivre Vert 208

Canard aux Ananas Reve
   de Balmain. 101
Plantation Eggplant. 177
Poitrine de Veau Farcie
   de Gascogne. 81
Pollo en Vino Tinto. 100
Pommes de Terre Souffles . . .175
POMPANO
   Pompano en Papillote . . .127
POTATO
   Pommes de Terre
      Souffles 175
   Potato/Cheese/Lobster
      Soup 57
   Special Stuffed Potato . . .174
Pralines 211
PUDDINGS
   Bread Pudding and
      Whiskey Sauce 189
   Bread Pudding with
      Rum Sauce 188,192
Puff Pastry with
   Caramel Sauce 200

Q
QUAIL
   Quail a la Bistro 108
   Quail with Wild Mushrooms
      and Thyme Butter 107
QUICHE
   Artichoke Heart Quiche . .181

R
RABBIT
   Le Lapin en Matelote 89
RACCOON
   Roast Raccoon. 90
Ramos Gin Fizz 215
RED BEANS
   Red Beans and Rice with
      Smoked Sausage 77
   Red Bean Soup. 59
Red Snapper "Dore". 130
REDFISH
   Broiled Redfish Fillets
      on Steamed Vegetables
      with Hollandaise 132
   Fish and Crab Boudin. . . .155
   Redfish Bon Ton 133
   Redfish de la Maison 134
   Redfish Valentine's. 135
RICE
   Calas 173
   Red Beans and Rice with
      Smoked Sausage 77

Roast Duck with Plum
   Sauce 104
Roast Raccoon. 90
Roast Veal Shanks 82
Roasted Duckling 105
Roquefort Cheese Dressing . . .68

S

SALADS
   Avocado Romanoff. 67
   Esquire Salad. 64
   Kolb's House Salad. 63
   L'Etoile de Melon au
      Jambon Fume 69
   Salad Savoyard 66
SALAD DRESSINGS
   French Dressing. 68
   Roquefort Cheese
      Dressing 68
Satchmo Punch 214
Sauerbraten. 73
SAUSAGE
   Andouille Filé Gumbo. 44
   Cajun Seafood Gumbo with
      Andouille Smoked
      Sausage. 41
   Chicken Andouille Gumbo .46
   Original Louisiana Cajun
      Boudin Pizza 76
   Red Beans and Rice with
      Smoked Sausage 77
Sauteed Mushrooms 172
Sauteed Shrimp 165
SCALLOPS
   Coquilles Saint-Ramon. . .148
Schwarzwalder Kirshtorte . . .199
Seafood Gumbo 40
SEAFOOD
   Andouille Filé Gumbo. 44
   Bayou Eggplant 176
   Bongo Bongo 56
   Bouillabaise. 149
   Broiled Redfish Fillets on
      Steamed Vegetables with
      Hollandise 132
   Cajun Seafood Gumbo
      with Andouille Smoked
      Sausage. 41
   Chilled Crawfish Curry 52
   Coquilles Saint-Ramon. . .148
   Corn and Shrimp Soup 53
   Crabmeat a la Julia 165
   Crabmeat and Artichoke
      Bottoms. 116
   Crabmeat au Gratin. .115,118
   Crabmeat with
      Grapefruit 117
   Crabmeat Yvonne 113

Crab Ravigotte. 32
Crab Sauce Piquante 114
Crawfish Bisque. 50
Crawfish Etouffee. 120
Crawfish Ravioli with
   Nantua Sauce. 123
Crawfish Versailles. 121
Creole Seafood Gumbo. . . .42
Crevettes a la Creole 161
Deep-fried Catfish
   Fillets 125
Escargot aux
   Champignons 33
Escargot Roquefort 34
Fettucini and Shrimp 164
Fillet of Snapper
   Rome. 128
Fillet of Trout Bayou
   Style 139
Fish and Crab Boudin. . . .155
Grenoille St. Michael 143
Gumbo Gouter. 43
Homemade Pasta with
   Louisiana Shellfish. 153
Hot and Juicy Boiled
   Shrimp. 168
Hot and Spicy Boiled
   Crawfish 124
Hot Boiled Crabs 119
Huitres Bienville 27
Jambalaya. 152
Kung Ming Shrimp 160
La Truite de Mer aux
   Champignons et Ecrevisses
   au Beurre Blanc 138
Les Merveilles de la Mer
   en Crêpes. 156
Marinated Shrimp 31
Original Louisiana Cajun
   Crawfish Pizza 122
Oyster and Artichoke
   Soup. 54,55
Oysters Hebert. 144
Oysters Maras 147
Oysters Rockefeller 29
Oysters Suzette 28
Oysters Trufant 145
Pâté de Poissons Marie-
   France 35
Plantation Eggplant. 177
Pompano en Papillote . . .127
Potato/Cheese/Lobster
   Soup 57
Redfish Bon Ton 133
Redfish de la Maison 134

Redfish Valentines 135
Red Snapper "Dore". 130
Sauteed Shrimp 165
Seafood Gumbo 40
Shrimp a-la-Pookey 157
Shrimp and Oyster
   Fettucini 154
Shrimp Chippewa. 169
Shrimp Italian 162
Shrimp Magnolia 163
Shrimp Neopolitan. 158
Shrimp Toulouse 159
Snapper a la King. 131
Snapper Fontenot 129
Spanish Shrimp 166
Soft Shell Crab and
   Crawfish Robert. 112
Stuffed Artichoke Bottoms.26
Stuffed Bell Pepper with
   Shrimp. 178
Stuffed Flounder 126
Stuffed Mushrooms 30
Trout Delmonico 141
Trout Lisa. 142
Trout Meuniere. 140
Trout Meuniere
   Amandine 137
Trout with Mushroom
   Sauce. 136
Turtle Sauce Piquante . . .170
Turtle Soup 47,48
Turtle Soup au Sherry. 49
SHRIMP
   Corn and Shrimp Soup 53
   Crevettes a la Creole 161
   Fettuccini and Shrimp . . .164
   Hot and Juicy Boiled
      Shrimp. 168
   Jambalaya. 152
   Kung Ming Shrimp 160
   Marinated Shrimp 31
   Sauteed Shrimp 165
   Shrimp a-la-Pookey 157
   Shrimp and Oyster
      Fettucini 154
   Shrimp Chippewa. 169
   Shrimp Italian 162
   Shrimp Magnolia 163
   Shrimp Neopolitan. 158
   Shrimp Toulouse 159
   Spanish Shrimp 166
   Stuffed Bell Pepper with
      Shrimp. 178

SNAPPER
    Fillet of Snapper Rome . . . 128
    Red Snapper "Dore" 130
    Snapper a la King 131
    Snapper Fontenot 129
Soft Shell Crab and
    Crawfish Robert 112
SOUFFLES
    Bread Pudding Souffle with
        Whiskey Sauce 190
    Lemon Tequila Souffle . . . 204
    Pommes de Terre
        Souffles 175
SOUPS
    Andouille Filé Gumbo 44
    Bongo Bongo 56
    Cajun Seafood Gumbo with
        Andouille Smoked
        Sausage 41
    Chicken Andouille Gumbo . 46
    Chicken Gumbo 45
    Chilled Crawfish Curry 52
    Corn and Shrimp Soup 53
    Crawfish Bisque 50
    Creme of Leek
        Chantilly 58,59
    Creamy Broccoli Soup 62
    Creole Seafood Okra
        Gumbo 42
    Flamingos Cold Cucumber
        Soup "Jordan" 61
    Gumbo Gouter 43
    Oyster and Artichoke Soup . 55
    Oyster Artichoke Soup 54
    Potato/Cheese/Lobster
        Soup 57
    Red Bean Soup 59
    Seafood Gumbo 40
    Turtle Soup 47,48
    Turtle Soup au Sherry 49
Southern Biscuit Muffins 183
Spanish Shrimp 166
Special Stuffed Potato 174
SPINACH
    Bongo Bongo 56
    Spring Rolls 38
SQUAB
    Pigeonneux Paradis 109
STEAK
    Steak Supreme 72
STEWS
    Bouillabaisse 149
    Fox Stew 88
    Le Lapin en Matelote 89

Strega Salute 212
Stuffed Artichoke Bottoms 26
Stuffed Bell Pepper with
    Shrimp 178
Stuffed Flounder 126
Stuffed Mushrooms 30

T
Tenderloin of Veal au Citron
    with Pâté de Foie Gras 79
TORTES
    Almond Torte 196
    Linzer Torte 197
    Schwarzwalder Kirshtorte 199
TROUT
    Fillet of Trout
        Bayou Style 139
    La Truite de Mer aux
        Champignons et Ecrevisses
        au Beurre Blanc 138
    Trout Delmonico 141
    Trout Lisa 142
    Trout Meuniere 140
    Trout Meuniere Amandine 137
    Trout with Mushroom
        Sauce 136

TURTLE
    Turtle Sauce Piquante . . . 170
    Turtle Soup 47,48
    Turtle Soup au Sherry 49

V
VEAL
    Kaiser Schnitzel 83
    Milk-Fed Veal Chop
        Francisco 80
    Poitrine de Veau Farcie de
        Gascogne 81
    Roast Veal Shanks 82
    Tenderloin of Veal au
        Citron with Pâté de
        Foie Gras 79
    Veal Braciuolini 85
    Veal Menefee 78
    Veal Versailles 84
VENISON
    Dutch Oven Venison 92
    Venison Lasagna 91

Z
Zitronen Rollchen 202

INDEX BY RESTAURANT

A
Antoine's 27,65,109,127
    161,175,201,213,215
Armando's Mexican Cuisine . .100
Arnaud's 28,31,193

B
Begue's 89,138,194
Benedict House. 154,177
Bienville's Courtyard 94
Bill's Seafood Restaurant 178
Bon Ton Café 50,133,189
Boudin King. 45
Brennan's 29,47,205
The Brent House—
    Tivoli 80,144,148

C
Café Rani 155,195
Carousel Cafeteria . . .96,172,180
Chez Pastor 72,129,192
Christian's 99,117,149
Commander's Palace . .79,145,190
Corinne Dunbar's. 43,60,97
Country Corral Steaks
    and Seafood. 151
The Court of Two
    Sisters 33,67,159
Covington Depot. 132,164

D
Deano's Pizzarama. 206
Delmonico. 49,128,141
Don's Seafood Hut . . .40,131,150

E
The Embers Steak
    House. 68,174
Emery's. 118,165

F
Fairmont Hotel—
    Sazerac. 69,139,143,209
Flamingos Cafe 36,61,181

G
Galatoire's. 113,137,203
The Gumbo Shop. 42,46
    120,152,188,198

J
Jackson Street Pizza &
    Spaghetti House 162
Jeffrey's Riverside
    Restaurant 44,125

K
K-Paul's Louisiana
    Kitchen. 41,95,173,183
Kolb's 48,63,83

L
La Coquille 56,123
The Landing of
    Lafayette 102
La Savoie 66,126,179,208
Leroy's Restaurant. 210
Les Chefs de Cuisine
    de la Louisianne. 88,90,91
    92,136,142,153,202
The Lion's Share. 157
Louisiana Restaurant
    Association. 74,119
    124,168,185

M
The Magnolia Plantation 163
Marriott Hotel—Riverview
    Restaurant. 26,58,130
Marti's 52,182,214
Masson's 112,116,156
Maurice's Bistro 108,158
Mayer's Old Europe . .73,105,197
Menefee's. 78,104,134
Mike & Tony's. 62
Mister Jay's. 76,122
Mr. B's 106,147,169

N
The New Orleans School
    of Cooking 211,216

O
The Oaks Plantation 57,207

P
Paddlewheel Express. 53,64
The Pepper Mill
    Restaurant. 55
The Plimsoll Club. 35,81,101

R
Ralph & Kacoos 30,140,184
The Red Onion 176
The Restaurant Angelle's 115
Restaurant Sclafani 37,85
Riverview Restaurant. .26,58,130
The Royal Restaurant. 86
    87,114,170

S
Saffron. 107,166,200
Sazerac. 69,139,143,209
Sheraton Inn Airport—
    Valentine's 135,212
Sheraton New Orleans Hotel—
    Saffron. 107,166,200
Stephen & Martin 146,196

T
Tivoli 80,144,148
Top of the Mart. 217
Trey Yuen 38,98,160

V
Valentine's 135,212
Versailles 59,84,121,204

W
Willy Coln's Chalet 82,199
Winston's. 32,34,75

INDEX 237

NOTES

CHEFS' SECRETS ORDER FORM

MAIL TO: TRIPLE M COMPANY, P.O. Box 720114, Atlanta, GA 30358.

Please fill in reverse side for your order.
Enclosed is my check or money order made out to the Triple M Company for $_____. (DO NOT SEND CASH.)

Name_____ Phone (___)_____
Address_____
City_____ State_____ Zip_____
Signature_____

Make sure amount of check matches amount added together on reverse side. Allow approximately 6 to 8 weeks for delivery. Add $3.00 per copy for orders for Canada and $6.00 per copy for orders outside North America.

CHEFS' SECRETS ORDER FORM

MAIL TO: TRIPLE M COMPANY, P.O. Box 720114, Atlanta, GA 30358.

Please fill in reverse side for your order.
Enclosed is my check or money order made out to the Triple M Company for $_____. (DO NOT SEND CASH.)

Name_____ Phone (___)_____
Address_____
City_____ State_____ Zip_____
Signature_____

Make sure amount of check matches amount added together on reverse side. Allow approximately 6 to 8 weeks for delivery. Add $3.00 per copy for orders for Canada and $6.00 per copy for orders outside North America.

CHEFS' SECRETS ORDER FORM

MAIL TO: TRIPLE M COMPANY, P.O. Box 720114, Atlanta, GA 30358.

Please fill in reverse side for your order.
Enclosed is my check or money order made out to the Triple M Company for $_____. (DO NOT SEND CASH.)

Name_____ Phone (___)_____
Address_____
City_____ State_____ Zip_____
Signature_____

Make sure amount of check matches amount added together on reverse side. Allow approximately 6 to 8 weeks for delivery. Add $3.00 per copy for orders for Canada and $6.00 per copy for orders outside North America.

ORDER FORM — CHEFS' SECRETS

NO.   TOTAL $

_____ CHEFS' SECRETS FROM GREAT RESTAURANTS IN LOUISIANA — $13.95. $_____

_____ CHEFS' SECRETS FROM GREAT RESTAURANTS IN GEORGIA — $12.95 $_____

Add appropriate sales tax if mailed in Georgia. $_____

Free postage and handling $___00.00___

Total amount of check or money order $_____

Fill out both sides of coupon and return to address indicated on reverse side of coupon.

- -

ORDER FORM — CHEFS' SECRETS

NO.   TOTAL $

_____ CHEFS' SECRETS FROM GREAT RESTAURANTS IN LOUISIANA — $13.95. $_____

_____ CHEFS' SECRETS FROM GREAT RESTAURANTS IN GEORGIA — $12.95 $_____

Add appropriate sales tax if mailed in Georgia. $_____

Free postage and handling $___00.00___

Total amount of check or money order $_____

Fill out both sides of coupon and return to address indicated on reverse side of coupon.

- -

ORDER FORM — CHEFS' SECRETS

NO.   TOTAL $

_____ CHEFS' SECRETS FROM GREAT RESTAURANTS IN LOUISIANA — $13.95. $_____

_____ CHEFS' SECRETS FROM GREAT RESTAURANTS IN GEORGIA — $12.95 $_____

Add appropriate sales tax if mailed in Georgia. $_____

Free postage and handling $___00.00___

Total amount of check or money order $_____

Fill out both sides of coupon and return to address indicated on reverse side of coupon.